LIVING & DYING

Living & Dying

MEANINGS IN MAITHILI FOLKLORE

Dev Nath Pathak

PRIMUS
BOOKS

PRIMUS BOOKS
An imprint of Ratna Sagar P. Ltd.
Virat Bhavan
Mukherjee Nagar Commercial Complex
Delhi 110 009

Offices at
CHENNAI LUCKNOW
AGRA AHMEDABAD BENGALURU COIMBATORE DEHRADUN GUWAHATI
HYDERABAD JAIPUR JALANDHAR KANPUR KOCHI KOLKATA MADURAI
MUMBAI PATNA RANCHI VARANASI

First published 2018

ISBN: 978-93-5290-215-6 (hardback)
ISBN: 978-93-5290-216-3 (POD)

Published by Primus Books

Laser typeset by Mithu Karmakar
mithu.karma@gmail.com

Printed and bound in India by
Replika Press Pvt. Ltd.

Contents

Preface

Nachiketa was very unhappy to witness his father's ethical decline, as his father King Vajashrava was donating unhealthy cows to the priests who had offered services in the *yajna* (sacrifice). The unhappiness of Nachiketa in the *Kathopanishad*—one of the ancient texts of wisdom in India—seems to be a nuanced expression of any growing child at any juncture in the history of human civilization. To cut the tall claim to size, Nachiketa's dissatisfaction on his father's cunningness is alike the critical sense of any growing child. In the story a son questions and resists an allegedly deviant father. Thus anguished by his son's unrelenting query, the father uttered the words which perhaps wrote Nachiketa's destiny. The child had to set on a journey to meet the god of death. The travail eventuated into a meeting with the god, after spending a long time knocking at the door of the god's abode. The clever and kind god allured him with many glittering gifts the mortals cherish. But Nachiketa only wanted answers to questions that could enable him to understand the mystery of life and death. The winsome innocence and disarming curiosity of the learner worked out, and the god relented.

This famous story from the *Kathopanishad*, narrated from my personal memory, was always in the backdrop of the research behind this book. My retelling of this tale serves me the purpose of making a statement on the self-reflexive underpinning of this work. Reflexivity is a radical necessity in Sociology to bring the self of the researcher on the anvil of interpretative analysis.[1] For me, reflexivity is also an inherently psychoanalytical process in which the personal and public intersect through discursive acts. In many ways, a retelling of this story constituted my reconciliation with biographical tumult, episodes of my personal tryst with the event of dying. Not that like Nachiketa I found absolute answers to questions pertaining to living and dying. I never witnessed a corporeal entity called the god of death. Instead death to my 'significant others', to borrow a phrase from the lexicon of social psychology, happened with due accompaniment of suffering. But there was a Nachiketa mode, so to say, at work when I had to make sense of the death and dying amidst emotional upheavals. Every time somebody died, I vicariously experienced my own death, something anthropologists have discussed as couvade syndrome in a different context. Simply put, it was an empathic experience of dying with the dying. It all occasioned a rationale for a quest, technically called research, on which this book thrives.

Dying is an extreme form of separation. The other myriad versions of separating may be equally potent and pertinent for the invocation of Nachiketa. I do not claim to be Nachiketa incarnate, but I believe anybody approaching the issue of suffering, separation, and ending with simmering conscience is likely to take a Nachiketa-route, consciously or otherwise. Be it the ethical decline of a father in a ritual performance of sacrifice or the father's willingness to die following the death of his wife, there occur moments of crises whereby agency shelters in liminality. The liminality becomes the womb of a research/quest, to know the unknown, even though the unknown remains as chimerical as before. Embarking upon such quests is perhaps an essential part of being even though the pursuit of knowing the unknown is only partial, and at best delusional.[2] Walking down the corridor of the All India Institute of Medical Sciences (AIIMS) in Delhi on several occasions built up for me a phase of 'neither here nor there' (the betwixt about which anthropologists have deliberated). It was no less than an emotive drama under the dictate of some divine conspiracy. The cruelty of the divine conspiracy is inexplicable and hence not a morsel for simple romantic imagining. Running around to have my father diagnosed with kidney failure and deciding on his behalf to put him on a regular dialysis was almost like nudging myself along with him towards the abode of death. Asking my father insistently to generate some life-force (the Freudian notions of Eros, against the death drive, Thanatos) and live for me for a few more years, and getting to see in response his helplessly blank face with moist eyes, happened to be an impetus for the eternally curious Nachiketa.

Then descended a night with an uncanny dream whereby the ailing father asked the unrelenting son whether he could take leave as nothing was holding him back. The son looked at him with his tearful eyes and said, 'May I accompany you to wherever you intend to go?' The father said, 'You cannot, for nobody can really accompany to that abode,' and he walked off the dimly lit stage. And the son could see with blurry eyes the merger of his father into a velvety darkness of the auditorium.

This was the closure in the script for a play titled 'Melodrama of Death' I wrote after experiencing the death of my parents. I must confess that the hypothetical assumptions that made the theatrical performance, elucidating the endearing cruelty of the melodrama of death, were not original. I had committed plagiarism in the sense that I picked them from myriad songs without acknowledging in any footnote. I grew up listening to them and they constituted the sonic background of my consciousness. When everything was rosy in my surroundings, I did not hear the pangs in those songs—they were only soothing. They also seemed irritating for my mother sang them a little too frequently and nobody could stop her. She was not a cassette player to be unplugged when a listener was bored. She sang at her own will and created a soundscape for the household. Even sadness did not hinder her singing. She sang songs of sadness to match her mood, time, and season. The repertoire of my mother's songs, unrecorded and unarchived, remained in my memory for ready reference. They appeared on my lips only occasionally so long as I was not curious about their meanings. In the spring of my upbringing when I was learning physics and mathematics those songs seemed to be insignificant renditions of a semi-literate woman. All those songs, however, magnified in meaning as nostalgia played uncanny tricks. After my mother's sudden demise, I did not seem to abort the effortless occurrence of those songs in my solitary humming. As a student of social anthropology, rather than of physical sciences, I grew curious about the songs. I began to ask questions from women of my mother's age in the villages, about the meanings of the songs and also the stories about my parents' lives. Perhaps this was my personal psychic arrangement to revive a sense of the normal in the face of the militant death and its after effects. Alongside my quest unfolded myriad stories, punctuated with songs, which became the skeleton of the research undertaken in this book. This was my Nachiketa pursuit, if it could be called so, of the meanings of the songs. Those songs and their varied meanings led me to comprehend the ideas of living and dying. Needless to say, this entails due limitations. The latter is aptly encapsulated in a verse in Isha Upanishad:

> *Into darkness enter those who worship ignorance,*
> *into as if still greater darkness enter those who delight in*
> *knowledge.*[3]

It is indeed this spirit in which this book joins in various already existent discursive frames. And hence the claim is not to lead anybody (from darkness) to the domain of light; instead, it is more to deal with various layers of darkness. A very thick kind of darkness perhaps arises from the domain of the 'known', and 'familiar', and consequently the convenient and comfortable. This predominant domain too has its failures.

There is something incredible about the failure of scientific-objective thinking. When it fails, it paves the novel ways for understanding. The failure of scientific-objective thinking, calculation, and certainty invokes a more sensible social scientist. When the intended consequences are superseded by unintended ones, science has to reorient itself. In the face of such situations my rational thinking faltered at many junctures as though it were a shock to a struggling doctor whose every bit of medical analysis is washed away by the tide of time. Somehow it dawned upon me that one cannot die until one wants to, almost like the Bhishma (the grandfather of the Kaurawas and the Pandwas) in the epic *Mahabharata*. Bhishma stayed on the spiky deathbed (made of arrows) for almost a fortnight and decided to die only at the right/auspicious moment. There is a moment somewhere in life where everybody instantly realizes the visibility of death in the shadows of life. As soon as it is accepted it becomes possible to die a happy death. Various Buddhist tales exhibit such an acceptance as a key to happiness. Acceptance of sorrow too becomes a reason for ecstasy, about which a distant observer may only wonder or turn cynical.

If I have to put the crux of this research, the kernel of this book, in one line I would say 'life and death unfold simultaneously and hence they are imagined in the same breath using the same set of metaphoric symbols'. The element of sorrow (especially pertaining to separation), widespread throughout life, is the best evidence of the interrelatedness. We learn to say 'yes' to an ending. Not that after this there is no continuity in the journey of Nachiketa, for the god of death was cunning enough to answer only three questions. And the questions cannot be only three; indeed questions cannot be limited to countable numbers.

My exposure to the anthropological and sociological literature on performative art and notions of life and death generated both an optimism to tell the tale in the language which offers objectivity, and a pessimism that everything that belongs to felt-knowledge of the folk cannot be put into the same language. Admittedly this work is also a compromise on the infinite possibilities as it restricts the articulation to the domain of the institutionalized. The bid to make everything fathomable relies on a compromise. But then, I do not regret this compromise as it is the only way to say the unsaid. I must not, for I am not a selfish mystic who revels alone in the trap of sublime psychic energy. Another level at which this work assumes distinction, to put it immodestly, is to do with a slightly unconventional interest in the folk imagination. While most of the a priori analyses have been focused on the ritualistic dimensions, or the institutional arrangements, or the socio-materialistic dimensions of ritual performances, in the studies of the folk literature or oral tradition, they fail to comprehend the philosophical import and the fluidity of imagination. This work is also an antithesis to the age-old social scientific prejudice that poetry is mere fantasy and thus, unreal; or that it is, as Freud felt, merely a neurotic articulation of the upset libido. If the whole of life is a work of art, everything people say and do are artistic expressions. While there may be occasional spectacles to remark certain ideas, there are more benign and ordinary expressions in everyday life as well. This work attempts at the totality with

unflinching interest in the ordinary and lacklustre moments in
the routine set up for human emotion does not conform to the
socio-structural restrictions, and often the former redefines the
latter. It was necessary to investigate the presence of sorrow in
everyday life, and its significance in the occurrences of life and
death. It was all supported by the conviction expressed in myriad
poetic expressions, such as a couplet from the rich anthology of
Mirza Ghalib:

> *Quaid-e-hayat Band-o-gham Asla mei dono ek hai,*
> *Maut se pehle aadmi gham se nizaat paaye kyu!*

Parallel are the two indeed; Prison of life and chain of grief;
Why would, thus, We shall be free, from sorrow before death; and
this is the decree.

Department of Sociology   DEV NATH PATHAK
South Asian University

Notes

1. See Gouldner 1970. Suffice to say, many interventions in the discourse
   on reflexivity have emerged ever since the discomfort with the
   conventional idea of self-free sociology and social anthropology. But,
   next to Alwin Gouldner in my scheme of inspiration are Michael
   Jackson (2013) and Avijit Pathak (2014, 2015). Both in different
   locations, dealing with different issues, perform one characteristic
   laying out a distinct pathway that this book treads—juxtaposition of
   personal, experiential, and existential with the objects of study.
2. This is an important lesson an anthropologist, interested in the
   significance of mystical experience qua dreams, can learn from
   Obeyesekere (2012).
3. This is translated and edited by Katz and Egenes (2015: 31).

Acknowledgements

This book has taken so long to come into the public domain that it needs a word of explanation. After a series of rejections and phases of silence from publishers of repute, the manuscript finally found two anonymous reviewers who suggested that with proper revisions in certain areas, the book could be published. However, up to the present time, I have not heard from the publishing house that had commissioned these two reviews. It was at this stage that my seasoned colleague Sasanka Perera, advised me that it would be useless to keep waiting for the elusive communication from the publisher. Aware of the politics of publishing, instead, he said that I should submit the book proposal with the existing review reports to Primus. I am thankful to Primus for the keen interest it has shown in the book from the very outset.

Here I would like to acknowledge those anonymous reviewers who delivered two wonderfully critical essays on my manuscript. Their comments have helped me to revise my work in significant ways, and I am indeed grateful to them. I also received detailed comments on earlier drafts of this book from N. Jairam and the late Hetukar Jha. I still read the handwritten comments of Hetukar Jha with great joy though also with strong disagreements. On a later occasion, Sadan Jha was generous enough to tender some useful comments towards tightening the manuscript. Also, I must thank Avijit Pathak who has been a perpetual source of feedback on my work in addition to being a storehouse of intellectual provocation. He persuaded me to believe in the merits of my work, despite my self-doubts. I can never thank him enough.

I have also received much encouragement to engage with this work in several fora in India as well as abroad. Some anthropologists inclined towards ethnomusicology at Queen's University, Belfast, found this work to be a significant departure in the anthropology of mourning. Scholars at Boston University as well as Brown University were curious about the philosophically significant roles played by women in the context of Maithili folklore. I thank them all, without performing the politics of naming, for inspiring me with their perceptive comments. However, it is pertinent not to forget a long-term friend and teacher at MIT, Jyoti Sinha, for bringing together the South Asian folks in Boston who wanted to hear about the research as well as hear me sing some of the songs I had recorded in my manuscript. I remember a similar situation, a demand to sing similar material, at a conference at School of Arts and Aesthetics, JNU in Delhi too. I had managed to narrowly escape such demands even though I was a confident actor with a theatre background. But I acknowledge those moments of awkwardness for a researcher of folk songs, which prepared me to be more sombre while speaking of the songs.

I am immensely grateful to Sasanka Perera for standing by me at a time when my authorial spirit had become low. He made me realize the importance of not giving up. We have done much work in collaboration, and I am deeply influenced by the diehard spirit and tough workmanship that he upholds. I am also indebted to his wife Anoli Perera for helping out with the designing of the jacket. Anoli Perera is a prominent name in the contemporary visual art scene in Sri Lanka, and her inputs have indeed been invaluable. Finally, I must thank Jagath Weerasinghe, an eminent archaeologist, artist, art-historian, and many other things rolled in one, who lent the image of his art work for this book's jacket. The fine blend of morbid and aesthetics, abstraction and emotion that Jagath chisels out in his craft is very much at the centre of this book, and pivotal in our friendship. Now I deserve to pester Jagath with demands to have more discussions over coffee and cigarettes.

In the process of becoming of this book, which spanned almost a decade, many of the great sources of my strength and weakness, instigation and inspiration, met with an untimely demise. I am not naming them since they have gone beyond naming, in the cosmological sense, but I will always remember the time spent with them, intellectually and emotionally, in sharing my pursuits.

Too many dramatic events of living and dying have fallen under the pale of this book. I acknowledge them all, humans and events, with due humility. And I thank all who huddled with me to help me cope despite our differences: Tuni and Bed, Badki and Chhotki Didi, Khusbu and Lali, Bhaiji and Ojha, Pankaj and Jhunna, Rikki, Bundul and Baua (Shlok), Pataniya wali and many others.

I shall duly acknowledge the assistance I received from some students, young scholars, who tend to look up to somewhat iconoclastic tendencies in teachers. Divyendu Jha was considerably helpful in getting copies of the maps done even though they were in tattered conditions in some of the premier institutions. I also thank Mithilesh Kumar Jha, a scholar on the Maithili language movement, for the discussions on the sources, and Vagish Jha for providing ignitions at the onset of the research. Many scholars from Mithila University, Darbhanga, were patient interlocutors during the research. I shall name Ramdev Jha, a living authority on Maithili literature, for generous conversations even though he had problems with my intellectual orientation. Towards the end of the research that led to this book, I presented a paper based on women's songs in Mithila in a conference convened by Lata Singh and late Biswamoy Pati, which translated into a chapter in the book edited by the conveners. The comments that came through the editors, Lata di and Bismoy sir (as I fondly call them), was truly a timely inspiration. I am filled with gratitude.

Finally, I shall be ever thankful to Priya, who grew almost fanatic about her surname 'Mirza' while the final version of the manuscript of this book was underway. No thanking will be sufficient for her being the most patient audience of my swaggy monologues, despite considering me a *kaafir*. To Chanda (Prabuddh), who has started asking me questions about death, and I have already announced: I have a book to answer your questions. I hope Prabuddh, with little Tara (Nargis), will use this book more for information on melody and the metaphors of living and dying rather than as a doorstopper or a paperweight!

DEV NATH PATHAK

from bygone times as one embarks on understanding meanings in the domain of folklore. It is also a need at this juncture in intellectual history where recognition of plural cultural scripts of meanings is a necessary point of commencement for any discourse. This is the mainstay of the second and third essays in this book.

Meanings in the folk world view indeed solicit an ability to comprehend, and be intellectually tolerant to a myriad criss-crossing of cultural forms and trafficking of contents. It would be impertinent to foreclose the possibility of, for instance, folklore and popular cinematic transactions, mutual influences, and reformulations of styles and content. This also underlines a possibly mediated character, rather than the pristine nature, of folklore. Consequently, this dents the cultural arrogance of folks from across the regions. This is another reason why the Kannada tale, borrowed from the compilation of Ramanujan, is pertinently insightful for the journey this book promises to undertake. The quest of meanings, or the veritable 'key' of meanings as in the tale, demands shedding the garbs of cultural, qua intellectual, superiority.

The cultural superiority manifests at various levels—generic-notional, conceptual-philosophical, and regional-geographical. We are aware of the rise of some of the overlapping trajectories of this superiority complex. The scientific epistemology, of promisingly emancipatory rationalist philosophy, is one key domain of superiority. It provides with methods, techniques, perspectives, and a value orientation for critical enquiries. Folklore studies too operated within this and placed the emotional content as being synonymous with the non-rational. In this light, we are aware of the politics of knowledge construction about cultural contexts. Knowledge about cultural phenomenon aids in understanding; but in historical context it has also played an instrumental role in the imperialist drive of colonialism. Closer to the various cultural domains we are aware of the sense of cultural superiority based on the distinctions of caste, class, and gender. They all shape the becoming of meanings, to say the least. In this wake, it is curious to visit a linguistic region, notorious for its own share of cultural superiority (glaring street light!, despite evident fragments within the whole). The third, fourth, and fifth essay ensure that we steer clear of superiority complex.

Context(s): Particular Location(s) and General Question(s)

The journey that this book invites the readers to is towards the
northern Indian linguistic zone and its collective memory. This
book seeks to unravel the world view constituted by Maithili
folklore. The latter—the mainstay of this book—is geographically
identified with the linguistic region Mithila, located roughly in
north-east Bihar, abutting Nepal. The ambiguous status of Maithili
language on one hand and the mythical significance of Mithila on
the other renders 'world view' into world views. Perhaps there
could not be one world view in Mithila. A pluralism of world
views and of contested meanings, however, does not deter an
engagement with Maithili folklore. Despite heterogeneity, there
are genres performed across social groups with a uniformity of
meanings. This is especially true of the Maithili folk songs of
everyday life in which notions of life and death figure prominently
and are sung across social groups. These songs are replete with folk
ideas, leading to a systematic body of 'folk philosophy'. It is not
philosophy in the typical academic sense of the term suggestive
of a sophisticated epistemological system of enquiry. However,
it is philosophy in a generic, semantic sense, with reference to
reasoning with cognitive and emotional categories. In the scheme
of folk philosophy 'reasoning' and 'doing' seem to overlap and
reinforce each other. Hence, ritual performances, singing, and
wailing—synonymously termed mourning and tuneful weeping
in anthropological texts—are significant aspects of folk culture in
Mithila. They occur on diverse occasions of union and separation
including the event of death, in the cycle of life. On all such
occasions of crying, a complexity of meanings, essentials of world
view, and constituents of folk philosophy become intelligible. This
book dwells upon the premium of the philosophical import in
the folk songs, by engaging with the notions of union-separation,
merging-parting, material-spiritual, divine-mundane, and broadly,
life and death. The philosophical temperament of this work
reaffirms the fundamental suggestion of sociology and social
anthropology that human social institutions are also reflective
of deep thoughts. This book ferrets out some of these crucial

characteristics of folklore through an interpretative engagement with Maithili folk songs.

This endeavour is premised upon a confluence of many ways of looking at folklore, emanating from folklore studies/folkloristics, ethnomusicology, social anthropology, and sociology. The format of this work is, thus, interdisciplinary. The Maithili folk songs sung in the rite of the passage and occasions in everyday life were gathered from the village named Fulhara in the southern part of Mithila located in Samastipur district. Research was also conducted in other villages such as Navtol, Beri, and Bhindi (located in the district of Darbhanga) for more clarity on the functions and renditions of the songs. Unlike the pre-existing anthropological works which focus on ritual aspects in the rite of the passage this book dwells upon songs sung alongside rituals as a more suitable domain of meanings. The discursive framework of this book departs from the usual positivistic doubt about the heard—hearing cannot lead to believing! This is ironical since methodological positivism more or less amounts to saying 'seeing is believing'. The supremacy of seeing over hearing in the hierarchy of the bodily/sense organs of a researcher ought to be questioned by giving ears their due. More discussion on it follows in the essay on methodology of being, where an attempt is made to restore a researcher's faith in the act of hearing, the heard, the act of understanding, and the understood. By disclosing key aspects of the Maithil world view through the method (or a humane attribute) of hearing and believing, this book seeks to unearth folk engagement with the ideas of life and death. How life with its various junctures marked by the rites of the passage is visualized and how death is perceived through the prism of life forms the centrality of this discourse. Death is not a separate phenomenon in the world view of Mithila as these songs reveal that departure of the soul from the body is similar to that of a bride from her natal home. The cognition of living and dying unfolds at the intersection between religious and social, metaphysical and material, and sacred and mundane. This complexity consummates the Maithil world view. The analytical understanding of the songs also establishes a notion of complementarity that rules the relationship between men and women in a patriarchal society such as of Mithila. Maithil women's songs, underpinning the social structure, open for a possible rethinking on the feminist arguments about women's position in a patriarchal society. This is however not to suggest an absence of power-relations within Maithili society. In a kinship structure and ideology that favours men folk, women are not merely either a subjugated agency lying as a dormant volcano of repressed anguish nor an unleashed agency seeking to demolish a structure. The research underpinning this book takes the onus of presenting women as a complementary partner, who can protest, plead, redefine, and reconcile with as well as without the 'freedom of agency' in a structure.[2] These issues, among others, dominate the sixth, seventh, and eighth essays in this book.

The reason why a research of this kind, and its textual consequence such as this book, assumes significance is mainly three fold—the singularity of focus on the thoughts of the folk and how these thoughts as expressed in their songs seem to regulate everyday lives; the focus here is beyond the spectacle of rituals, which may be an occasional phenomenon, and is on the repeated renditions and circulation of motifs; the thoughts of the folk also influence their practices and social institutions. Additionally, the relentless suggestion in social anthropology to draw the totality of the world view with respect to the gendered roles and performances also flags the significance of this research. By researching into tradition without dismissing the ambiguous presence of modernity, this work produces knowledge that is rife with the possibility of conceptual regeneration. The conceptual dichotomy between tradition and modernity takes a rest here to allow their intertwined nature to surface. In a socially globalized world, allegedly homogenizing as well as hybridizing in effect, when the intellectual and imaginative realm is restricted to predominant notions of our time, a study of folk songs, its meanings and philosophy in association with the folk practice assumes significance for a researcher of indigenous tradition.

A few questions gaping in the face of this book are worth recounting. Why to make meanings of living and dying so prominent? Why Maithili folk songs? And how could they be relevant in social anthropology? The book tends to deliver an answer, overtly as well as covertly. It is worth, briefly, reflecting upon them in a manner to satiate impulsive curiosity and fulfil introductory basics.

More than once I was asked this question, a daunting one, by both friends as well as foes. Why to think of the meaning of death? It looked like a downright case of necrophilia to many. The well-wishers, sympathizers, and even academic friends were not quite sure about the meaning of death. For death was a taboo stronger than sex in the world of non-academic common sense; and it was an alleged hobbyhorse of myth-mongering godmen, as the academic common sense suggests. One could watch 'pornographic stuff' but could not consider contemplating about death. On a lighter note, it was acceptable to fantasize about the opposite sex, singing one of the famous Sahir Ludhianvi lyric *Chaudhavin ka chand ho* (you are the lunar beauty of the resplendent waxing moon) (Sadiq 1960). But it was bizarre to use similar lyrical tenor for death and dying. One of my colleagues once gave me an unsolicited nugget of wisdom worth unalloyed mention, 'make love with as many women as possible and you would forget about death!' Barring the bluntness of expression, making love seemed parallel to the other part of my quest, namely meaning of life. However, the latter was never divorced from the tabooed part, meaning of death, in my contemplation. And that was a serious issue as per the popular observation. To my academic peers the whole formulation, meaning of life and death, seemed a little like the title of a godman's sermon. There are way too many godmen around and they invariably talk about living and dying. There is no longer a divide between the East and West as far as popular appearances of the godmen is concerned. They are the most circulated commodities, promising packaged spiritual salvation, from India to the United States of America. Amidst the bewildering abundance of packaged sermons, one is always wary of echoing the populist spiritual ideas about the secrets of life and death. While my academic friends and foes were not sure about the academic credence of the thematic issue of my interest, some odd non-academic curious folks deemed me to be a mystique in the making. They raised intriguing questions about 'after-death' and I obviously had no interest in the after-death. The question about the validity of the research, and by the same breath that of this book, is always susceptible to dubious attitudes and questions. This trope of questions and doubts also opens up a window to the idea of living and dying. Why do we think in the way we think about death? Why is it a taboo? If not a categorical taboo, this is perhaps something about which one cannot speak freely. Why is it only associated with the notion of after-death? Why is there not much thinking on the ordinary and aesthetic speculation about death in relation with life? Curiously enough, this is so despite the popular cinematic imagination of death and dying that places death in the realm of ordinary experiences. The dominant popular cultural trope, heavily determined by the cinematic medium, presents an abundance of acoustic propositions. A generation heard it, and sang it for the youngsters, *admi musafir hai, aata hai jaata hai, aate jaate raste me yaade chhod jata hai* (humans are merely travellers, in the flux of arriving and departing, and in this course of being, they leave behind memories) (Om Prakash 1977).[3] Many among the Hindi cinema viewers grew up singing a popular lyric among many others, such as *Rote huye aate hain sab, hansta hua jo jayega, wo muqaddar ka sikandar jaaneman kahlayega* (all arrived crying, those who leave with a smile, will be hailed by all, as the conqueror of destiny) (Mehra 1978).[4] If one adds more regional varieties of cinema, the richness of the popular cultural trope is further enhanced and the abundance of meanings in the sonic surrounding becomes evident. Despite the ubiquity of popular cinematic notions of living and dying, there is a queer attitude toward death.

The paradoxical significance of death today makes it even more important a muse in social anthropology. Death, dying, and living have been some of the key coordinates in the anthropological understanding of primitive society. There is, however, an interesting challenge in discussing these coordinates in the context of a society which is not primitive in a typical anthropological sense. One such sociocultural context, namely of Maithili folk songs, occasions a possibility of some debates. There could be many more similar sociocultural contexts used as an analytical premise. This book centres the Maithili case for a few curious reasons. One is that it has been relatively under-researched in India. There are reams of writings mostly by scholars of Maithili languages and cultural historians. Some of these writings are in English, while a larger proportion of the writings are in Maithili and in Hindi. With a few exceptions, a common and dominant motif has been a celebration of the cultural superiority of Mithila. These celebratory accounts present Maithili culture and practice as superior fossils of a past in the scheme of cultural glorification. They use history and mythology to create a heady cocktail of 'my superior Mithila!' And indeed everybody seems intolerant to even the slightest of criticism about the fakeness of such celebratory accounts. I grew up listening to all versions of the celebratory accounts making me more sickly curious until they became sources of research questions for critical enquiry. Moreover, in recent times there has been narcissistic mobilization on the idea of the state of Mithila.[5] It dwells upon a hyper-emphatic invention of Maithili heritage and development. It seeks to present an overly simplified idea of Maithili culture that is conducive for the tourism industry and dominant model of development. Political groups vie with each other to 'encourage' Maithili culture through various funded *mahotsavas* (state-sponsored festivals).[6] The postcard image of Maithili culture may have adverse political implications for the cultural complexities in the region. Also, it may not convey the deeper interpretative meanings of the cultural performances in the wake of the political window-dressing and crescendo of cultural nationalism. This book seeks to present a discussion on the songs from Mithila while being conscious of the cultural politics lurking in the background.

Departures in the Quest of Meanings

The brief outline above hints at the messy realm of meanings which this book seeks to engage with. In this scheme, it is imperative to stress on the importance of departing from the clinically clean domains of enquiries that have occupied social anthropologists ever since the beginning of classical anthropology. The area of life wherein emotions confuse formal patterns is what becomes important in a work which this book aims to present. In this regard, it seems urgent to recall Veena Das:

Anthropologists have been very successful in studying formal aspects of life when individuals can be shown to be playing their roles, or when they are

engaged in formal exchanges or when people are acting out rituals whose
format is collectively agreed upon. But in the entire mushy area of life
when the individual emotion seems to confuse the formal pattern or when
the context is not formally structured as in Levi-Strauss'[7] example of two
strangers sharing a restaurant table in Paris, the models of the anthropologist
begin to falter. (Das 1986: 185)

It is the domain where 'individual emotion seems to confuse
the formal pattern' that renders this book and the underpinning
research relevant. It makes a conscious effort to look for meanings
beyond the familiar way of fathoming the Hindu world view.
The most familiar way has been allegedly restricted to the
categories arising from the 'cognitive structure of Hindu society'
(Das 1987). The categories pertaining to the classical texts, e.g.
dharma, karma, moksha, have dominated our understanding of
Hindu belief and practices.[8] The bifurcation of the classical Hindu
religion and its counterpart, alternative Hindu dharma, seems to
facilitate a systematic knowledge about a particular version of
Hindu world view. But it also delimits the exploration of the
folk world view and of social philosophy.[9] This was the reason
why the ethno-sociological approach of Mckim Marriott put the
categories from the classical texts as the only set of indigenous
cognitive categories of Hindu society. This facilitated a very
neat conceptualization of Little tradition and Great tradition
on the one hand, and Universalization and Parochialization, the
processes of social change in traditional society, on the other
hand (Marriott 1967; 1990). This discursive trope seldom makes
visible the widespread significance of 'folklorization' in the Indian
context. With excessive attention to the ritual performance the
available discursive tropes rarely arrive at the totality of folk world
view, let alone *folk-philosophizing* that deals with finer nuances
attached to the events of life, including death. The possible
improvization of the classical Hindu categories of dharma, karma
and moksha in folklore, which resists as well as reconciles with
the Brahminic-Sanskritic textual ideas, seldom surface in the
conventional anthropological discussions. They shed little light
on the instrumental role played by the category of emotion in
framing the folk world view and formulating folk philosophy.
Perhaps, this also explains one of the reasons why intolerant

religious sentiments have emerged in the politics of Hinduism. This sentiment seeks to put Hindu dharma into pure (classical) and impure (folk). The public sentiment similar to the academic bifurcation precludes a possible comprehension of the fluidity of Hindu belief and practices. This is indeed the need of the time to reason with Hindu dharma beyond the familiar bifurcation in academic discourse and emphasize the perpetual negotiations between the binaries in the realm of folk performances.

Along this line, Wendy Doniger's proposition is significant. Showing that 'Hinduism has porous margins and is polycentric' (2011: 29), she underlines that:

Hinduism is composed of local as well as pan-Indian traditions, oral as well as written traditions, vernacular as well as Sanskrit traditions, and nontextual as well as textual sources. The first (often marginalized) elements of each of these pairs tend to reinforce one another, as do the second elements, the dominant elements, but there are important distinctions within each of the two groups. For these contrasting pairs did not translate into polarized groups of people; a single person would often have both halves (as well as non-Hindu traditions) in his or her head; a Brahmin would know the folk traditions, just as, in the Euro-American world, many people study paleography and then go to church and read Genesis. (Ibid.: 32–3)

This is the scheme that aids in fathoming the interactive framework of folk culture in which the 'written' and 'oral' interact. Elsewhere, Gananath Obeyesekere dwelt upon a similar interactive framework to show that 'little' (of the unreflective many) and great (of the reflective few) parts of a tradition does not mean a disjuncted existence of tradition. Robert Redfield's binaries for understanding peasant societies underlined that the two traditions are interdependent. In the context of Sinhala Buddhism, thus, there is a perplexing paradox. Obeyesekere suggests that:

the paradox is a result of the synthesis or fusion of pre-existing beliefs or later diffused beliefs from the great tradition. These beliefs are contradictory to the great tradition, but from the point of view of the people, they are resolved and explained in terms of a single tradition. (1963: 150)

This is the reason why the common worshippers, irrespective of caste groups in the social hierarchy, persist with their belief in the contradictory aspects which arise from the ceaseless interaction between the two aspects of a tradition. And in this wake, there is seldom a recognition of the divide between the belief and practices of the literate or illiterate, elite or masses, and scholars or ordinary folk. This indeed paves the way for envisaging a consolidated body of thought, corpus of idioms and metaphors, and imagination to emerge from the expressive domain of folklore.

Another key issue which this book grapples with is the impact of modernity in conditioning our thinking of life and death. Death figures as a 'sequestered reality' (Clark 1993), with loneliness of dying in the modern society as an absolute reality apprehended in the framework of sociology of death (For example, Elias 1985; Kearl 1989). The polemical understanding of the experiences of death in the contemporary world enables us to find ways forward. One of the many such ways forward is the recognition of plural cultural script of experiencing death and dying.

A validity of pluralism summons a return to the anthropological accounts of death in various cultural contexts. In the anthropological literatures, the cultural imagination of dying has been largely captured through the performed rituals in rites of the passage.[10] These works are fair antitheses to the dead-end of individualized-atomized experience of death as 'sequestered reality' in the postmodern condition. The conventional anthropological account, however, also tends to reduce the phenomenon of death into performance of mediated rituals. Does death also not constitute social philosophy? How do folk express their philosophy, or thoughts, of death? What are those thoughts, the epistemic units of the folk philosophy of death? To turn to the Indian context, there are Indological works dealing with thoughts on death.[11] They derived largely from the classical literature from textual tradition of India to unearth the cosmological imagination of death and the phenomenon of after-life. Needless to say, anthropology and indology in India have shared interest in this regard despite the difference of truth-claims and veracity of materials.[12] But then, it was also delimiting due to the preoccupation with the textual tradition. The fluid relation of text and context, in the folk world view, could not assume centrality in discussions on the cultural imagination of death and dying in India, barring a few exceptions.[13] It becomes challenging indeed to understand the traditional social structure by fathoming the acoustic dimension vis-à-vis folk songs, and arrive at the folk notions of living and dying. It is imperative while doing so to not fall prey to the conceptual divides such as folk and classical, folk and popular, and in short Little tradition and Great tradition. Instead, one has to operate by viewing tradition as an integrated whole in which intermixing brings about paradoxes even as the belief system still remains intact.

The conventional way of studying tradition has been prepossessed with the notion of order and disorder. Everything that belonged to tradition has been looked at with the objective of discovering the structure of order, and how disorder is avoided or coped with in a traditional society. Studying death meant understanding the issue of order and disorder. While it is a valid concern of a study on traditional society, it somewhere lost the basic prerequisite to understand the inherently fluid structure of traditional societies. Let alone the dynamics of day-to-day social relations and occurrences, the studies on traditional society and of meanings did not move away from the classical/Sanskritic texts and the social exotica of rites and rituals. The prepossession with the issue of order and disorder vis-à-vis the phenomenon of death and dying in traditional society has reached a stage whereby sociologists perceive a modern society where death is a sequestered reality and dying is a lonely act. In this light, it is significant to notice the recurrence of traditional notions of death and dying in the folk society in modern times, where doctors are an important part in the folk society. But the modern-medical injunctions are almost same as the classical-textual ones, as they are both subject to folklorization. Folk philosophy works in close collaboration with other sources of insights and ideas without compromising on its own accord. Hence, in our times, the study of tradition demands an orientation towards neither modernity nor the traditional elements. The study of tradition could, as an aspired departure in this work, be beyond the binary opposition of conceptual categories. An event in the life cycle finds cultural expressions according to the world view of the folk which may be inclusive of the features of both tradition and modernity or hybrid, or something that is beyond such categorization. The present work intends to discuss 'folk philosophy' vis-à-vis perceptions/

beliefs about life and death as found in narratives within folk songs without simplifying the complex of emotion and participation of both men and women. Moreover, one must emphasize that this research evaluates women's position in the Hindu society on the basis of the songs they sing. As already stated in the beginning, the context of the work is Mithila.

Mooting Maithil Contexts

Mithila and Maithili have been awfully intriguing for ethnologists in colonial India (Burghart 1993). Perhaps the intrigue resonates in the fact that 'Mithila' is more mythical than historical in terms of territory, for it was never a politically demarcated geographical territory, an explicit import in the chapter five that places Mithila in historical framework. It may not go well with the sense of cultural superiority in the prevalent common sense in Mithila that views mythical as opposed to real, and Mithila and Maithili identity as an eternal reality. The claim of eternal reality however solicits a critical discussion which this book offers. This is not to deny the reality, so to say. Instead, the attempt is to substantiate it with the world view of the Maithili speaking people. Perhaps this was one of the reasons why 'speech marks' rather than 'landmarks' are more important to understand Mithila. The heterogeneous composition of the region and its people and language assume importance in this scheme. This also entails an acknowledgement of the peculiarity of social stratification along caste lines within Maithil society. For all ritual purposes, superiority of status lies with the Brahmins. The powerful position in terms of land and property ownership is with the 'forward castes'[14] such as Brahmin, Rajput, Bhumihar, Kayastha, and Bania. The anomalies of caste structure are manifest in Mithila too. Instances of caste violence, marginalization of lower caste, and also caste-based vote-bank politics are regularly reported in newspapers. In the daily encounters too, I have personally come across various modes of humiliation along caste lines. I have heard sayings, which target caste groups, belonging to both forward and backward castes. A famous saying, which was a colonial construct according to hearsay, is: kill a Maithil Brahmin first if you spot both at once, a Maithil Brahmin and a black cobra! The idea is that all the Maithil Brahmins could be more venomous and deadlier than a black cobra. Similarly, there is a saying targeting Kayasthas: *Lala ka bachcha kabhi na sachcha* (a Kayastha is too cunning to be trusted, and if he is trustworthy, it means he is a mixed breed)! This saying is used, replacing Kayastha with Bhumihar, to target the latter too. All these caste groups are apparently upper caste in Bihar in general and in Mithila in particular.[15] There are several such sayings that target lower caste groups as well. One saying blends casteism with racism: a black Brahmin and a fair Chamar is suspicious character! Apart from the deeply entrenched caste hierarchy, the villages in Mithila also exhibit the secondary status of women. Patriarchy underpins the social structure of Mithila society. The line of inheritance and kinship is patrilineal. The notorious line from Tulsidas' *Ramayana* is known and uttered every now and then: *dhol, gamar, shudra, pashu, naari, ye sab hain taran ke haari* (a drum, a rustic, a lower caste man, an animal, and a woman is to be treated with stringent measures). In this wake, combining caste and gender discriminations, Mithila too exhibits the regressive social politics of inclusion and exclusion. In other words, the land of pride and prejudices pertaining to the Maithil common sense is not devoid of the peculiarities of social inequality. If one adds the secondary status of Muslims in contemporary Mithila, the mirror image of the region will perhaps reflect more of the cracks than of the proudly proclaimed 'civilizational harmony'. It hence becomes quite daunting a task to discuss the folk world view of a community. The central question of this book, folk world view, and its philosophical engagement with death and dying, demands a drift away from the familiar 'sociological trope of discussion'. The latter in inverted commas could be significant exploration on some other occasion. However, a brief awareness of it enables this book to hint at the totality of the Maithil world view optimally including caste and gender dimensions. Aware of the socio-political dynamics of the divides along caste, communities, and gender, this book unravels Maithili folk world view of the Hindus. There is, however, a conscious effort to ensure that such an awareness does not eclipse the central objectives. This is a point at which this book may disappoint many of us who hold our sociological sense of social divide as superior to the notions, ideas, and thoughts of the folk. This book indeed restraints from feeding into identity politics, be it of Maithil Brahmins or of the other politico-ethnic groups. To reiterate, this is not to suggest that these are less important issues and it ought not to be erased even in this book.

It is important that the heterogeneous constitution of the Maithil, Mithila, and Maithili precedes the discussion on Maithili folk songs in this book. It is in this scheme that the book factors in the intermingling of a variety of sects, religious influences, historical encounters, and philosophical transactions in the shaping of the world view. There is also a conscious effort to engage with the idea of the exclusive space of women in the song culture of Mithila. 'The exclusive privilege of women in rendering these songs without any formal training, mainly in terms of creation and recreation of the stories of Sita's marriage, on several occasions, like marriage and other rituals, (which) make the Maithil folk songs distinctive' (Jha 2002: 14). Such an assertion has to be taken with a pinch of salt and therefore the book tends to unravel such claims without undermining the possibility of a space for women. The framework of discussions on the folk songs is not unaware of the larger trope of songs in Mithila. The latter encapsulates songs among the Brahmins, as well as folk songs and ballads among other caste groups, such as the Salhesa songs of the Dusadhs, the Deenabhadri of Musahars, the Loric of Yadavas, the Jat-Jatin of Mallahs, among others. Some of the common found categories of folklore in Bihar (in Mithila in particular) are cumulative songs, non-sense rhymes, pastoral songs, and folk plays. Cumulative songs are various integrated songs, which give an impression of a rhythmically moving tale. Non-sense rhymes are yet another element of folklore of Bihar, which are often used to lull the child in to drowsiness and finally to sleep. Pastoral songs occupy a great deal of space in the folk life. These songs 'express the thoughts, aspirations and sorrow of the villagers' (Roy Chaudhury 1980: 36). Folk plays are not plays in a typical sense. These are often aided by cumulative songs in association with real life performance of the social actors. The example from Maithili folklore is of 'Shama-Chakwa' and 'Bhaiya Duj/Bhardutia (Bhratri Dwitiya)'.

are the characteristics of religious structure in Mithila? What is the nature and scope of interaction between religions and sects intertwined in the sociocultural context of folklore in Mithila? On account of world view in folklore, the question would be with regard to the performance and meaning. How do the folk make sense of their performance, the context and the text that they deliver? What are the coordinates in the meaning-making exercise? What are the avenues of conflict and reconciliation in the making of meaning within world view(s)? All the above stated questions point to the neologism I began with, i.e. folk philosophy. In the context of Maithili folklore, folk philosophy is a confluence of diverse notional categories. It is the operational version of world view that brings about a parallel between their theory and praxis. In other words, what they communicate in their songs, in their crying, and in their practice, characterizes the concept of folk philosophy. It entails numerous folk ideas/ unstated postulates/taken-for-granted assumptions on the basis of which the folk reason with matters of everyday life. It is widely accepted among the various communities of the followers of Hinduism that everything is religious and philosophical. Religious and philosophical aspects of the folk, as articulated in their songs, offer a vast array of meanings, and it figures in the outcome of this work. This book, in a nutshell, aims at the folk philosophy of the Maithili-speaking folk. With these objectives, questions, and hypothetical assumptions the research underpinning this book not only deciphers the narratives within each song, instances of crying, and performances in context, but also seeks for an interpretation and explanation of the folk in the context.

Scheme of the Book

With this introduction on what this book is about, the following essays unfold elaborate accounts on the central issues of the book. The very next essay presents a discursive reflection on the unbecoming of the idea of death. The alleged 'death of death' in contemporary sociology of death emerged in a specific sociocultural context. But the recognition of ambivalent modernity, and the possibility of plural cultural scripts, enables us to further explore the social imagining of death and dying. One of such cultural scripts is folklore in the age of polyphony, discussed in the subsequent essay laying out the prerequisite discursive framework for the whole book. The discursive framework underlines the archaeology of knowledge on folklore, and location of world view, role of folk, and issue of living and dying in the centrestage of folklore. This essay is a thick perusal of literatures, with an irreverence to the notions of pastness and monolith associated with folklore. This is followed by a discussion in the fourth essay on the way the research underpinning this book unfolds in the field. However, this essay defies the conventional ways of discussing methodology by connecting the processes of learning, unlearning, and relearning in a relational framework. This is intended to establish the significance of a dialectic between book view and field view of hermeneutics, for a more thorough idea on 'interpretative understanding'. This entails a synoptic discussion on hermeneutic philosophy to devise the methodology that could help arrive at the folk world view and the folk philosophy of living and dying. The dichotomy between subjectivity and objectivity, the researcher and researched, which has ruled the roost of methodological reflections in social science in general and in sociology in particular, is questioned. A research of this kind warrants this critical orientation, as part of methodological preparation, so as to render the hidden and the obvious in juxtaposition to arrive at the meaning. The second, third, and fourth essays, largely based on the perusal of literature, underline the schematic predisposition of the book characterized by swing between micro-context and macro-questions. It begins to incline more toward the micro-context in the following essay.

The fifth essay questions the three predominant categories of Mithila, Maithil, and Maithili with critical readings of historical accounts to elucidate the broad realm of micro. It is in the background of history with recurrent mythology that the broadness of the notions become clearer. Dispelling the ethnocentric air, without indulging in the never-ending glorification of Mithila or even denigrating the same, this essay discloses the limits of the glorification. Here we get a glimpse of the formation of Maithil pride in a historical as well as mythological context. It also underlines the misplaced Maithili pride, a case of cultural arrogance in the wake of multiple undercurrents. Various religious denominations, nurtured in the historical contexts of Mithila, also express multiplicity of versions, and thus humility rather than arrogance. This essay also reveals the polysemy in the categories of Maithil, the people of the region who belong to various caste groups rather than only the Shrotriya Brahmin, and the pluri-vocal character of the language Maithili, which is not only the chaste (pure Sanskritic) Maithili of the Shrotriya. It is in this broadened framework that the wide ambit of Maithili folk songs makes sense. This essay also establishes the significance of Mithila where the rulers were as much into philosophical, poetic, and artistic vocation as were the courtiers, patronized, and non-patronized scholars. Besides, this essay highlights the missing link in the conventional historiography between the historical accounts based on the deeds of the mighty and the contributions of the unsung ordinary people. This is ironical because the region of Mithila has been described as that of unconventional kingship: any politically ambitious king met with utter failure. The reason why an essay of this kind is significant is mainly three fold:

1. It helps in understanding the inner dynamics of the region vis-à-vis thereof people, socio-religious varieties, stratification, linguistic complexity, and over all the contributions of history and mythology together in the evolution of Mithila;
2. It offers a continuum on the timeline to imagine past and present of the society, thereof people, their religious belief and practices, thereof language and knowledge; and
3. It lays out the context in which the field work in one of the villages of this region can be presented for microscopic analysis. In other words it also bridges the gap between the historical and the sociological.

The sixth and seventh essays zero in on an even more focussed part within the micro-context of Mithila, with the two essay complementing each other in drawing the cultural landscape with sound and sight, and the renditions of songs in the village of Fulhara. The two essays are therefore put as two parts with the same title. They present a descriptive glimpse of the everyday life in the village, the calendar of festivity, and the events in the rites of the passage. They chart the demographic composition, spatial arrangement, main occupations, agricultural as well as otherwise, of the people to render the ethnography into a narrative of pulsating lives. The presentation of songs is peppered with slices of biographies and everyday living as part of the ethnographic details along with the spontaneous interpretation offered by the singers. Through these songs, consisting of innumerable genres, the seventh essay extends the interpretative analysis by connecting the loose threads. The interpretative analysis in this essay aims at drawing the totality of world view. It emerges that the Maithil world view, elucidated in the songs, projects a particular notion of dying and death in the folk context. Hence, the eighth essay specifically discusses this notion, which is conceptualized as art of dying, returning to the creative swing between micro-context and macro-questions. The intent here is to elaborate upon the holistic idea of death, without resorting to the generic binaries often apparent in the common sense. In association with the events of life, the imagination of death involves emotional responses of the people to it. It is not bereft of, what this essay conceptualizes as *emotional truthfulness* of the folk. Thus, the ubiquity of metaphors of death seems to be artistic expressions of the folk connecting living and dying in the rite of the passage. This is where the interplay of emotions, classical categories, and a negotiational process becomes intelligible. In this essay, 'art of dying' thus forges a connection between the special events of life and the ordinary everyday life. In addition to the songs, everyday life conversations aid to the folk philosophy.

The conclusion is an attempt to summarize the book with a proposition that the key thesis of the book emanates with support from significant peripheral expositions, which ought not to be put into oblivion. Also, the conclusion is not drawn in theoretical vacuum. This is evident as the essay tends to place them in the larger, theoretical discourse to make sense of the sociological implications of these findings. The conclusions leave room for further research by stating the futuristic dispositions behind them.

Notes

1. For another version of this tale in which the elderly lady is replaced by Mulla Nasrudin, the famous eccentric thinker, see Doniger 2011: 17. Wendy Doniger's reading of the search of the lost key in the street light (outside) whereas the key was lost in the dark house (inside) questions the divide between insider and outsider. The contact with outsider (foreigner) may be heuristically useful for the insider (native) in the quest of the lost key.

2. A preliminary essay on this note is available elsewhere, see Pathak 2013.

3. This was a song in a musical hit.

4. There are many such songs in popular Hindi cinema expressing engagement with death and dying using melodramatic lyrics.

5. See http://news.webindia123.com/news/articles/India/20130801/2233768.html, accessed 5 January 2017.

6. See http://zeenews.india.com/news/bihar/nitish-kumar-inaugurates-mithila-mahotsav_1562220.html, accessed 5 January 2017.

7. Veena Das, here, refers to the example of strangers in a coffee house from Lévi-Strauss's 1969.

8. See for example, Kakar 1978; Madan 1991, 2006; Srinivas and Shah 1968; Doniger 2011.

9. M.N. Srinivas hints at the potentially distinguishable version of Hinduism, emerging from the practices of the people rather than the ancient texts. It, however, fails doubly to note that Hinduism is not either textual or practical. It may consist of both in perpetual negotiation.

10. The anthropological trope is too thick to be encapsulated, but a few could be quickly mentioned: Gennep 1960; Turner 1969; Hertz 1960a, 1960b; Parry 1981; Vitebsky 1993; or Myerhoff 1984, among so many others.

11. To mention a representative few: Schombucher and Zoller 1999; Filippi 2005; Saraswati 2005, from a fairly huge corpus of published literatures.

12. See Tambiah (1987) and Dumont (1970) on the confluence between Indology and Sociology.

13. Blackburn 1988 is one of the exceptions.

14. I am using the term 'forward caste' in accordance with the general usage among the people of the region, rather than meaning any conceptually clear term, to indicate those caste groups who are socially perceived to be higher in the caste hierarchy, as opposed to the 'backward caste'. Both the groups in question and the perceiving groups share the perception of location in the social hierarchy.

15. This is well recognized in various works such as Sachchidananda and Lal 1980; on the dominant position of Maithil Brahmin in general and Shrotriyas in particular, see Jha 1974, 1977.

16. In this regard the only exception is the collection of songs by Anima Singh (1993), wherein among more than a thousand songs three songs are under the category of *mrityu geet*. I draw attention to the fact that this category of song is conspicuous by absence. The meaning of this absence is twofold—singing in typical form ceases in the face of death, and that ritual wailing substitutes singing.

17. Most of these assumptions are gathered from the respondents in the field. I am using them to support my hypothetical points and research questions. *Nepobhatin* is somewhat akin to *Syapa* in Punjab and *Rudali* in Rajasthan. The institution of *Nepobhatin* is said to be extinct now. But then, social wailing by the kith and kin along with family on the event of death is still prevalent.

2

Living and Dying in the Age of Plural Cultural Scripts

As Gregor Samsa 'awoke' one morning from 'uneasy dreams' he
found himself 'transformed' in his bed into a 'gigantic insect'![1]

—FRANZ KAFKA (1996: 1)

How necessary it is to die each day, to die each minute to
everything, to the many yesterdays and to the moment that
has just gone by! Without death there is no renewing, without
death there is no creation!

—J. KRISHNAMURTI (quoted in Weeraperuma 1996: 38)

An idea has a life as well as death. The idea of death is no exception.
It has a discursive trajectory coming to a stalemate, the death
of death. However, a possibility of the resurrection of the idea
of death exists in the wake of plural cultural scripts. To narrate
the story about the idea of death, its becoming and unbecoming,
this essay does not follow the conventional manner of perusing
literatures. Instead, in the manner of storytelling, it eclectically
connects threads from literatures and common sense. For in
common sense too, we express an aversion to death-related talks.
But it is not a plain aversion. We tend to speak of death as a joy of
the grotesque, much like a conventional anthropologist's fondness
for the exotic. We tend to imagine it with all possible creepiness
as though it were the most bizarre thing in the face of humanity.
This juncture in human consciousness, as well as in the discursive
trajectory, is a cumulative culmination. It has happened through
a vast tract of time, experience, and evolution. But then, every

stalemate could have a possible way out as life is not a plain game of chess. The death of death is not final. This essay humbly posits that the pluralism of cultural scripts could offer a much needed way forward. This is about showing that the idea of death has been a source of cultural imagination in poetry, philosophy, aesthetics, and narratives as much as in social anthropology. So much so that medical practitioners are beginning to admit the significance of the cultural imagination of death (Gawande 2014).

For a provocative start, let us reflect over a common sight revealing our common sense: on the sixtieth birthday, the grand old man announcing to his peers, 'I am only a sixty-year old young man!' It is not merely an announcement. It suggests a way of living, structured by a range of youthful and simulated activities, and a gamut of consumption entailed. The tacit implication is a denial of aging, leave alone dying. Critically reflecting on it, Atul Gawande says, 'when the prevailing fantasy is that we can be ageless, the geriatrician's uncomfortable demand is that we accept we are not' (Ibid.: 46). The bestsellers, visible all over the pavements in the global market, with titles such as 'Younger Next Year', 'The Fountain of Age', 'Ageless', 'The Sexy Years', and many more, allude to the social craving to deny aging.

The political economy of anti-aging, and by implication anti-dying, is revealed in numerous advertisements of products that promise delayed aging or preventive measures against aging. These advertisements—from life insurance to cosmetic products—dwell upon people's fear of aging, and subsequently dying. They capitalize on this fear, and shield it behind the idea of well-being. Is it merely for well-being? This probing question requires a more thorough analysis on another occasion. Suffice to flag that we tend to hail such human attributes, of staying youthful until the inevitable end, due to the negative notions attached to aging and dying. We perceive a sense of heroism in it and we solicit social adulation for the same. This could have qualitative differences along class and gender lines, but despite variations it tends to be a characteristic feature of our disposition. We do not intend to be associated with the morbid ending. This is what has been termed 'death taboo', more stringent than 'sex taboo', in contemporary societies all over the world. These notions have emerged from particular contexts and are hence laced with particularities of cultural imagination.

This essay attempts to eclectically read discursive slices, in the light of the common sense experiences, to discern the (un)becoming of the notion of death and dying in the contemporary world. The objective, as stated earlier, is to see the possibility of resurrection in the wake of plural cultural scripts of death and dying. The attempt is not to exhaustively reproduce the debates on the issue; it seeks instead to pithily narrate the story about the idea of death.

Modernity, Creative Ambivalence, Inter alia

It is almost a truism—albeit a useful one—that every cognitive development draws from the scheme of modernity. Much water has flown in unravelling this scheme. One could briefly surmise about the emergence of binaries and ambivalent disposition from this scheme. Allegedly, these cognitive binaries condition the ideas of living and dying. One perceives the negative in ending, dying, separating; one imagines the positive in living, meeting, starting, continuing. Death thereby (un)becomes a monstrous reality, a spectral entity, and an undesirable eventuality. Modern knowledge system combats it and yet maintains little room to engage with it. After all, modernity is known for inherent ambiguities. I suggest this be read as modernity's 'creative ambivalence' towards death.

Using the metaphors of friends, enemies, and strangers, Z. Bauman deliberated upon the lurking ambivalence in the ambit of modernity. The antinomies, such as negative and positive, friends and enemies, were easier to cope with than the ambiguous entities—the strangers. The modern nation-states attempted to ensure that the officially enforced process of assimilation disarms the strangers. In this wake, as Bauman remarks:

the history of modernity is one of the tensions between social existence and its culture. Modern existences force its culture into opposition to itself. This disharmony is precisely the harmony modernity needs. The history of modernity draws its uncanny and unprecedented dynamism from it. For the same reason, it can be seen as a history of progress: as a natural history of humanity. (Bauman 1990: 166–70)

Seemingly, in Bauman's schema, the ambivalence of modernity unfolds with creative motives. Taking this line further, the present essay employs the notion of creative ambivalence to underline the discursive metamorphosis of death. By the virtue of this ambivalence, there have been attempts to transform death from 'what it is' to 'what it could be'. It suggests that we have sought to accomplish in myriad ways the death of death, and thereby the birth of a sociologized or philosophized notion of death. This is the process, which we propose to call discursive taming of the unwanted-inevitable death. This had led to the lamentation for the 'death of death'. Be it as it may, it enables us to not only fathom the cognitive crises of the modern minds, but explore a possibility of departure from the mode of lamentation.

Uneasy Dream(s) and Transformation(s)

Groping in the dim passage of slumber, Kafka's protagonist (Gregor Samsa in *The Metamorphosis*) encountered many 'uneasy dreams'. So did early human civilization in the slumber of modernity. The uneasy dreams, of existential complexity eventuating into death, have inspired further dreaming—philosophically, mythologically, aesthetically, and anthropologically. There is an abiding aspiration, on the part of those who were having those 'uneasy dreams' and those who were interpreting the same for the modern world, to 'transform' the 'uneasy dreams' into an acceptable narrative. The necessity to know about death arose from existential anxieties, inquisitiveness, and the sociocultural arrangement around it. This stems from a unique paradox of humanity, which has been discussed aplenty by various thinkers, philosophers, psychoanalysts, and, least to say, shamanic visionaries. What is the paradox?

An instance in the epic *Mahabharata* vividly elucidates this paradox. The Pandwa brothers, except Yudhisthira, had refused to answer the questions of Yaksha (god of death) and were cursed to death. Yudhisthira, the eldest brother, answered all the questions, including what is the most striking paradox of humanity. Yudhisthira answered that the most striking paradox is that humans know that death is ultimate truth of life, yet they refuse to believe that it is ultimate truth of their lives! This instance from the epic sets one way of reasoning about death.

There is another way of reasoning, which occurs in the scheme of modernity. E. Becker suggests that the human paradox refers to the knowledge that she/he is unique in the kingdom of species, and simultaneously aware that she/he will die. The awareness of uniqueness, with peculiarly human attributes propels human adventures and the ability to prove oneself. But the simultaneity of the awareness of finitude engenders stoicism. An individual is aware that all the efforts to immortalize oneself could eventually be of little avail. Hence in the paradoxical disposition, there is on the one hand a conviction that one can be master of one's own destiny, and on the other there is a sinking feeling that one cannot escape the end of existence. In this light, Becker agrees with Eric Fromm, 'all human strivings are an attempt to avoid insanity in the face of the contradictions of man's existence, all man's passions are an attempt to relieve the terrible paradox of his nature, the existential dilemma of what we might call his individuality-within-finitude' (Becker 1971: 144–5).

Both ways of engaging with the paradox, pertaining to the epic *Mahabharata* and Becker's insightful reflection, are at the root of the mythological and philosophical approaches. It also influences the sociological and social anthropological reasoning with death. In this regard, on a lighter note, it should be mentioned that the possible advent of the idea of death also underpins a paradox. James Frazer noted that the divine messenger committed an error in delivering the right message to the humans awaiting a confirmation of immortality, 'Death came into the world because of the mistake made by the messenger bearing the gift of deathlessness, who either garbled the message out of forgetfulness or malice or did not arrive on time' (quoted in Choron 1963: 14).

Consequently, mortality was the fait accompli of human beings while the mythological windmill has been producing multiple narratives to soothe the troubled souls, or to engender a convincing cosmological explanation about the inevitable endings. Through these mythological instances humanity has been approaching the question of death and its inevitability.

If it is inevitable, how to make it more liveable? This is where a host of imageries, tales, and legends from mythology become crucial components in the world view, a sacred canopy (Berger

1990). There is a curious coincidence here: the advent of the early human imagination of death and dying occurs in this sociocultural scheme of cosmology, and on the other hand social anthropologists, traversing the terrain marked by sociocultural cosmology and socio-religious eschatology, begin to decipher the same. Reading between the lines, one could suggest that the social anthropological attempts aimed at solving the enigma of death for modern humanity in industrial society. Death assumed the notion of a socially functional event in these significant endeavours. Be it for regenerating 'solidarity' or 'sacred', or reaffirming 'communitas', an imagination of death through mortuary and piacular rituals involved significant transformations (Durkheim 2008; Turner 1969; Gennep 1960). The latter implies interpretative politics of the functionalist sociological studies of the phenomenon of death. It amounted to a reasoning with death that was appropriate for the society.

In this regard, it is worth paraphrasing one instance of the social imagination of death, configured through the functionalist scheme. B. Malinowski's detailed examination of the release and relocation of *baloma* among the Kiriwina in the Trobriand Island is typical of the functionalist scheme. *Baloma* is the spirit released by the body of a person who dies. The mortuary rites are aimed at helping a smooth passage of exit, an acknowledgement of the dislocated spirit and hence due propitiation of the soul, and finally a relocation in the sacred domain beyond the sociocultural sphere. This new location of *baloma* is imagined after the image of society. The body may end after releasing *baloma*, but what persists is the recognition of the individual through an invocation of *baloma* on all the ceremonial occasions. It means that the ancestral spirit descends on all auspicious occasions to bless the living. *Baloma* can attain rebirth too. In this scheme of interpretation, of the Kiriwina as well as of Malinowski, the pain and suffering of death and dying are transformed into a socially functional prerequisite. As Malinowski notes:

Death affects the deceased individual; his soul (baloma or balom) leaves the body and goes to another world, there to lead a shadowy existence. His passing is also a concern to the bereft community. Its members wail for him, mourn for him, and celebrate an endless series of feasts . . . but these social activities and ceremonies have no connection with the spirit. They are not performed, either to send a message of love and regret to the baloma (spirit), or to deter him from returning; they do not influence his welfare, nor do they affect his relation to the survivors. (Malinowski 1916: 353–4)

As evident, Malinowski tends to discern social, and needless to say sociological, significance of the activities around the released soul, *baloma*. This is achieved by the way of according the sociocultural structuring to death and post-death enactments of rituals priority over the individuated experiences of horror, mourning, and the sense of irredeemable loss. Despite the inherent limitations, it aids in convincing of a possible sociocultural imagination of death, mostly in relation with society and community after death. This is the focus of the predominant paradigm of comprehending death in social anthropology. As has been adequately recognized, the primitive imagination of death and cosmological arrangement hinges on the notion of cyclical time. Similarly, R. Hertz (1960), following the fundamentals of the Durkheimian sociology, narrated the release of human soul from finite body to a domain which society imagines as its own replica. Hence, the social rules of left hand and right hand corresponding with the performance of negative and positive rights become unimpeachable.[2]

The harbinger of change in the imagination of death descends when the notion of time changes. It arguably impacts not only the world view of people but also the schemes of the interpreters— in philosophy as well as in sociology. The change is not without continuity. For instance, the influence of the primitive-mythological idea of death causing the release of spirit from the entrapment of the body does not disappear altogether even in the wake of the advent of scientific epistemology. The prophetic proclamation of Socrates for his pupil, which Xenophanes represented in his report on Socrates' trial was, 'Have you not known all along that from the moment of my birth nature has condemned me to death?' Furthermore, Socrates attempts to soothe his beleaguered pupils by suggesting that death would only bring about liberation from the body. This does not change even in the Cartesian scheme, yielding a curious sense of ambivalence. On the one hand, Descartes would plead for the supreme ability of cogito in relation with intellect to arrive at truth. This would dismiss the sensuous body as a source of spurious feelings, an impediment in the pursuit of knowledge. This is a key characteristic of the scientific epistemology that emerges from the Cartesian philosophical scheme. On the other hand, while thinking about death, Descartes would suggest that the 'heat of body', ubiquitously present in all the bodily organs, releases upon death. The whole of the body, without the divide between sensuous body and capable mind, is entailed in the phenomenon of death. And as Choron would suggest, this is what sets the tone for modern philosophical postulates on death. A dispositional ambivalence could, arguably, give way to the primitive-mythological imagination of the release of *baloma*, or Cartesian heat of body, or Brahminic *aatma*, upon the occurrence of death. However, it was not devoid of the scepticism and stoicism that emerged in the body of Western philosophy. And the major epistemological shift, as it were, has been associated with the changing notion of time. 'Not until linear time replaced cyclical time did every event received the character of uniqueness and of unrepeatability, and it is its combination with the already dawning individualization of the members of the primitive group that makes death appear as a real threat' (Choron 1963: 25).

With the change of the notion of time, an idea that death could be a source of total annihilation dawns upon human imagination. The terror of finitude and the futility of life brings a self-reflective Tolstoy (1987) back to the idea of faith that is amicable to the modern sense of rationality. Curiously enough, faith for Tolstoy is not the same as belief configured in the Durkheimian sociology of religion or in the functionalist scheme of ritual performances. This is a rediscovered faith by a modern-independent mind out of a sheer imperative to understand the significance of living, if any, in the face of inevitable dying. In other words, this shows the juncture in the trajectory of imagining death where necessity to engage with death, without illusions/make-believe and mythology, assumes preponderance. It reminds one of an insightful rumination by Max Weber on the significance of death for men who died old and satiated, 'Whereas civilized man, placed in the midst of the continuous enrichment of culture by ideas, knowledge and problems, may become "tired of life" but not "satiated by life"

. . . and because death is meaningless, civilized life as such is meaningless' (1970: 140).

The divide of the meaningful past wherein humans were 'satiated by life' and meaningless present wherein humans are 'tired of life', determined the novelty of imagining death and dying. This, once again, disclosed the sociological imperative to find a way for modern humans in industrial society to deal with the phenomenon of death. However, there was a caution against returning to the primitive imagination, and mythological refuge. One could delve into the reservoir of existentialist philosophy and substantiate this further. One representative thinker, G. Bataille, adequately engaging with the issue of death reframed the old issue, 'We cannot escape our desire to be everything, to identify with the entirety of universe. The wish to surpass our limited existence may be satisfied in numerous ways—among them there is the illusion of never dying, or the wish to be read and esteemed as an author' (1988: xi).

Furthermore, it seeks to de-intoxicate oneself, freeing from the illusions of the mythological-cyclical appearance of life. It evokes the idea of being aware and suffering the gradual decay of the body until its total annihilation.

An acceptance of the inevitability of death comes with an inherent scepticism towards the mythological stance and of imagining death in a cyclical sense. And 'with the realization that death is total annihilation, man's discovery of death becomes complete, the sense of the futility of life overwhelms man with unprecedented force' (Choron 1963: 25). It is in this wake that Bataille seeks for an individuated reinvention of the 'sacred' (1988: 53), of living and dying, of inner experiences without taking refuge to the mythological idea or conventional romanticism. The notion of sacred, akin to Tolstoy's notion of faith, solicits a great deal of human ability to suffer rather than escape the inherent pathos, agonies, and shock of death and dying. The human ability to suffer requires having faith in the sacredness of human existence, profound experiences, and the significance of living and dying. This is the juncture at which creative ambivalence towards death solicits an individual's imagination rather than of collective-communal and religio-mythological imagination.

The above narrative reflects on the various ways of transforming death into an acceptable entity. They are the philosophical ambivalence, which retains the mythological idea of the release of the infinite from the finite body; the anthropological attempts to transform death into a socially functional phenomenon; and the literary-philosophical attempts to transform it into an entity without mythological-cosmological explanations. It also shows the effect of creative ambivalence toward death, either within, what P. Berger (1990) called 'sacred canopy', or without it. The 'sacred canopy', which alludes to the world view and its religious-spiritual dispositions, aided in imagining and transforming death into primitive-mythological as well as philosophical imaginings. The decline of the sacred canopy in modern philosophy and the urge of individuals to find a way of coping with death in its fulsome manifestation is followed by another instance of transformation. The notion of death does not prefigure in the sociocultural framework alone. Death now appears in conjunction with industry, market, culture, and society at once. This is the imagination of death, fraught with the connotation of denial, in a society which has been amply characterized as a 'risk society'. In this wake:

Classical distinctions merge into greater or lesser degrees of risk: Risk functions like an acid bath in which venerable classical distinctions are dissolved. Within the horizon of risk, the 'binary coding'—permitted or forbidden, legal or illegal, right or wrong, us and them—does not exist. Within the horizon of risk, people are not either good or evil but only more or less risky. Everyone poses more or less of a risk for everyone else. The qualitative distinction either/or is replaced by the quantitative difference between more or less. Nobody is not a risk—to repeat, everyone poses more or less of a risk for everyone else. (Ulrich 2009)

The discursive life of the idea of death gathers a different kind of momentum, arising from the recognition of the newly discovered maladies in a society where ontological security has been transformed. To be precise, the traditional ontological security pertaining to the sacred canopy has been replaced by a new system of ontological security pertaining to market, industry, medicine, inter alia.

'Gigantic Insect', Death Denial, and Ways Forward

For the sake of the temperament of storytelling, it is imperative to return to the Kafkaesque imagination. The protagonist(s) woke up, after having an array of disturbing dreams. Those dreams were sufficiently interpreted. But then, a new crisis was afoot. It was the metamorphosis of an entity into an unrecognizable beast indicating an unbecoming of death. What to do with the beast? It is not a mere bad dream, which could be interpreted and the dreamer could be calmed. The social response, thus, is to deny it, sweep it under the carpet, and hide it in a closet, just like Kafka's protagonist tries to hide himself in the bedroom. The epistemological taming of the phenomenon of death culminates into what has been discursively called a 'denial of death'. It alludes to our common practices of hiding death, or diseases leading to death, or even aging that has become a quasi-disease in the late modernity. The lifting up of one kind of system of 'ontological security' (Clark 1993: 15), mostly conjured by the sacred canopy, leaves the dying or the bereaving without many moorings whatsoever. For:

(t)he effectiveness of a religious antidote to death (that is, the cogency of religiously founded meanings of life) is not a simple function of the determination, ingenuity and acumen of its prophets, codifiers, preachers and vigilantes. It depends closely on the type of society, which it addresses, and the human experience prevalent in that type. For most of human history, up to the rise of the type of society and the kind of human experience which came to be known as 'modern', the timelessness of the religious message chimed well with the stagnant, self-repetitive life routine. (Bauman 1992: 91)

The timelessness of the religious message has dissipated and so has that of the human soul. The new social situation solicits a reinvention of mortality and immortality, which does not depend upon the timeless notion of the soul. In this wake, many other factors assume significance, primarily in the framework of late modernity, which promises yet another variety of ontological security. The metanarrative(s) of modernity, with a pluralism of factors, is the only refuge in this wake. The medical institutions, a wide range of medical professionals, drug industry, insurance market, etc., are the newfound coordinates for imagining death. However, in a confessional tenor, a sociologist of death suggests:

The more diverse are the approaches to death in modern societies, the more difficult it becomes to contain it within a communally-accepted framework, and thus the limit the existential anxiety it potentially offers to the individual. The apparent cultural diversity and flexibility in modern approaches to death can be explained as being consistent with the sequestration of death from public space into the realm of personal. (Clark 1993: 19)

The privatization of the experience of death, dying, and bereavement has been a constant refrain in the contemporary sociology of death. Needless to say, these experiences, discussed in the available literatures, arise from Euro-American contexts. But they all point towards an ultimate manifestation of creative ambivalence towards death—death denial. All the energies of individuals, with the tools and techniques purchased from market, are to render death invisible. Crichton suggests:

In Australia, for instance, there are strict rules about transporting coffins: they must be placed in boxes or wrapped in heavy protective paper, and outside must be marked with the sign of an empty champagne bottle so that nobody will know that they are coffins. In America the funeral industry makes great endeavors to ensure that a corpse does not look as though it is dead. (1976: 12)

In the same vein, P. Aries (1974) argues that people do not get to see death in modern society in its magnanimity, and hence, have little socio-psychological arrangement to cope with death. This becomes even more intense with atrophied death rituals in modern society causing the prolongation of melancholia and a failure to regenerate—in a functional sense—the social order. It is in this wake that loneliness becomes an essential accompaniment of aging and dying. J. Baudrillard suggests that death has been thrown out of the symbolic system and ceases to exist in the sense that nobody really imagines it in elaborate details. As though it were a 'pornography of death', it is hidden away in the private chambers/ wards of hospitals, 'To be dead is an unthinkable anomaly; nothing else is as offensive as this. Death is a delinquency, and an incurable deviancy. The dead are no longer even packed in and shut up, but obliterated' (2011: 126).

And in the continuum it appears that aging too becomes an anathema, and hence to be eliminated from the sociocultural scheme.

Since the discovery of death (and the state of having discovered death is the defining, and distinctive, feature of humanity) human societies have kept designing elaborate subterfuges, hoping that they would be allowed to forget about the scandal; failing that, hoping that they could afford not to think about it; failing that, they forbade speaking of it. (Bauman 1992: 15)

To make it gorier, Bauman depicts the pre-modern and modern scenarios with the imagery of cannibalistic practice: tribes ate up their dead enemies with the logic to incorporate their enemies' lives into the life of the living victors, but modern people spew them out by designating them as the other, deemed separate from the living. It is in this sense that humanity seeks to invent new notions of immortality, in liaison with the market and professional experts, in relation with consumerist practices of devouring in the here and now. In the contemporary social situation, and this means a comparative view with the pre-modern condition in mind, it is impossible to tame death. The taming of death in the pre-modern sociocultural situation did not mean ignorance of the fear and shock of death. It suggested a possibility of encountering it, negotiating with it, and imaginatively transforming it. Such a taming is not possible in the contemporary milieu for a variety of reasons—a linear sense of time, replacement of the sociocultural by market-based agencies, and consumerist practices among others. While Bauman notes it as absurdity determining immortality/ mortality, there are a few who celebrate it. In an uncanny attempt to underline merit in the techno-market driven arrangement for death and dying, C. Seale suggests that there is a newfound optimism about death in late modernity. Arguably, 'Medicine and systems of social security, then, provide people with many of the comforts previously only available through religious belief since, like religion, they help to contain anxieties about the future' (1998: 4–5). It furthermore attempts to imagine the 'imagined community'[3] invisibly coalesced by the various insurance agencies, advertisements about health and hygiene, services for dying and bereaving, popular media, and the like.

To understand the vulgarity and implausibility of this optimism, it is imperative to turn to Bauman once again:

Eschatology has been successfully dissolved in technology. It is 'how to do it', not 'what to do', on which the survival concerns now focus; not what is to be done, but 'how well' it has been done, is the measure of each episode in which the struggle for survival now splits. Transcendence of mortality has been replaced with the mind-and-energy-consuming task of transcending the technical capacity of living. This is a triumph of mundane life-size instrumentality over metaphysical purpose inscribed in eternity. (Ibid.: 141)

Given the near Kafkaesque (un)becoming of death, excruciatingly privatized and individuated with the aids of secular agencies of medicine and market, it seems relevant to revisit Illich's thesis. Ivan Illich stressed that death has become a commodity, a fetish in the form of what the bourgeoisie called 'natural death'. What is natural death? It is the imagined end, which comes to a person when the person is hale and hearty, at their job, and is quietly put to sleep by the blow of death. No pain, no suffering, no volte-face involved in this bourgeoisie imagination of death; indeed it is a 'happy death', devoid of the essential pain and suffering. Illich further suggests that this notion of natural, qua happy death, arises from clinical, social, and cultural iatrogenesis, the over-determinacy of the biomedicine as it were. The dominant medical metanarrative disabled humans at various levels: it attached negative connotations to the idea of aging, suffering, and dying, it rendered the sociocultural arrangement for coping with death and dying into secondary or worse, inferior status. In this wake, 'People die when the electroencephalogram indicates that their brain waves have flattened out: they do not take a last breath, or die because their heart stops. Socially approved death happens when man has become useless not only as a producer but also as a consumer' (Illich 1977: 206).

Mechanical death has seemingly conquered all other forms of death; the variety of cultural scripts have become redundant or have been looked at with suspicion, and suffering is thereby either an illusion of romantics or a superstitious entity.

It is not far-fetched to suggest that the imagination of death, propelled by a creative ambivalence towards it, has reached the limit of transforming death from what it is to what it could be.

This brings us back to the imagery from the opening line of Kafka's novella. The initial discursive tendency was aided by 'uneasy dreams' of the horrific and inevitable ending. It was crucial in the primitive imagination as well as in the creative engagement with death in philosophy, poetry, aesthetics, and social anthropology. However, the sceptic engagement with death tore away the manifold subterfuges—what was left was a bare experience of death. Only able-minded humans could cope with it, by duly suffering the tyranny of finitude. Curiously enough, this ends with a stalemate whereby death denial is seemingly the only way to deal with death. Death does remain a haunting idea, felt and coped with only privately.

Conclusion: Auguries for Further Quest

It is to be reiterated that the above argumentative trope consists of the peculiarity of cultural contexts. To be precise, it bears the germs of Eurocentric reasoning, and hence thrives on only one side of common sense. The history of modernity is not devoid of appeals for the pluralism of many scripts.

In this wake, Göran Therborn makes sense when he suggests that modernity, in 'non-Eurocentric sense, entails several different, competing master narratives, different social forces of, and conflicts between, modernity and anti-modernity, and different cultural contextualization of the past–future contrast. But these different varieties do not simply coexist and challenge each other, they are entangled with each other in various ways' (2003: 293).

This warrants making a quick note of the possibility of plural cultural scripts. It is imperative to turn to non-European contexts and its intellectual resources, particularly at the time when the imagination of death and dying has met with a potential dead end vis-à-vis a denial of death. In this scheme, this essay turns to the Indian context where various narratives contain a surplus of reasoning with death. A brief glimpse of the variety of narratives could be obtained by taking note of traditions as a process rather than as a finished product. That is the scheme in which the RgVedic hymn could be juxtaposed with a Kannada folk proverb in the cultural landscape of India, 'The Rg Vedic hymn: (To the dead man) May your eye go to the sun, your life's breath to the wind. Go to the sky or to earth, as is your nature; or to the waters, if that is your fate. Take root in the plants with your limbs' (Dharwadker 1999: 83).

A Kannada proverb, 'The one who eats once a day is a yogi; the one who eats twice a day is a bhogi (enjoyer); the one who eats thrice a day is a rogi (sick man); and the once who eats four times a day- take him away to the burial ground.'

The two instances from A.K. Ramanujan's compendium pave the way to propose that the sociocultural imagination of death and dying traverses various tropes—the cosmological, eschatological, and the ordinary-mundane. This is also explicated in the exhaustive poetic terrain. The Tamil classical poetry, classified in *akam-puram*, inside and outside, systematically captures living, loving, and dying. Furthermore, there is a possibility of unearthing a cultural engagement with death in the saint-poet tradition too. Ever since Prince Siddhartha's anguish about the sick, aged, and dying and his becoming of Buddha, there has been a bewildering variety of saintly-poetic deliberation on death. A long list would include Kabir, Basava, Mahadevi, Vallabha, and many others in the Bhakti tradition (see Schomer and McLeod 1987). At the risk of a little oversimplification, they all attempted to reconfigure death and dying in juxtaposition with moments of life through the notions of bhakti (broadly meaning devotion). Similarly, the 'divine love' of transcendental devotion in Sufism presents conjunctions of living and dying through a variety of metaphors (Green 2012). Death continues to appear as an issue of poetic engagement in Persian and Urdu poetry too. Names of the poets such as Mir, Dard, Ghalib, Shah Zafar, Momin, Dagh, among others frequently appear for poetry about death, dying, and the ultimate physical demise. One could perhaps recall, for example, Mirza Ghalib from the anthology of Persian/Urdu poetry, and particularly the couplet, *Quaid-e-hayat, Band-o-Gham, Asal me dono ek hain; Maut se pehle admi gham se nizat paye kyun* (the prison of life and the chains of pathos are akin; no riddance as such before one dies indeed). And Nazeer Akbarabadi's *Banjara Nama*[3] is famous for the poem *Sab thaath pada rah jayega jab laad chalega banjara* (everything will stay still behind, when the wanderer will depart) puts the motif of dying succinctly. Furthermore, the history of modern poetry in Hindi reflects a sustained creative engagement with the idea of death. Names of the poets such as Sachchidananda Vatsyayan Agyeya, Gajanan Madhav 'Muktibodh', Kunwar 'Bechain' to name a few, surface. Agyeya's *Ur chal haril liye haath me yahi akela ochha tinka* (take a flight holding the tiny straw)[5] presents a testimonial for the interface of living and dying. One may also add that there were many social thinkers in modern India who ruminated on death and dying. They were hailed as exemplars (Shah 1990), opposed to ideologues, in the sense that they did not only theorize but also practised their ideas. It is in this scheme of modern thinking on death and dying that names of Sri Aurobindo, Mohandas Gandhi, Rabindranath Tagore, J. Krishnamurti, and many others surface frequently in academic discussions in India.

The many ways of engaging with death and dying seems befitting the socio-religious backdrop. Myriad religious traditions have a great deal to offer on the idea of death and dying in the region of South Asia. It is, therefore, not surprising that the cultural imagination of death and dying is a refrain in popular musical and cinematic constructions too. The vast domain of popular culture reinforces the traditional imaginations. For example, Kabir becomes cotemporary with Kumar Gandharva's classical rendition of *Ud jayega hans akela* (the swan will fly alone eventually).[6] Or the Sufi notions assume the significance of popular lore with Nusrat Fateh Ali Khan's renditions. Popular cinema too has played a role in the perpetuity of cultural imagination of death and dying. Anand, the protagonist in the film *Anand*, is appropriate in this frame when he sings along the seashore: *zindagi kaisi hai paheli haaye, kabhi to hansaye, kabhi ye rulaye* (such an enigma called life, it makes one smile, and it makes one cry)! (Mukherjee 1971).

To surmise, the sociocultural framework tends to place living and dying in an interaction whereby fear of aging, suffering, and dying as well as a self-reflexive acceptance seems plausible. These auguries, emanating from the cultural landscape of India, solicit more detailed explorations on some other occasion. Suffice to say, the pluralism of cultural scripts ought to be juxtaposed with the discursive trajectory, which this essay has succinctly sought to explore. And this enables for further exploration along a particular part of cultural script, i.e. Maithili folk songs.

Notes

1. The inverted commas are added to highlight the crucial components in the opening line of Franz Kafka's novella; awoke, uneasy dreams, transformed, gigantic insect, are incidentally motives in the discourse that this essay seeks to generate.

2. This is worth noting that anthropological works on death, through mortuary rituals, in India have been preoccupied with the material aspects of ritual performances as well as the classical Sanskrit texts. The predominance of the Sanskrit texts was in continuum with the relation of social anthropology with Indology. See Perry (1981); Marriott (1990); and Das (1987), for example. The objective is not to offer an exhaustive perusal but to engender a synoptic view of the predominant way of thinking.

3. Elsewhere Chatterjee (1991) has eloquently posed a question to Anderson's thesis: Whose Imagined community!

4. A personal communication with Dr Irfanullah Farooqi aided in understanding the engagement with death in the Urdu poetry. See for a rendition of Akbarbadi's poem, see https://www.youtube.com/watch?v=R7DyYAr-5VY, accessed 4 April 2017.

5. See http://kavitakosh.org, accessed 4 April 2017.

6. See https://www.youtube.com/watch?v=kY2k0JcfByg, 4 April 2017.

3

Discursive Framework:
Probing Folk and Seeking Lore
in the Time of Polyphony

An utterance of the term folklore conjures a curious sense of a
disappearing pristine entity from the past. One grows nostalgic
and invariably begins a liturgy of lament. This is what seems
dominant in the SAARC (South Asian Association of Regional
Cooperation) version of South Asia and its culture. The approach
of SAARC Cultural Centre's intellectual mouthpiece, a journal
named *SAARC Culture*, to the question of folklore largely
resonates this sentiment. A special issue of the journal bemoans in
its title: 'Diminishing Cultures in South Asia!'[1] It seems impossible
in the predominant discourse to think of folklore in the scheme
of contemporary myth-making, singing and sharing, narrating,
and circulating. It is disturbing to think of folklore in terms of
the past—about to be forgotten, exotic, and thus a thing for
heritage, grotesque and hence to be placed safely in a museum!
It is imperative to unravel the possibility of contemporariness
in folklore, and also the complex undercurrents of approaches
to folklore. This solicits a discursive dissection of the becoming
of folklore studies in general and of interest in folklore in India
in particular. The following essay does a partial archaeology of
folklore with an appropriate focus on the region of South Asia,
specifically India dwelling upon the corpus of available literature.
Such a critical engagement seems essential, an intellectual
preparedness for a thorough engagement with Mithila, Maithili,
and Maithil. By doing so, this essay aids in underlining the cardinal

presence of the category of world view and its emotional and cognitive constitutions in folklore. The question of death surfaces as a leitmotif in this discursive framework. And thereby, this essay paves the pathways for a sonic anthropology of death, rather than the conventional ritual performance based anthropological approach to the same.

Issues at Inception and Beyond

Recalling the Kannada folktale from the introductory essay, we find that folklore studies since its inception has been preoccupied with 'street lights'.[2] A little too much of dependence on the classical and modern sources of information, a kind of predetermination, led to what R.M. Dorson (1978) has called the quest for the hidden, forgotten, and backward, bound by exoticism, romanticism, and evolutionism. Folklore was considered a preoccupation of primitive people, signifying an epoch of savagery. In the nineteenth century, synonyms of folklore such as 'bygones, popular antiquities, and survivals' figured frequently. Still later, Dorsan suggests that terms such as simple, unspoiled, pastoral, and close to nature viewed them in nobler light. Whether admired or despised, the folk represented a world different from the centres of power, wealth, progress, and industrial, intellectual, and political activity in the metropolis. In the late-eighteenth-century Germany, philosopher and poet Johann Gottfried Herder called for volunteers to collect what he called 'songs of the people'. Jacob Grimm and Wilhelm Grimm responded to this call and began to enrich the treasure. Brothers Grimm popularized the intellectual value of folklores. Their examples and concepts inspired nascent folklorists in other European countries to emulate their models of collecting and interpreting folk traditions as an emblem of people's proud antiquities. As a ripple effect, John Brand in 1777 in England titled his miscellany of notions, customs, and practices 'Observations on Popular Antiquities'. Many antiquarians in England followed this trend and Europe was inclined towards this new-found vogue. By 1846, another antiquarian, John Thomas, perceived in Brand's accumulated mass of folk materials the subject matter of a separate branch of learning, which he proposed to call 'folklore—the lore of the people'. Like the term 'popular antiquities', the new term too stressed on the notion of pastness. The classic cliché of the folkloric enterprise was, Dorsan notes, 'The old traditions and rites are disappearing; hurry up and collect them as fast as you can' (Ibid.: 13).

There have been rivalling echoes of the death of folklore, a diminishing of cultures in the wake of modernity. Max Müller propounded the concept of the 'disease of language' according to which in the mythopoeic age of the Aryan race men forgot the original meanings of the words and used them metaphorically.[3] E.B. Tylor formulated his doctrine of survivals according to which the folklore of today represents the survivals of animistic thinking of humankind. Apart from seasoned philologists and ethnologists, many contributors to the survivalist theory were also British colonial administrators, their wives and daughters who explored about peasants in India and tribesmen in Africa. Interestingly, the survivalist assumptions, Dorsan informs us, were coupled with romanticism in American folkloric approaches. The romantic view associated with an evolutionary understanding is at the base of Cecil Sharp's folklore studies. In the first issue of the *Journal of American Folklore* in 1888, William Wells Newell echoed the very same European concepts by restricting folklore to the past, as illiterate and oral. American anthropological folklorists, under the influence of Franz Boas, continued with the historical approach that presupposed folklore as a 'people's autobiographical ethnography' located in the past, to be fathomed with the help of given text, in search of origin.[4]

Allen Dundes (1961) argues that this tendency ignored the fact that folklore entails a present as well, which is exhibited in the context where it is performed. For literary and anthropological folklorists, 'folklore has been thought to be ruled by laws which operated independent of individuals. In theory, one could discover these laws and mechanics without reference to the humans who were subject to them' (Ibid.: 243). A recognition of context renders folklore broad and alive despite potential changes in form and content. This is a line of proposition that is central in this essay. According to Dorson, there are two sides to the historical development of folkloric studies:

Folklore studies have been associated from their beginning with antiquities and 'primitive' country folk. But another side of the story depicts folklore studies in quite a different light, presents them as contemporary, keyed to the here and now, to urban centers, to the industrial revolution, to the issues and philosophies of the day. (1978: 23)

Hence folklore, even though being a prerogative of the folk, need not apply exclusively to the country folk (peasantry and rural masses), but rather signifies the anonymous mass of tradition-oriented people. The 'contemporaneity'[5] as opposed to the antiquity of folklore is the latest development in the folklore studies (Dorsan 1973). Dorsan also reckons the presence and prevalence of 'fakelore' in urban centres (1963). Fakelore are artistic creations in the age of mechanical reproduction, which unlike folklore have great finesse and are pleasing to the audience. They do not belong to folk, but sound like folklore. Many of the recorded songs in vernacular languages popularized by the cassette culture belong to the domain of fakelore. Whether fakelore has any implication whatsoever for folklore is another issue worth probing on some other occasion.

Indian folklorist A.K. Ramanujan also targets exoticism and romanticism in the conceptual formulation of folklore studies. The sharp distinction between *marga* (classical) and *desi* (folk) or between great tradition of the reflective many and little tradition of unreflective and anonymous lot is misleading. When cultural performances are looked as texts, says Ramanujan, 'we need to modify terms such as "great tradition" and "little tradition", and to see all these cultural performances as transitive series, a "scale of forms" responding to another, engaged in continuous and dynamic dialogic relations' (1991a: xviii). In this way texts are also contexts and pretexts for other texts. This scheme puts the classical, folk, and popular on an interacting continuum, bridging the conceptual divides of folklore and fakelore. Hence, one cannot approve of the line of difference between literate and non-literate pertaining to the attachment with folklore. Ramanujan argues, 'In a largely non-literate culture, everyone—whether rich or poor, high caste or low, professor, pundit or ignoramus, engineer or street hawker—has inside him a largely non-literate subcontinent' (Ibid.: xiv). And in this line of argument, none of the societies is without connection with a non-literate past. Jawaharlal Handoo (1999) goes to the extent of tracing many methods of mass-mobilizations to folk culture, marking the pervasiveness of folklore even in literate societies. The study of folklore in India began with an evolutionary stance, largely due to vested interests.[6] One of those was to rationalize colonialism and the civilizing mission in the colonies (see for example, Dorson 1966; Raheja and Gold 1994; Blackburn 2003). Guy Poitevin (2003) talks about the superstitions, beliefs, and practices of tribes and low castes and the elaborate rituals of the twice-born as the 'empire theory of folklore'. The empire theory classified folklore in a colony as indigenous knowledge that disabled the cognitive abilities of the natives. R. Carnac and W. Crook were the pioneers among the British officers, civil servants, scholars, civilians, and foreign missionaries who assumed the role of folklorists in the last decade of the nineteenth century in India. George Campbell, an ethnologist and later the governor of Bengal (1871–4) was a vocal proponent of this and requested The Asiatic Society to add an 'exhibition of aborigines' in the agricultural exhibition where the specimen of tribes would sit in a demarcated space. The English visitors would converse with the specimen of aborigines on exhibit and photograph them. The colonial construction of the other, the folk, entailed exhibitionist and classificatory motives, and had an underpinning evolutionary logic (Prakash 2000; Chatterji 2003). Some of the native folklorists continued with the colonial schema, especially with regard to the respect for the Brahminic perspective and practices. Pundit Ram Naresh Tripathi and Shiv Sahay Chaturvedi, followers of Mahatma Gandhi and champions of upper caste views, echoed such a stance through the magazine *Braj Bharat* published by the Braj Bhasha Academy in 1940.[7]

The colonial folkloric ventures were carried out under the anthropological instructions on scientific methods. These methods were devised on the Cartesian philosophical tenets, which eventually resulted in to the construction of the 'Orient'. In agreement with Edward Said, Handoo says that the 'Orient' was seen as fixed texts. He elaborates:

it was also felt that by doing so, it would be useful for understanding the past, present and perhaps, the future of mankind and will thus accelerate the process of transformation of these primitive societies and usher them in the world of the civilized. (1999: 2)

Dynamics of Folklore

While the empire theory of folklore in colonial India narrates the folk becoming the other, it also underlines the dynamic characteristics of folklore. As a counterargument to the pastness of folklore, Roma Chatterji (2003), in agreement with Dundes, offers a novel perspective.[8] In any temporal sphere there is a shared expressive tradition qua folklore. It manifests on the occasion of sentimental-ideological mobilization of the masses. Chatterji tends to believe that the very archaicness of folk vis-à-vis community life, the sentimental bent and oneness has been instrumental in whipping up the sense of nationalism among people under political leadership. She says, '. . . in the nationalistic discourse the term folk carries the connotations of primordial essence and is seen as the expression of an unselfconscious and timeless community life' (Ibid.: 568).

By the frequent use of the folk categories, a curious process of 'mythicisation'[9] occurs. This renders the leadership extraordinary and in many cases charismatic. Chatterji looks at the examples of Nazi Germany and Stalinist Soviet Union to corroborate her point. The nationalistic movement in Bengal presents similar features. There is nevertheless an intrinsic ambivalence of folk culture and folklore; on the one hand it generates legitimacy for a given regime, and on the other it constructs an ideology to subvert another or the same regime. Elsewhere, Chatterji (2004, 2012) discusses the perpetuity of folklore in the wake of hybridity of cultural forms. The Chho dance of Purulia as well as the contemporary pata-painting in Medinapur are instances of continuity of the folk and their lore *in the age of the mechanical reproduction of art work*.[10]

The issue of archaic, authentic, original, pristine in the folklore, against the notion of fakelore, solicits a mention of Ramanujan. To quote, 'The signifiers, whether they are images or characters or episodes; or even so called structures and archetypes, may be the same in different periods and regions, but the signification goes on changing . . . (Because) meaning of a sign is culturally and contextually assigned'.[11] (1991a: xiv)

Folklore, hence, possess a transformative character of a significant kind, which can be best understood by an anecdote Ramanujan shares. A philosopher meets a village carpenter who had a beautiful antique knife. When asked by the philosopher as to how old the knife was, the carpenter says, 'Oh! The knife has been in our family for generations. We have changed the handle a few times and the blade a few times, but it is (still) the same knife' (Ibid.: xx).

From the aforementioned arguments placed in a sketchy trajectory, it is obvious that folk as a category and folklore studies as a systematic search of knowledge has come a long way. In South Asia specifically, the study of folk expressions and performances has indeed come of age whereby it is no longer limited in terms of method, complexity of data, and subtlety of interpretations. As Arjun Appadurai remarks, 'South Asian folkloric studies no longer occupy that strange semiperiphery between the studies of folk phenomena in Europe and America on one hand and of native performances and practices in allegedly untouched small scale societies on the other' (1991: 467). Appadurai questions the validity of terms like 'folk' and 'lore'. Like the word 'belief', he says:

lore is a term that implies knowledge that is somehow more weak in its epistemological foundations, more evanescent in its relationship to social life, and more hazy in its grasp on history, than words like knowledge, theory, and world view . . . lore is a poor word to describe the very rich variety of texts and practices, of strategies, of structures, of arguments, and of counterarguments. (Ibid.: 468)

Similarly, the term folk continues the conventionally attached romantic values and it is also 'intrinsically self-referential and essentialist idea, which did facilitate the kind of fantastic and horrifying spectacle of nationhood which the Nazi regime erected around the German term volk' (Ibid.: 468). This underlines an iota of self-critical tendency, a later development in folklore studies. Folklore studies have, to a great extent, exorcised the master terms such as folk, primitive, and native that created an illusion of synchronic homogeneity and historical and geographical fixity.

An implicit move from text to contexts, occasions what Appadurai calls 'the variety of regimes of reception', which augurs well for folklore studies. In this variety of regimes of reception one finds that the contemporary writings on folklore do not show cultural consensus, but debate on central matters of power, status, gender, genre, and reality itself. The polyphonic situations depicted in these analyses remind us that the folk (themselves multiple) have many lore and forms of representation. This indeed suggests that folkloric texts are translucent rather than transparent, entailing inner dynamics of prose, parody and meter, of tone or style, of structure or ethos. Appadurai does not find folklore fading even 'in the age of mechanical reproduction'. Rather:

[t]here is a great deal of evidence to show that indigenous traditions have always been plastic and pluriform, that certain forms and texts were standardized over large spaces and long periods, and that individual 'signatures' and prestige are not wholly a product of the new mechanical age. (Ibid.: 473)

Similarly, Appadurai (1986) postulates the idea of 'hybrid forms and popular culture', which by and large, envelop the life of the middle class.

Folklore studies took a turn to the contexts of performance, broadening the framework in which not only 'verbal art' but also non-verbal aspects of performance assumed intellectual significance. Dundes draws a long list of what can be called 'lore' including:

myth, legend, folktale, joke, proverb, riddle, superstition, charm, blessing, curse, oath, insult, retort, taunt, tease, tongue-twister, greeting or leave-taking formula, folk speech (e.g. slang), folk etymologies, folk similes (e.g. as white as snow), folk metaphors (e.g. jump from the frying pan into the fire), names (e.g. nick names or place names), folk poetry . . . epitaphs, latrinalia (graffiti) . . . ractical jokes (or pranks), and gestures . . . the comments made after body emissions (e.g. after burps or sneezes), and sounds made to summon or command animals. (1966: 238)

The coming of age of folklore studies entail not only a recognition of diverse subject matter but also an acceptance of the folk in literate as well as non-literate society, the relation between the oral and the written, printed, or recorded, individual and communal authorship, survival as well as revival.

Mazharul Islam (1985), amending the old and essentialist definitions of folklore, proposes:

Folklore is the creation of people who live in a particular geographical area, share the same language, culture, mechanism of livelihood and living conditions; whose way of life and traditional heritage are bound by a common identity. Folklore is the outcome of the creative ideas of people expressed through verbal art as well as material forms—it may originate from a community or an individual, it is transmitted orally or through written process from one generation to another and from one country to the other—it exchanges its position from written and oral tradition . . . folklore may belong to a non-literate or literate society, to a tribal or non-tribal community, to villages or town-dwellers. (Ibid.: 6)

In the contemporary condition of a polyphony of folklore, as 'folklore is everything' (Bendix and Hasan-Rokem 2012), there is an evident tendency to unearth folk motives in the modern cultural forms of expressions such as cinema, drama, music, and literature (Dalmia and Sadana 2012).

Folklore, thus, consists of not only oral but written, not only the tradition of past but of the present and contemporary, not only text but context, not only cultural but political, not only continuity but changes, not only collective but individual performance and authorship. Second, the folk is not necessarily the category of the unreflective, non-literate lot confined in the self-subsistent little tradition. In a broader sense it is everywhere in a dynamic relation with the classical lore, fakelore, and the most recent mediums of expression. Folklore is characterized by 'where it lived and lives' (Bendix and Hasan-Rokem 2012).

Given the shifting grounds of folklore, with its inherent dynamics as well as its manipulations in nationalistic fervour, it seems difficult a task to discuss a singular way of understanding it. The specific contents of folklore, however, connote a world view. It is generally believed that folklore of a region is descriptive of the world view of the folk (see Dundes 1971, 1995; Jones 1972; Degh 1994). The following subsection reflects an imperative to persist with a quest of meanings through the category of world view in the domain of folklore.

Folk Songs, World View, and the Feminine

W.T. Jones (1972) dismisses the scientific behaviourism allegedly found in the anthropological works since it restricts the concept of world view to a sociocultural collective system of beliefs. This is allegedly manifest in an anthropological preoccupation with rituals to arrive at the system of belief. Raising a vital question, Jones suggests that world view is termed so variously that it is certainly doubtful to believe in one concrete all-pervasive meaning of it.[12] This vagueness of the term accords a chance to enlarge its scope, thus incorporating the collective and individual in a dialogic relation. On the other hand, there is a consensus in defining world view in association with community. *The Penguin Dictionary of Sociology* defines world view as:

> the set of beliefs constituting an outlook on the world characteristic of a particular social group, be it a social class, generation or religious sect . . . However the analytical problem consists in what justification the sociologist has for putting particular elements into a world view, for it will never be the case that all members of a group believe all elements of the world view that is ascribed to them. (Abercrombie et al. 2000: 398)

The question of group and individual creates a space to reflect on the dynamics of the concept of world view in its fullest, contextual sense. In fact, folklore studies, as discussed in the preceding section, are studies of folk world view (Degh 1994). L. Degh argues that folk narrative study[13] brings about context and text in relation with humans (the folk). Thereby 'observed live narration led to the introduction of the concept *homo narrans*: the idea that *homo sapiens, fabers* and *ludens*, is by nature also a narrator' (Ibid.: 245). *Homo narrans* observe verbalization of distinctive mental (spiritual) attitudes as a creative force. Degh quotes Kurt Ranke, 'as long as human being perceives, thinks and represents the world, as long as he creates the world primarily in his own language, he will have given his various emotional and mental processes a form of expression corresponding to them' (Ibid.: 245). Thus, their world view is not an ideal type, a cognitive construct in abstraction for scholars' analytical purpose. It is instead a natural type with all practical vagueness and confusions. As a natural type, world view has ethnic/native/local variants of perceptions. The vagueness of the term, as found in the context, holds a blessing in disguise as it enables a researcher to abstain from a certitude that is typical of the dominant anthropological perspectives. World view, thus, means:

[a] sum total of subjective interpretations of perceived and experienced reality of individuals. Any human action is motivated by such a perception. It contains beliefs, opinions, philosophies, conducts, behavioral patterns, social relationships, and practices of humans, related both to life on this earth and beyond in supernatural realm. World view then permeates all cultural performances, including folklore. Narratives, in particular, are loaded with world view expressions: they reveal inherited communal and personal views of human conduct this is their generic goal. (Ibid.: 247)

Degh, furthermore discusses genre types, essentially legend-tale types, which yields narratives that point to the folk world view. Interestingly, a narrator may offer a sense of two world views at once, 'The one inherent in the traditional type, and the other, the specific world view of the narrator. Evidently, the individual's world view is revealed already by his or her choice of stories from the available repertoire and further shown by the creation of new variants' (Ibid.: 249).

Dundes (1971, 1995) steers clear of the confusions arising from the taxonomical and classificatory concerns of the folklorists about world view and proposes two separate notions. The first suggests world view to be synonymous with cosmology, a man's view of his place in the world. The second, a more modern one, suggests world view to be cognitive and structural. It refers to the way people perceive the world through native categories or unstated premises or axioms. The elements of world view are present in tales, songs, and other contents of folklore. Dundes emphasizes that genre is not important in this regard. While the primary concern of folklore studies may be classification and taxonomical ordering of genres, the study of world view in folklore can dwell upon *folk ideas*. Dundes incisively argues, 'by folk ideas, I mean traditional notions that a group of people have about the nature of man, of the world, and of man's life in the world. Folk ideas would not constitute a genre of folklore but rather would be expressed in a great variety of different genres' (1971: 95).

Folk ideas are found in folklore as well as non-folkloristic genres such as cinema and popular literature. In Dundes' schema folk ideas are akin to the terms popularly used in anthropology such as 'basic premises', 'cultural axioms', or 'existential postulates'.[14] Furthermore, 'all cultures have underlying assumptions and it is these assumptions or folk ideas which are the building blocks of world view' (Ibid.: 96).

Dundes offers a twofold warning in relation to folk ideas. First, folk ideas are not traditional stereotypes. The idea, for example, that 'the French are great lovers', is a stereotype, a folk fallacy. They are demonstrably false and the folk are mostly aware of them. In contrast:

folk ideas would be more a matter of basic unquestioned premises concerning the nature of man, of society, of the world, and these premises although manifested in folklore proper might not be at all obvious to the folk in whose thinking they were central. Folk fallacies would therefore be part of the conscious or self-conscious culture of a people whereas folk ideas would be part of the unconscious or unself-conscious culture of a people. (Ibid.: 101)

The folk use folk ideas the way we all use language (speaking and understanding) efficiently without an authenticated knowledge of the grammar of the very same language. As an analogy, it is like a fish which is unaware that it is in water since it knows no other medium.[15]

The second point to remember in the process of understanding the world view of the folk through folk ideas is about a potentially conflicting heterogeneity of folk ideas. 'One need not assume that all the folk ideas of a given culture are necessarily mutually reconcilable within a uniform and harmonious world view matrix' (Ibid.: 99). For example, in the American world view linearity is valued more than the non-linear scheme. In fact, anything circular, curvaceous or crooked is despised as undesirable. But both, linear and non-linear, exist as indispensable denominators of folk reasoning. It is beyond imagination to reconcile pure capitalism and pure socialism, as much as linear and non-linear. Nevertheless, Dundes argues, 'both principles are taught to American children and the fundamental opposition is left unresolved' (Ibid.: 100). Furthermore, folk ideas cannot be restricted to certain genres. At this point Dundes breaks away from other folklorists and argues, 'proverbs would almost certainly represent the expression of one or more folk ideas, but the same folk ideas might also appear in folktales, folk songs, and in fact every conventional genre of folklore, not to mention non-folkloristic materials' (Ibid.: 95).

The main emphasis so far has been on a few important characteristics of world view. First, it functions both at the level of the individual and the group/collective. Second, it entails an important aspect, folk ideas, which are unstated and the folk are not fully conscious of it. Third, these ideas may be myriad and in conflict and thereby not form a harmonious whole. Fourth, it may be comprehended through any genre because folk ideas or such postulates or axioms recur across diverse genres of folklore. After offering a synoptic view at how folklore studies conceptualizes world view, in agreement as well as disagreement with anthropology, it is important to take note of the way it is understood in phenomenological (in sociology of knowledge in general) discourse. The description of everyday-life world entails people's world view. In agreement with Max Sheller, T. Luckmann carries forward A. Schutz's proposition of world view as a relative-natural domain. In simpler terms it means that world view is relative to a people and most of it is taken for granted as if it were naturally pre-given. It does not form 'a closed, unequivocally articulated' and clearly arranged provinces. Its validity is beyond questioning 'until further notice'. Reasoning (Luckmann calls it 'explication') with issues, objects, events of the world is through a host of a priori knowledge within world view and the individual experiences. As Luckmann remarks:

Each step of my explication and understanding of the world is based at any given time on a stock of previous experience, my own immediate experiences as well as such experiences as are transmitted to me from my fellow men and above all from my parents, teachers and so on . . . In the natural attitude, I only become aware of the deficient tone of my stock of knowledge if a novel experience does not fit into what has up until now been taken as taken-for-granted valid reference schema. (1974: 7–8)

In the face of a problematic/unfit experience of an individual, a further explication (reasoning) by the concerned individual takes place, and due to such possibility a world view is often subject to diversification and individuation despite its collective nature.

Notwithstanding, no amount of questioning on the validity of a priori dismisses 'socially transmitted traditional solutions of problems'. Driven by pragmatism in everyday life and in terms with the paramount reality of relative-natural world view, social actors have to follow an intersubjective format to put forth their subjective explications. For every individual seeks to ensure meaning of social existence. 'In short, within the natural attitude I do not act only within a biographically determined hierarchy of plans. Rather, I also see typical consequences of my acts which are apprehended as typical and I insert myself into a structure of incompatibilities that is lived through as being obvious' (Ibid.: 20).

The phenomenological conceptualization of world view concurs on the issue of meanings with Dundes and Degh discussed earlier. With this broader understanding of world view and its relation with folklore it is imperative to turn the focus towards women's association with folklore. By the virtue of singing the songs women establish a social order which permits resistance as well as reconciliation in the folk society.[16]

World view in folklore, as reflected in diverse genres and elements of folklore, brings about an interaction between perspectives of diverse social groups across caste, religion, and gender.[17] While both male and female social actors use certain genres, there are some which are specifically identified with women (Jordan and Caro 1986; Henry 1988, 1998). The *akam* (inside the domestic domain) and *puram* (outside the domestic domain) division of genres in the folklore from south India establishes that women narrate stories from *akam* genre.[18] This genre consists of narratives on child rearing, moral tales, love poetry, and devotional songs. A.R. Jordan and F.E. De Caro (1986) suggest that women's association with folklore is twofold. One, what and how much is the space for women's participation in folklore; two, how are women figured in the folklore. Jordan and Caro classified the folkloristic literature into three broad areas of concern. First, the projection of women in folklore, which initially was mostly negative; second, the roles of women in the social order, which was mainly patriarchal and their influence on female creativity; third, whether women are recognized as artists or not. In this wake, it is curious to note that there are literatures in the Indian context that depict women in stereotypical roles (Upadhyaya 1970, Deva 1989), as goddesses (Bachofen 1977, Wadley 1988), and ideal types and scare warnings to make women accept sex roles (MacLaughlin 1974). On the other hand, some of them also present the narratives of struggling women, as heroines who may destroy the threatening male villain.[19]

Therefore, it is not unusual that women hold a place of significance in the song culture of Maithili and Bhojpuri speaking regions (See Upadhyaya 1970; Henry 1988, 1998; Deva 1989). No wonder that Ved Prakash Vatuk dedicates his *Studies in Indian Folk Traditions* to his mother, who in his words 'was the best carrier of village traditions particularly of rituals and folksongs' (1979: 6). Notwithstanding the nostalgia, it helps us to understand women's engagement with folklore, which on the one hand socializes them for their roles and on the other hand, provides them an exclusive space. Ramanujan emphasized the instrumentality of folklore, saying, 'the aesthetics, ethos, and world view of a person are shaped in childhood and throughout early life, and reinforced later by these verbal and non-verbal environments'[20] (1991a: xiv). Women's world view is shaped and reinforced time and again by folklore that they have been exposed to since childhood. This is equally true for men who learn their way of 'doing' and 'not doing' in the same context.

Women, as Sudhir Kakar (1978, 1989) suggests in his psychoanalytical discourse on femininity, motherhood in relation with child and inner world, attain cultural consummation in the form of motherhood in Hindu society. The mythological icons surround Hindu women and orient them in typical value configurations. Studies in oral tradition in south India, especially in the Tamil context, have been centred on women, considering women as 'Sakti', the power or energy of the universe.[21] In the same line of arguments, suggestive of folklore's instrumentality in socializing women, Veena Das (1988) elucidates the orientation of women and the development of femininity. The body of women receives characteristic fundamentals throughout the life cycle, until the end of life—which is death. Based on the study of Punjabi kinship, Das underlines the 'double register' of law and language, and, of poetry and metalanguage in this context. Women's subversive assertions against the official kinship ideology

are in the 'register of poetry and metalanguage'. The latter yields
wider morality that is sensitive toward biological bindings. This
is apparently dominated and set off by the 'register of law and
language', the mainstay of masculine domination in the patriarchal
structure. The register of law and language, arguably, determines
the inheritance principle in the kinship structure and constitutes
a closed morality. But both closed and wider morality coexists;
registers of law and language, and, poetry and metaphysics cannot
be denied. A proposition of this effect emerges in Ann Grodzins
Gold's reading of song culture in north India (2003) that accords
a premium to women's assertions in their folk songs. Gloria
Goodwin Raheja and Gold argue that women's songs from north
India are not only a counterargument to the colonial construct
of meek and silent women of rural India but also a source of
complexity in the patriarchal social structure. The duo established
that the inherent ambivalence/ambiguity in women's songs is
arguably strategic on the part of women, as it facilitates alliances
with the male partners.

If women's place is significant in folklore as not only performers
but as characters of the narratives, then women's contribution
vis-à-vis performance of songs and perpetuation of meanings in
the world view is a foregone conclusion. It is however debatable
whether the functional significance of folklore is only for the
socialization of women. And if it is so, what is this socialization for:
conformity or resistance, or for both! More importantly, what role
do women play in folk world view which envelops both men and
women? These are a few questions undertaken for substantiation
in the latter essays on Maithili folk songs.

Toward a Sonic Anthropology of Death

Having underlined the relation between/among categories of
folklore, world view, and the feminine, it is interesting to turn
towards the domain of singing and expression of the notions of
separation and union in the performance of folklore. The extreme
of folklore performance, arguably, is when songs are replaced by
crying. It is an improvisation, in sync with the event at specific
junctures of life. It has an evolving script as the performers, the

crying social actors, voice it with sobs and hiccups. Within the
domain of folk songs, this subgenre, ignored until late,[22] was of
ritual lament song. Also called tuneful weeping and ritual wailing,
these are performed across folk cultures the world over. They
manifest during painful separation from the family, kith and kin
after (during) marriage or on the occasion of greetings, or as an
extreme example on the occasion of death.[23] The tuneful weeping
is performed by the women folk. It is significant to note that
in such instances of women-specific performances the men folk
sombrely accept the vulnerability of social order. This subgenre of
folksong in the ambit of folklore, like any other, entails narratives
vis-à-vis statements. These 'wept statements', akin to statements
in poetry or sung statement, carry emotive power of the women.
K.M. Tiwary suggests, 'It is institutionalized weeping prescribed
as a right kind of response to given social situations' (1978: 25).
As found in the Magahi, Bhojpuri and Maithili region of Bihar
in north India, these wept statements express memory of the past,
the fear of an unknown future in an unknown place, apologies for
any guilt, plea for forgiveness, and urge to not forget the weeping
person. Tuneful weeping, invariably deemed as ritual mourning,
takes place not only during a marriage, while bidding farewell to
a daughter and during the arrival of somebody after long time
but also is performed on the occasion of death. For the latter, the
content and style of renditions change. In many contexts, ritual
mourning has been associated with male folk.[24] But there has been
an instance of *Rudali* in Rajasthan, performed by professional
female mourners.[25]

   In the context of ritual wailing by womenfolk in Amerindian
Brazil, Greg Urban (1988) argues that it serves to reaffirm social
order and acceptance in the audience. By the virtue of musical
design, icons of crying such as creaking voice, voiced inhalation,
falsetto vowels, cry break, with proper intonation implicit in the
wailing, 'one emotion (sadness) points to or "comments upon"
another emotion (the desire for social acceptance)' (Ibid.: 386).
This amounts to a meta-affect because other actors find the
rendition appropriate and intelligible. In this the 'hearer', an
'over-hearer', and men, are passive participants without joining
them. Urban concludes that it shows the socialization of affects

and hence wailing contributes to social order and social control. On the other hand, C.L. Briggs highlights the polyphonic and intertextual character of laments that also plays a role in the cultural construction of women's social power. On the basis of a study among Kwamuhu and Murako in the delta of Amacuro of Venezuela, Briggs uncovers the musical and emotional construction of social disorder, which can be also read as social order due to the polyphony of texts.

Wailing exhibits a double relationship to agency. The content of textual phrases draws attention to agency by providing a comprehensive account of the way that particular words and actions contributed to death. Nevertheless the dynamics of lament performances transform the individual agency of particular wailers into a shared sense of agency. The performance dynamics of wailing thus create a sort of inflation in the economy of agency such that agency becomes highly diffuse and can no longer be attributed to a single individual. (1993: 949)

The subversive narrative of wailing inverts the discursive power equation between the male and female participant at the event of death. While anthropological texts have enhanced our knowledge of people's engagements with death, they have not established the essential relationship between the event of death and the folk engagement with the same beyond the rituals. A notion of cosmology has been predominant over the emotive actions of the bereaving. Death has, thus, been a focus only because of the associated rituals rather than the folk imagination, cultural aesthetics, and the usage of metaphoric expressions. The ritual performance and idea of cosmology are largely conditioned by the injunctions of the classical texts. The distinctions of metaphors borrowed from the social situations to imagine death renders death as a phenomenon larger than mere ritual performances.

The conventional anthropological works on people's perceptions of death largely attempt to deal with the issues of social order and disorder, collective representations, structures of cognition, and taxonomy.[26] Apart from detailed description and analysis of piacular rites, these works highlight the beliefs associated with death. According to R. Hertz (1960), these are threefold—beliefs pertaining to the body of the dead, soul of the dead, and the mourners.

Two broad exegetical points befitting the present work emerge from the fairly huge corpus of anthropological knowledge. First, life and death are conjoined realities in people's perception. J.J. Bachofen (1967) demonstrated it in his analysis of Greek and Roman mortuary symbolism. Hertz (1960) pointed out signs of fertility and sexuality in the mortuary rites among Malayo-Polynesian people. Studies on death have used symbols of sexuality and fertility to derive common conceptions which strike a connection between death and many other events of life. 'It is clear that such conceptions imply that death is a source of life. Every death makes available a new potentiality for life, and one creature's loss is another's gain' (Bloch and Parry 1982: 8). Second, mourners are considered only as functional tools in the course of the last rite of the passage, preparing the body of the dead for funeral rite on one hand and helping the family of the deceased reintegrate into society on the other. Das (1986) extends this line of thought by drawing a cognitive/structuralist conclusion as she argues, 'rituals of mourning have to provide mediation between these two opposite poles in which life and death are seen to be completely conjoined and which are seen to be in complete disjunction' (1986: 197). Though Das considers women's/mourners' noise and silences meaningful and points out the dialogic format of the performance she falls short of carrying it forward to locate it in the matrix of life. It is further revealed in the analyses of the symbolic representation of death in the Hindu world view and the rules in the piacular rites amongst the Hindus[27] (Das 1976, Kaushik 1976). The process in the last rite, to which the dead as well as the living are subjects, is in sync with the classical injunctions. The functional significance of the rite is that the dead and living are reincorporated into the social, the dead in the socially envisioned domain, and the living in the society. The last rite is thereby focused on the attributes of liminality that the incident of death brings about. There is little dispute about the functional and structural significance of the last rite and associated activities in the pale of the normative social. But the probing question is: does the sociocultural engagement with death have nothing more to offer than the elaborate normative-ritual performance and phenomenon of liminality? Is death an idea confined to cultural liminality alone? What is the role of the whole of world view in it? Do the classical and folk reconcile on the issue of death?

Conclusion

The discursive framework in this essay underlined the polyphony of folk, their lore, and thereof world view. Polyphony is a metaphorical expression, in this essay, indicative of currents and counter-currents, probing questions, and intellectual anxieties. This is to show that the folk and their lore are fraught with a multiplicity of notions. In this wake, a recognition of the contemporariness of folklore also amounts to understanding its perpetuity. This solicits an orientation towards comprehending folklore in conventional as well as in unconventional domains. It also suggests that folklore exists in an intricate relation with other forms of cultural expression. A basic caution thereby is that folklore is not exotic!

With a recognition of the inherent fluidity of folklore, this essay attempted to establish the imperative of exploring world view in folklore. There has been ample engagement with world view in folklore. It seems that world view could not be considered in the singular in the wake of a generic milieu of polyphony. But then, it is not necessary that genres of songs, tales or other components of folklore be always distributed along the divides of social groups. Informed by this challenge, it is relevant to engage with the idea of world view in folklore to critically approach the questions that emerge from the fields of enquiry in social anthropology. Anthropological understandings of death and dying, of sociocultural imaginations, have been determined by the performance of rituals. This may have aided in understanding the social imagination of living and dying. However, this essay proposed to draw a sonic anthropology, based on folklore, to understand the social imagination of death and dying. It is perhaps in sonic anthropology that the divide of classical and folk resources comes for a dialogic negotiation. This discursive framework also enables us to argue that women sing their songs not only to perpetuate stereotypes but also to reinforce world view, which envelops men and women alike. Many of these issues resurface for more field-based substantiation in the essays on songs from Mithila. The next essay presents a methodological preparation that is essential for making an inroad into the villages of Mithila for understanding songs.

Notes

1. See http://saarcculture.org/images/stories/publications/2011_vol_2. pdf, accessed 2 February 2017.
2. Here the use of 'street light', obtained from the Kannada Folktale retold by A.K. Ramanujan, is metaphorical. It stands for those influences that make us perceive folklore as a set of knowledge of 'the other'.
3. Max Müller's 'disease of language' is best explained in the term 'good morning', in which Müller found the metaphoric use of 'morning' is to express a wish. Müller also called it 'solar myth'.
4. Ruth Benedict wrote an article on folklore for the *Encyclopedia of the Social Sciences*, in 1931, and argued that folklore is a dead trait in the modern world.
5. R.M. Dorson explores the contemporaneity of folklores under four categories—the city; industry and technology; the mass media; and nationalism, politics, and ideology. Besides, Dorsan attempts to distinguish between folklore and fakelore where the latter stands for folksy songs or stories recorded, printed, and sold in the market.
6. Allen Dundes (1966) talks of the use (or abuse) of folklore. Its falsification serves the purpose of the capitalist in the US while its distortion serves that of communists. In similar fashion, Guy Poitevin discusses the folklorization of politics in India in an unpublished paper.
7. Poitevin mentions these instances in an unpublished paper. Pundit R.N. Tripathi valorized the practice of sati, using folk songs, in an article 'Sati Dharam' in *Braj Bharat*.
8. Roma Chatterji agrees with Dundes that among physicists, 'it is not their shared scientific knowledge that makes them a "folk" but rather a shared expressive tradition'.
9. By 'mythicization', Chatterji means a process in which, by the frequent use of folk categories, individuals are accorded religious sanctity and political legitimacy.
10. Folklorization of art forms in the domain of popular culture briefly refers to the perpetuity of an aura of collectivity, and thus continuity of mythic sacredness.

11. Note that Ramanujan underlines continuity and discontinuity in the folk on the one hand and attributes the changes to the process of signification, on the other hand, which is largely a process of consciousness, whereas there may be images pertaining to unconscious.

12. Baidyanath Saraswati (1991), Robert Redfield and others deemed world view synonymous with 'primitive categories', 'cognitive maps', 'ethos', 'forms of life', 'ideology, theme', 'style, super-style', and 'ultimate cosmology, pattern'.

13. By folk narrative study, L. Degh means folklore study concerned with folk narratives.

14. Dundes (1971) draws a parallel between his notion of folk ideas and Clyde Kluckhohn's 'unstated assumptions' and H.E. Adomson Hoebel's 'cultural postulates'.

15. Dundes does not use the idea of the unconscious in the Freudian or Jungian way. Another allusion, to understand the usage of folk ideas by the folk in their folklore, Dundes cites Benedict's idea that 'we do not see the lens through which we look'.

16. The instances of resistance in women's songs are not radically nihilistic. As it would appear toward the fourth essay of this book, the resistance is for reconciliation with the folk society including men, with emotional appeals. For more see Pathak 2013.

17. See works in ethnomusicology—Lomax 1962; Blacking 1973; and Feld 1984. Edward O. Henry (1988) propounds a counterargument to the conventionally forgone conclusion on the relationship between social categories/groups and genres of songs/folklore.

18. George Hart III (1973, 1999) classifies the ancient Tamil poetry into *akam* and *puram*. The former comprises those poems, which deal with life inside the family, and specifically the love between men and women, while the latter comprises those songs, which deal with life outside the family and, usually with the king. Ramanujan (1991b) too uses similar classification.

19. A.R. Jordan and F.E. De Caro (1986) argue that reinterpretation of folklore offered a categorical picture of women.

20. Here verbal and non-verbal environment, discernibly, is constituted by the symbolic language of non-literate people and their culture.

21. For more along this line, see Hart 1973; Wadley 1980; Egnor 1980. Susan Wadley terms Sakti as power or energy of the universe. This idea of the power of women breaks the misconceived notion of women's passiveness arising from the sacred power of goddesses. As the Tamilians believe, women are controlled by the male authority as well as by themselves to contain this sacred power in order to bring about good fortune for their family. This containment is, interestingly, also meant to enhance her same power.

22. Of late in ethnomusicology, studies were conducted to understand the significance of tuneful weeping as one of the categories of folklore. Not only intonation, melisma, and the musical structure over all but also the narrative in the wailing were analysed. The narrative of this genre offers a potential alternative to that offered so far in anthropological texts as people's perception (largely mythological) of death and life.

23. This has been discussed variously. See Alexiou 1974; Tiwary 1978; Briggs 1993; Urban 1988; and Magowan 2007.

24. See for example, in Tamil context (Blackburn 1988) and in Yolngu in Northern Australia (Magowan 2007).

25. A short story titled 'Rudali' was printed in Mahasveta Debi's collection of stories in Bengali titled *Nairetey Megh*, adapted into a Hindi film by Kalpana Lajmi (1993), and also appeared in English as a drama directed by Usha Ganguli (1997).

26. For example, Malinowski 1926; Hertz 1960a, 1960b; Parry 1981; Bachofen 1967; Levi–Strauss 1969; Das 1976, 1986; and Gennep 1960.

27. Both Veena Das and Meena Kaushik separately share the main interest of discussing the symbolic significance of the rules: lateral, spatial, and acoustic. Somehow the last, the acoustic dimension is understated in their analyses; it seems only about the pundits and the chief male-mourner voice. What assumes centrality are the distinctions of left hand and right hand, the categories of profane and scared, and the debate on the Durkheimian distinction. Das's discussion is based on the scriptural injunction in the *Garud Purana* and the *Grahya Sutra* (1976), and Kaushik's on the ethnographic study of the Doms of Varanasi (1976). The appearance of these works is at the juncture of sociological studies in India when the debate on the sociology of India was rife with validity claims of diverse kinds. It shows that the notions from the classical Hindu texts were employed as though they are absolutes.

4

Methodology of Being: Ruminations on the Field-Hermeneutics

If I limit myself to knowledge that I consider true beyond doubt, I minimize the risk of error but I maximize, at the same time, the risk of missing out on what may be the subtlest, most important and most rewarding things in life.

—E.F. SCHUMACHER (1990: 11)

Reality can be found only in understanding 'what is'; and to understand 'what is', there must be freedom, freedom from the fear of 'what is'.

—J. KRISHNAMURTI (1995: 32)

The world we have created today as a result of the thinking thus far, has problems which cannot be solved by thinking the way we thought when we created them.

—ALBERT EINSTEIN (Quoted by Bhaskar 2002)

The category of *Being*[1] of the researcher, and the *Field*[2] inhabited by the respondents interact and shape a research project. This is not a rhetorical, wishful thinking, smacking of naïve sentimentalism. This emerged as one of the takeaways from the tiring range of debates on the ways of doing anthropology, to be precise ethnography, known as the writing culture debate in 1980s.[3] At this juncture of the century, this essay need not exhaust space in recapitulating the issues, arguments, and propositions stemming from the writing culture debate. Instead, it seems worthwhile to explore the intriguing process of becoming a 'being in the field'. This essay offers an embodied expression of the anxieties that the writing culture seemed to represent, and offers more field-based answers to them. Such an endeavour aids in understanding the passage to the domain of meaning, the field of the folk and their lore.

The Field, a village called Fulhara, is roughly located in the southern part (sharing borders with two districts of Darbhanga and Samastipur) of the north-east of Bihar. It is yet another village with the peculiarity of sound and sight displaying folk ideas, the constituents of the world view. In this essay, an attempt is made to understand the ways of making inroads in a village, which are seemingly familiar for the researcher and yet fraught with methodological challenges. The attempt here is in establishing the significance of a discursive paradigm of understanding a cultural region and its folk materials.

In Fulhara, the women are largely housewives, while some of them are employed in various government schemes such as *Angan Baadi*, teaching in a local school, or simply as an aide in agricultural occupation along with their male counterparts. All the inhabitants of the field are here potential informants; women who are known for their singing consist of the main pool of the informants. To begin with, interviewing them seemed to be the best way of gathering data. In the course of the fieldwork, freewheeling conversation became a more efficient mode of data collection. The songs were recorded during the contextual renditions as well as on the insistence of the researcher on various occasions during conversations. As we proceed, this essay presents the nitty-gritty of interaction between the researcher and the villagers, a crumbling of the romanticism attached to field work in the familiar place, a love-hate dynamic with the field, a reading of the hermeneutic philosophy in the face of field-based methodological crisis, and a re-evaluation of the hermeneutic insights in the field leading to what I have modestly termed a methodology of *Being*.

Some Questions

More often than not our understanding of hermeneutic philosophy and of methodology arises from textual deliberations. A field view[4] of hermeneutics and consequent amendments in methodological orientation is, in diverse ways, distinct from the book view of the same. Most importantly, it facilitates an exercise in critical appreciation of the technical training in close encounter with the field and its elements. It is painful insofar as it impels for a heuristically important unlearning of the technical training and pleasant as it endows, or could endow, a research with optimum reflexivity. This essay intends to evaluate the book view of hermeneutic methodology from the perspective of the Field. While it constantly pricks the pride of a theoretically-oriented researcher by taking into account the challenge of the Field, it also enables to adjust to the emotional constitution of the Field. A book-view based methodology, no matter how free of doubt, is volatile if a researcher intends to be just to the field. If the intricacies of a field are bypassed by shielding a research with a straitjacket of methodology, the results are likely to be fraught with the delimiting impacts and interpretative politics of the researcher. Thus, some of the probing questions are what constitutes meaning in the field, the researcher's academic-intellectual world view or that of the listed as well as unlisted inhabitants of the field? The interpretative politics of a researcher largely stands on his or her academic-intellectual world view. And hence, it is necessary to question it. Who imputes meaning, the social actors of the field or the researching actor? Most importantly, how does such a researcher deal with the emotional content of the expressions of social actors in order to arrive at intellectually intelligible content? Is it like fishing the fishes suitable for the theme of a research from the muddied water of emotion in which units of knowledge breathe like small and big fishes?

This essay attempts to address such questions by bringing about an interface between book view and field view, between the hermeneutics of the field that a researcher stumbles upon and the textually elaborated hermeneutic philosophy. It is a practical appraisal of the textual knowledge in the field where we encounter not academic peers trained in critical debates and advice but reflective as well as not-so-reflective laypersons. An interpretative understanding that this essay arrives at discloses a twofold proposition—every field paves the way for an emotional reading of hermeneutics; and thus every field, in totality, is a *foundation*[5] for anti-foundational sociology. An important rider, though, is that the emotional reading is by no means a counterpart of the rational/reason-based one. The emotional reading, instead, facilitates to perceive the decimating dichotomies of reason and emotion, and intellect and sentiment. This essay, thus, arrives at an idea of a holistic paradigm of hermeneutics premised upon the unison of book view and field view. Thereby, the essay also departs from the vexed separation of the two, which scuttles the growth of a holistic hermeneutics.

Inroad(s): Context of Questions

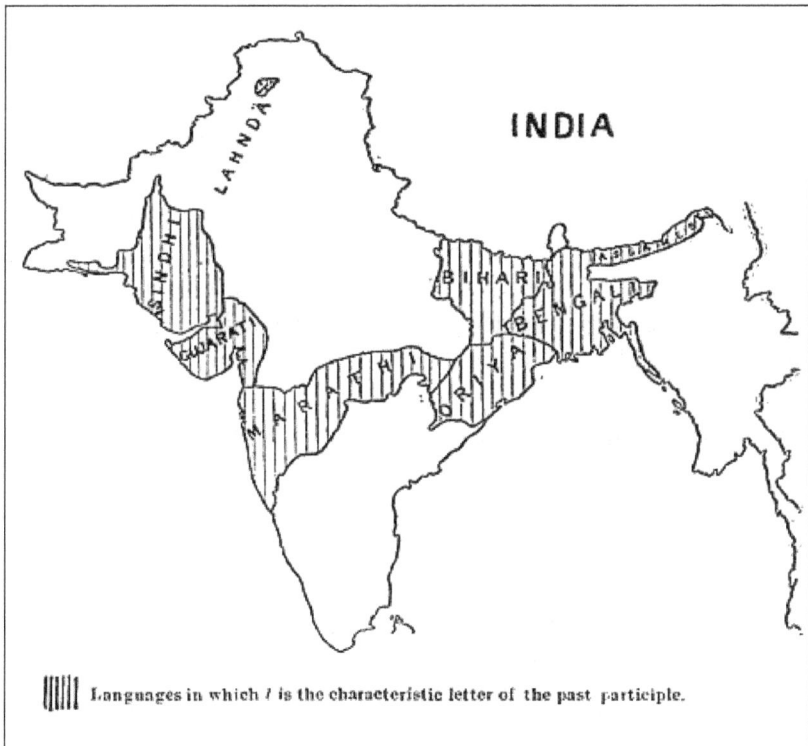

MAP 4.1: Map of Mithila
Source: *Linguistic Survey of India*: Introductory by
George Abraham Grierson, vol. 1, pt. 1, Calcutta: Government of India,
Central Publication Branch, 1927.
Courtesy: Nehru Memorial Museum & Library.

I have had an avuncular relation with Fulhara where my mother's natal home was located. Incidentally, I never visited this village with my mother. The only familiarity with this village was through oral sketches of it that had emerged from my mother's memory. After the death of my mother her stories as well as songs became a source of intellectual curiosity. I took to explore this village and began by delving into the maternal mystique attached to it. The images of the many faces of my own mother, readily singing the songs of an unknown past soon met with a reality check. Nostalgia died in the face of practical inconveniences and the real face of the village. It was replaced by sheer scepticism of a university-bred researcher.

The first time I entered the village with research intents, while riding an old Hero Honda motorbike on a stretch of tarmac road matching with irreparable ditches and holes on the roads traversing bamboo grooves and sideways of the fields, I thought I had stepped into a real mystical world. The only link alive in the village was my deceased mother's widowed sister-in-law whose son-in-law, also from the same village, had promised to help in my research. Never had I been to Fulhara before and hence was not able to locate my facilitator's house. I traversed the entire village in an hour as if on a wild goose chase, and returned to where I had started my journey. Setting aside my urbane certitude that I could find the place by myself even though it did not show on Google Maps, I stopped by the village tea shop for some help. Hastily I moved within the earshot of some villagers near the bamboo-roofed tea shop and overheard them talking about me, the stranger in the village! Now that the questionable stranger was available in front of them, intrigue was writ large on their faces. However, I was given the luxury of asking my question first, and I enquired about Puna Misar's[6] house in Maithili. They were stunned at the revelation that the stranger speaks in Maithili and his fatigue-clad urbanity was not a marker of his identity. Their surprise was perhaps also due to my right way of calling somebody's name in the village. Rather than answering the question, one of them took the baton, and counter-questioned: *who are you*?! This was an irritant for my mind as I expected them to straightaway answer my question first. He like other men in loosely tucked *dhotis* (a wraparound) and *ganji* (vest) intended to know everything about me—my name, relations, pedigree, and the place I came from. To each question I delivered curt replies expecting them to stop asking me any further questions and answer my question instead. But then, they continued their questioning and further asked who my father was, what he did in his life, how I was related to Puna Misar, the purpose of my visit to the village and so on. With my greed to find an answer to my simple question I maintained my poise and answered them as gently as possible, hiding my exasperation. Each question laid me bare in front of the villagers and I became a subject of their scrutiny. When it became intolerable to disclose myself any further I kick started my bike in an indignant gesticulation and this yielded the answer to the mere question I had asked: 'keep going on this road, turn to east on the northern *tin-muhani* (trifurcation), and near *puranka inar* (old-abandoned well) find the house in the south.' My mind, accustomed to the instructions with 'turn left and right', went tizzy at the 'turn south and north' type of instruction. I moved ahead, in confusion, until I saw a man standing in the verandah of the house with a *lota* (a brass pot) in his hand and his sacred thread slung from his right ear. Apparently, he was on the way to the field, or the bamboo grooves where people go for this purpose (defecating), to do what I am habituated to do in the enclosed toilets with running taps. I thought he would not take much time in telling me the way to the mysterious abode of Puna Misar. To my surprise, he withheld *his nature's call* and gave me the same trial once again by asking all the questions I had answered at the tea shop. Once he was satisfied he gave me the direction which was of little avail, for it was again in terms of 'south-east-west' rather than the left-right-centre that I was habituated to. The clash of everyday geographical instructions was evidently impeding my modest search. On my humble insistence he translated the whole 'direction-based instruction' into 'side-based instruction', replacing a south with a left and a north with a right. I rushed to Puna Misar's house as soon as I grabbed a sense of the direction, and I was there parking my dust-clad bike with muddied wheels in the shade of a *dalan*, the outer chamber of the house meant to accommodate male guests, which also accommodates elderly people of the household who have to maintain distance from the women of the family.

As Puna Misar appeared, a yellow dhoti clumsily wrapped around his waist, totally naked, with a pot-bellied torso, a yellowish sacred thread slinging across his chest, and chewing areca nuts in his mouth, my pretense to be a mere researcher was cast aside. I was instantly reminded of the distant relation with him from my mother's side. He was my mother's brother in the sense that they both belonged to the same village, and second, he was father of Putur Misar with whom my mother's brother's widowed wife (maternal aunt addressed as *maami*) married her daughter. Though my urbane mind denied any significance of such distant relations, I gingerly bowed to touch his feet, as I knew the significance of this custom. It perhaps may also have been because the younger ones touched my feet on the spur of moment out of their habit. Having asked for my well-being and that of my family, and exchanging sweet memories of my mother and my father, he called out for Radha. Radha is the granddaughter of my *maami,* and daughter of Putur and his wife Baby. Radha, a ten year old girl in a well-worn frock appeared with a *lota* of water for me, touched my feet in respect and called me *mama* (maternal uncle), which reminded me that I am maternal cousin of Radha's mother Baby; I am Radha's mother's sister-in-law's son; she is my mother's brother's daughter's daughter. It seems quite confusing, but very simple for an anthropologist used to drawing rather more intriguing kinship charts. Every child who came to touch my feet called me *mama* and thus I was catapulted into the matrix of relationships, a web-of-significance, rendering me as a 'significant other' in the village. I generally intended to avoid this status as though it were a precondition to be a dispassionate researcher. I have been generally very hesitant about 'touching feet', and did it only to please my parents or very close relatives. But then it seemed imperative at this occasion to establish that I am a nicely behaved man and I deserve all the help from them in my research. My submission to this seemingly indispensable part of the folkways was by and large a calculated move to garner maximum favour from the folk. And hence I did it willy-nilly creating a long chain of feet-touching exercise. In a while Radha ushered me inside the home, from the *dalan* so that I could meet her mother Baby and *maami*, my maternal aunt whose name is Gulab Devi. It appeared that this facility of going inside the household was available only for the visiting guest who has a particular kind of relationship (siblings, children of the siblings, cousins) with the women of the household. Not everyone is ushered inside the home. A round of 'feet-touching' ensued and placed me in the household as a guest who deserved attention. But then the researcher in me, subjecting everything to critical enquiry, hardly found any coherent meaning in such things, and thus only faked around touching feet for 'ulterior research motif', in a manner of speaking.

Listening to the Ladies; *courtesy* author

I disclosed my intention of the visit to my *maami* and subsequently to her son-in-law Putur. I also revealed that I was equipped with a camera to record the live performances. The news that a guest had come over from the town with a video camera to record performances spread like wildfire across the village. Putur and his family took pride in spreading the message as they all thought it would help me find women and men willing to sing for me. They were right indeed however, with mixed consequences because it amounted to the folk perception of me as somebody from a television channel. Some men, mostly adorning the public spaces such as *dalan* or teashops also thought of me as a scientist trying to understand the intriguing songs of the village. Another rumour wafted through the wind that the camera-clad man would select the best singer who may be invited to the town for some mega performance. Thus, towards the afternoon there was a bevy of women in the *aangan*, the interior of the house where visiting women sit. Each of them was in a garish saree, colourful bindi with proper make up, as they vied with other to appear the best. They had indeed come to perform 'for the camera' as they sang, especially those songs which they thought would earn them instant recognition. Those were the songs of popular choices, in Maithili, and often appreciated by the listeners in the village. Singing in groups as well as individually, they maintained that the effect of their throats is sweet enough. They displayed the varied quality of their vocal chords and knowledge of songs. Some of those songs they sang were from the compact discs available in the market. Radha and other kids whispered in my ears the hidden intent of the singing women who sang songs in Maithili to the tune of *filmi* (Hindi cinema) songs. These were songs in Hindi laced in Maithili timbre. The lilt, stress, and musicality were local while the songs were inspired by some of the popular films the women may have seen on television in the village. As a generalizing principle, it seemed mostly young singers liked to sing popular songs they had heard on microphones or on CD players. They also heard songs played on tacky MP3 player devices or on cellular phones. Some of the young singers seemed oblivious of the songs their older generation knew and sang on various occasions. It was, by and large, a sight of a visiting guest being entertained and impressed by the host women to prove that they are no less than their urban counterparts.

As evening dawned, I took a break from the recording that had unleashed a shock on me in more than one way. A string of thoughts clouded my mind: 'song culture is not fossilized', 'folk songs that defined oral culture are subject to dramatic changes', 'songs I had heard from my mother and which drew me to this research were almost forgotten', 'technical aids such as camera and other devices may be detrimental to research', 'it is well-nigh impossible to be a guest and a researcher at once', and so on. When a researcher is a fashionable guest, the yield is only fashionable stuff. And when the guest is a researcher it summons folk-doubt, as the former is a downright outsider trying to pry into the informal domain of the village.

To shrug off the intrigue I had stumbled upon, I took a walk in the village and at every step I discovered meaninglessness vis-à-vis things unfit for my research. These were practices of everyday life, people's general talk, rural factions and politics, and strands of religious beliefs. I was filled with disgust when I had to go to the field with a *lota* filled with water in the absence of a proper safety toilet; I wondered how people can manage with a single fill of *lota*.[7] As I waited for the evening tea at the *dalan*, I discovered that a man is about to visit me. Named Chandruji, he was a butt of ridicule among the villagers as well as a free-floating entertainer due to his strange singing abilities. I was told that he was a social misfit, accommodated in the social structure only at the cost of general social prestige. He was unmarried at the age of fifty, lived on other's offerings as he did not earn his living by himself, and pleased the men folk of the village by singing on their *farmaish* (request). My facilitator thought it pertinent to record Chandruji for my research, and I humbly obeyed albeit with a great deal of reservation. His performance ranged from old Hindi film songs to Maithili chartbusters on which everybody generously clapped, even as they secretively laughed at him. Coincidentally, one elderly villager present, turned his salvo towards me, and began to enquire about my economic status: do I earn enough, do I own immovable and movable properties, do I belong to the category of elite Maithil Brahmins, etc. It just did not fit the village common sense that a man of my age was collecting songs in a village for a doctoral degree. For them it was a sheer waste of time and resources, and they felt that I was just ruining my life. My facilitator somehow defended me and I fell short of being dubbed as another Chandruji.[8]

Adding to the whole experience was the incompatibility between my notion of time and that of the village. My body clock was still very urbane causing me great difficulty in adjusting to the rural time, which was characterized by the 'early to bed and early to rise' principle. Not that the villagers had any conscious notion of the productivity of time. It just happened to be part of their everyday life. While for me rural sense of time was intellectually unproductive, for them it was highly pivotal to maintain a rhythm of mobility.

The recording spanned a week causing me dissatisfaction that I was not about to find what my research required. The notion of village had undergone a sea change. Fulhara was no less networked and 'materially progressing' than district towns. It has the tower of Airtel cellular phone service provider and almost everybody has access to cell phones. There is no good roadways connecting villages yet every household has a motorbike. There is no safety toilet in every household but there is at least one television set with one Delhi-made video cassette player. Electricity is abysmal, but there is a small battery in every household, which gets recharged in the nearby low-key Dudhpura baazar on the power generator. The familiar materiality of Fulhara and the mediated existence of the folk seemed to be a serious challenge to my monolithic expectation from a village.

On my expressive disappointment, my facilitator Putur took me to several individual households. Everywhere I was a prized guest at the receiving end of their respect and offerings. Everything I exhibited was in perfect conformity with the social expectations from a guest. Since most of the hosts were aware of the purpose of my visit, they sang for me when I visited them. I gingerly took notes on such occasions though I could see that my notes were replete with question marks on the songs, which were largely exhibitory and hardly of my research interest. Notwithstanding, in the same series of songs I stumbled upon a woman by the name of Sulekha Devi who added, perhaps unwittingly, a pinch of emotion to her renditions. While singing she broke into a melancholic pause with her tone trembling as though she intended to weep. The song was of the genre known as *Nachari*, sung in devotion to Siva, wherein the protagonist complains to the god that the latter has never turned his kind glance and thus this worldly life is so woeful. At the end of the song I impatiently asked for the meaning of the song and she balked at me saying: 'Meaning! what meaning do you want?' She perhaps deciphered some baleful intention in my pursuit of meaning, and snapped at my curiosity. On my unrelenting insistence she gave me some idea about the song. It left me irredeemably curious about the melancholic pause in her songs. It had triggered my tendency to read between the lines. Then on, she sang all kinds of songs in as emotionally flat a manner as she could manage to, as though she performed to amuse the visiting guest. She became cautious about the emotional display in her songs. I could experience her cautious performance that sanitized the emotional intent of the otherwise emotionally truthful woman.[9] She sang well for my camera and notebook rather than for me who was in quest of finding meaning of those songs.

How to get the meanings attached to the songs sung by the emotionally truthful singers remained my pivotal concern throughout my first stint in the field. My pursuit of meaning met with resistance, ridicule, and refusal. Women made fun of my insistence for meaning, as they smelt something fishy about my intentions. They thought I was not only prying into their personal domain, I was also not quite an able-minded man who could understand the meanings of the songs. At the tea shop people jeered at me as someone looking for meanings in the meaningless stuff, such as women's songs! They opined that the village is only a source of ignorance, without any knowledge-value whatsoever, and a researcher after meaning is clearly on a wrong path. Paradoxically, coded meanings seemed to be strewn all around awaiting an interpreter. It was beginning to unfold to me after my encounter with Sulekha Devi and the subsequent trail. It was, in bits and pieces, in villagers' acute social habit of narration. For example, my facilitator Putur is habitual of saying *hey suna*! (listen to me). Almost everybody, men and women alike, have a similar urge; they have so many tales to tell. Anybody who listens to them belongs to them; anybody who belongs to them understands them! While I am in pursuit of meaning perhaps I am not a good listener! For everything they speak does not make sense to me. What makes sense to me, or what is meaningful to me, is determined by my own academic world view, which is tightly defined and defended by the methodology of the research. Operating within the framework of my research I would remain an outsider; no matter how efficiently I fake and feign to be an intimate insider I would be nothing more than a respectable guest.

At this juncture of my visit to Fulhara I took a break and went back to the district town where I mulled over the intricacies afresh. I thought of visiting some other villages before my disappointment became conclusive. Another contact person Dheerendra Jha (nicknamed Dheero), a distant relative (my mother's cousin sister's son), took me to his village called Dekuli Dham. Situated right by the side of the main road that connected with the district town Darbhanga, it was one of the most 'advanced' villages I had seen, especially in north Bihar. It was impossible to spot a single *kuchcha ghar* (un-cemented house)! All the households had practically manageable toilets. There were well-built roadways even inside the village. Notwithstanding the apparent advancement, it was no different from Fulhara as far as basic folkways were concerned: I had to answer the same set of questions as to *who I was*. This time I was with Dheero who answered any such query on my behalf quite efficiently and saved me from the embarrassment of laying myself bare for social scrutiny. He also ushered me to the innards of the households where I could manage to steal glances of the daily chores of the women. Mostly, these women were related to Dheero and being brotherly to him I was also considered as 'somewhat' of an insider. It was only 'somewhat' so, because my space was beyond questioning until I opened my mouth in curiosity. An act of asking for an explanation for anything translated me into a 'slighted stranger' or in euphemism 'a curious guest' who knows nothing about the village life. In Dheero's presence women sang songs while they continued with their chores. After spending some days in Dekuli and recording almost similar kind of songs laced with religious overtones, I became a little sceptical about the much-talked variety of Maithili folk songs. It was also a déjà vu in the sense that the pursuit of clearer meaning was extremely impeded by the folk reluctance to divulge. On this note of my doubt Dheero took me to another village, called Bhindi, about 5 km. off the railway station of Rambhadrapur en route to Samastipur and Darbhanga. It was yet another village along the bumpy brick-pathways, away from the railways and roadways. Of all the singers I heard in Bhindi one, Surdas, merits special mention for the specificity of performance. Around sixty, he easily finds audience for his famously catchy renditions, while he is also jeered at and chased away by the village boys. As a regular consumer of marijuana, an addict so to say, he gives into singing for anybody who provides him with a shot or two. Considering me his prized guest he also breaks the folk rule about the times of singing categories of song, which encapsulated in the folk proverb: *saanjh parati bhor mei sanjha, ei sab chhi mair khai ke dhandha* (songs of evening singing in the morning, and songs of morning in the evening; incur wrath for such doings). After taking a long shot of marijuana one evening, Surdas broke the rule and sang some of his favourite *Parati*, a genre of songs to be sung in the morning. Most of them were *Nachari*. Surdas was however no different from the women of Bhindi, or for that matter that of Fulhara and Dekuli, in carefully selecting songs to entertain and appease 'the guest'. On the occasion of a *mundan samskar* (tonsorial rite) in the village the same bevy of women were less guided by the presence of the visiting guest. They sang songs meant for the occasion irrespective of the likes and dislikes of the audience. I need to mention here that the male audience is never a directly active audience. They may be seated outside, at the *dalan* or on the veranda along the *aangan* (open space in the middle of the house). The songs will continue while men of the household may frequently come inside for some work. They however do not pose to be a formal audience like I greedily did. In the flow of the songs I noticed them taking a pause here and giggle there, and also to make sure that folkways associated with the *mundan* are discharged properly. It was in this hurly-burly, I could not resist my need to find meanings of the songs they were singing. As and when any woman came out from the site of ritual performance and singing, I scurried to her and asked if she could offer me an explanation on the songs being sung. Each woman I encountered for the meaning gave me a disapproving gesture, a mellow ridicule, and only a wishy-washy explanation. I certainly irritated them as a curious guest and they in turn debilitated my faith in intellectual pursuit.

The encounters in the villages Dekuli and Bhindi warranted another break from the field and a thorough stocktaking for which I went back to the district town of Darbhanga. A methodological realization was that a 'researcher as a curious guest' in the eyes of the folk could access only songs of certain kinds, other than ridicule and disapproval. These were songs of popular choice. Second, the songs of everyday life are sung individually by men as well as by women as they carry out their daily chores. Third, as a researcher I have to be one of them if I intend to understand the meanings of the songs. It indeed required a 'becoming of the being' of a researcher, whereby I could truly be one of them. Only two options heralded my mind: either give up the whole research on folk songs or throw myself in the tidal ocean of meanings. I chose neither and decided to give a chance to the field to decide the course of this research. After a while, I returned to Fulhara with renewed aspirations to rediscover the village and its song culture, though not before a thorough intellectual soul-searching in the field.

Intrigued *Weberian's* Turn to Hermeneutics Philosophy

Fulhara is very much like Arvind N. Das's *Changel* (1996) as far as its connection with the cities is concerned. As a researcher my instant experience is not much different from that of *bachha* (an affectionate address for a man characterized by the innocence of childhood), a student of St. Stephen's college in Delhi who went on to understand his village Changel and found that the village is same but he has changed in terms of perspectives. Thus, he has mixed feelings of nostalgia as well as intellectual remoteness toward his village. In Das's biography of Changel, the researcher is also a protagonist or social actor himself located in the field. The location of researcher-cum-protagonist-social actor in the familiar field casts a complexity of experiences and offers broadly two methodological options: either to become a romantic researcher nostalgically describing everything of the field or a rationally guided researcher in search of befitting information in order to impute meanings and draw conclusive judgements. Das apparently allows the confusion to become a methodology par excellence.

The first step for a research concerned with interpretative understanding would be to begin with Max Weber's methodological suggestions. Weber suggests that the meaning of social action, subjectively imputed by actors in society, is of two kinds—one is 'actual existing meaning' and the other is 'theoretically conceived pure type of subjective meaning'. The dual aspect of meaning solicits interpretation for understanding in two ways. One is rational understanding based on logic and mathematics, while the other is 'emotionally empathetic or artistically appreciative quality'. As Weber argues, 'Action is rationally evident chiefly when we attain a completely clear grasp of the action elements in their intended context of meaning. Empathic or appreciative accuracy is attained when, through sympathetic participation, we can adequately grasp the emotional context in which the action took place (1978: 5).

Weber does not distinguish between understanding and interpretation of meaning. He often uses the word 'irrational' as opposite to rational in understanding the emotional part of meaning. However, rational understanding yields causal explanation along the means-end line. Against the dominant positivistic-empiricist trends of his time, Weber attempted to establish an explanatory-empathic type of understanding. On the question of unclear motive and intention of the actor, Weber argues, 'every interpretation attempts to attain clarity, but no matter how clear an interpretation as such appears to be from the point of view of meaning, it cannot on this account claim to be causally valid interpretation. On this level it must remain only peculiarly plausible hypothesis' (Ibid.: 9).

The Weberian pendulum vis-à-vis interpretation and understanding of meaning disparagingly oscillates between the rational-causal and empathic-explanatory types. The latter only delivers a hypothesis to be verified by the former. Weber too subscribes to the foundation of social science that rejects the validity of emotional understanding of meaning and seeks for causal explanations to make knowledge doubt-free, verifiable, and objective.[10] Let alone the terse exclamation of my female singers, a Weberian enterprise would fall flat in the face of the melodramatic twists in the stories such inhabitants of the field unfurl. Would a Weber be able to comprehend a sociologically significant meaning of crying and sobbing in the middle of a conversation? In the want of more discursive thrashing, I turn my attention to the hermeneutic tradition where the interpreter and interpreted are put on the anvil under the same hammer.

To map the historicity of hermeneutics we can cite broadly three strands (Bleicher 1980, Muller-Vollmer 1985). First is the Hermeneutic theory, with a predominant purpose of devising methodology that is restricted to philology, theology, and jurisprudence. Second is the Hermeneutic philosophy (Giesteswissenchaften[11]) with a predominant purpose of developing a philosophy laced with idealism, with formerly implicit and latterly explicit methodological implications. It arose as a philosophical critique of the positivism of social science and the dominant methodological propositions of the Enlightenment. It had an overt orientation towards history in particular and social sciences in general. Though generally traced to Wilhelm Dilthey, and before him to Friedrich Schleiermacher, Anthony Giddens (1976) dates its advent back to Johann Gottfried Herder and Friedrich Wolf. Third is the critical hermeneutics, with a clear bent to balance philosophy and methodology. It continued with the critique of the limiting methodological notes of the Enlightenment, but on the whole it was wedded to the latter insofar as acceding to the supremacy of reason and rationality is concerned. Paul Ricoeur, following Jürgen Habermas, serves as a methodological signpost for critical hermeneutics.

Instead of unravelling each strand in the historical trajectory it is important to highlight the key issues that are relevant to the discussion in this essay. The earliest usage of hermeneutics[12] rendered it as a technique with three features of efficiency: it assisted in discussions about the language of the text (philological), facilitated exegeses of the Biblical literature, and guided in jurisdiction. Johann Martin Chladenius[13] in the eighteenth century set the tone by stating, 'the completeness of the account can be ascertained only by referring to the author's intention' (Mueller-Vollmer 1985: 4). It means that meaning lies in the author's intentions. The catch however lies in the suggestion that the author's intention can be deciphered because of 'the presence of rules and reasons in the author's utterances' rather than comprehending the author's orientation. Schleiermacher, hailed as the founder of modern hermeneutics, introduced a romantic linguistic paradigm, and its key paradigms of interpretation—grammatical and technical. While one was to serve philological needs the other was to explore the author's intention with psychological tools. The grammatical interpretation, according to Schleiermacher, is objective but also negative as it indicates the limits of understanding. It is only with the technical, synonymously psychological, interpretation that we can reach the subjectivity of the one who speaks. The author's/ interpreter's intention thus assumes significance. Johann Gustav Droysen added to it what is popularly known as the hermeneutic circle. According to it, 'the part is understood within the whole from which it originates, and the whole is understood from the part in which it finds expression'[14] (Ibid.: 19). It is however Dilthey who brings about a watershed moment by stepping away from romanticism and making 'understanding' a central issue in hermeneutics. The key maxim for him is 'life expressions', that emerges from 'life experiences'. One expresses what one is; in other words, there is proportional relation between essence and appearance. Dilthey clarifies, 'By "life expressions" I mean not only expressions which intend something or seek to signify something, but also those which make a mental content intelligible for us without having that purpose' (Ibid.: 152).

Two broad points stemming from Dilthey are important. Understanding requires not only comprehending the expressions of others but also a simultaneous understanding of one's own self. A researcher himself/herself becomes a part of the scrutiny. To understand is as much an inward process as it is outward. Second, life expression is in unequivocal sync with life experience. It means what I articulate is actually what I am. Despite these potentially promising postulates, Dilthey runs a risk of obscurity due to the lack of connection between 'my knowledge' and 'my existence'. In other words, Dilthey's conclusions are only partially ontological and more occupied with the epistemological implications. It does not divulge the intricate details of my 'existential and contextual complexity'. Third, it has a microscopic reliance on an individual life experience for the evolution of understanding. It also has a psychological dimension to it, reducing an individual into a unit of analysis. In case I am a researcher with sadist tendencies, say for example, how would I make sense of a female singer's outbursts, or songs soaked in tears? My emotional limitation will obscure the possibility of a fair understanding.

At this point it is curious to note that Martin Heidegger brings Dilthey face-to-face with Edmund Husserl's transcendental phenomenology to fulfil the most felt need: ontologizing understanding. Dwelling upon the ontic character of understanding, Heidegger highlights 'preunderstanding' or primordial mode of understanding that underlies *Dasein*—Being-there and Being-in in the world. It means what is out there is also in here. Understanding occurs in an intriguing way to my being as Being-there always discloses itself to Being-in. To quote, 'Understanding is the existential Being of Dasein's own potentialities-for-Being; and it so in such a way that this Being disclose in itself what its Being is capable of' (Ibid.: 217).

In a more accessible sense, I can understand what I am because I understand what my world is. Both my world and I disclose to each other in terms of potentialities and possibilities. It takes place in this way because we are situated on a timeline with the past, present, and future as coordinates. But an understanding, curiously, does not guarantee meaning. Says Heidegger, 'Meaning is that wherein the intelligibility of something maintains itself. That which can be articulated in a disclosure by which we understand, we call meaning' (Ibid.: 224).

Meaning is an *existentiale* of *Dasein* that emerges from interpretation. We can hear, converse, and thereby interpret the meaning from our understanding. We can do so because we all have in common Being-there and Being-in, disclosed and disclosing *Dasein*, and the basic minimum pre-understanding. Interpretation, carried out in the form of assertion, is 'derivative mode' as it is based on 'fore-having/fore-sight/fore-conception'. The latter is actually the existential foundation of interpretation, arising from *Dasein*. Thus, as an offshoot of understanding, interpretation—through explication and assertion—is only the fulfilment of understanding. Similarly, discourse that hinges on understanding and interpretation is ontologico-existential in nature.

Two significant hermeneutic strands based on the philosophical fundamentals of Heidegger are Rudolf Bultmann's methodology of 'demythologizing' and Hans-Georg Gadamer's 'fusion of horizon'. Accepting that any understanding, in science or history, of natural phenomenon or historical events, presupposes pre-understanding and personality of the observer, Bultmann takes a quasi-theological turn. The abiding question as to how to understand the apparently religious texts, particularly mythology, in the wake of modern science guides this strand. The methodological significance of 'demythologizing' is evident when Bultmann argues, 'I take the term "demythologizing" to mean a hermeneutic procedure which inquires after the real content of the mythological assertions or texts' (Ibid.: 248).

This however does not mean a rational and secular elimination of mythology under the influence of modern science. Instead, it means extricating its true and symbolic meaning that could make sense to humans even in the wake of science and technology. Mythology ceases to be an explanation of the physical phenomenon, associated with the primitive and hence a counterpart of science. Instead, it becomes an expression of what it feels like living in the world across time and space (Segal: 2006). The human life has a ground in transcendental power, which lies beyond human control. How to make sense of this power when we are in one way or another a buyer of scientific knowledge is a question that makes Bultmann argue, 'Since God is not an objectively ascertainable phenomena in the world, it is only possible to speak of His activity in such a way that one is speaking simultaneously of our existence, which is affected by God's activities' (Ibid.: 253).

The process of such an understanding is paradoxical in the sense that it entails inwardly occurrences and the other-worldly God eventuating into a relationship between the two. Furthering the Heideggerian project of ontological-existential notion of understanding, Gadamer offers a critique of the enlightenment and its methodological preoccupations. Gadamer points out the methodological 'prejudice' of modern science against the 'prejudice' of sociocultural thoughts. Thereby tradition, religion, and everything that belongs to social thought appeared as an inferior counterpart of Reason. The German romantic reaction to the prejudice of Enlightenment resulted in the resurrection of the past, Christianity, and tradition. This however only exalted tradition as opposed to reason. But methodologically, it remained akin to the scientific epistemology. For example, Schleiermacher's view that narrowness of vision and over-hastiness cause misunderstanding is only slightly different from Descartes' emphasis on the same. Gadamer acknowledges the potential pitfall of the romantic hermeneutics and cautioned against endless relativism and subjectivity. Gadamer suggests, 'the focus of subjectivity is a distorting mirror. The self-awareness of an individual is only a flickering in the closed circuit of historical life' (Ibid.: 261).

Similarly, Gadamer departs from imagining an unconditional antithesis between tradition and reason. The object of study/understanding and the person seeking it are in a historical continuum. This is what Gadamer calls 'effective history', and the success of hermeneutical enterprise depends on the development of one's 'effective historical consciousness'. By virtue of this, an individual can understand his/her horizon. 'A person who has no horizon is a man who does not see far enough, and hence overvalues what is nearest to him' (Ibid.: 269). We could comprehend each other's horizon because no single horizon is fixed and final. Curiously, 'the horizon is, rather, something into which we move and that moves with us' (Ibid.: 271). It is not mere empathy because we are in a reciprocal relationship that leads us to understanding, leading to the 'fusion of horizon'. A tradition is, in fact, a site of perpetual fusion of horizons. As Gadamer argues:

In fact, the horizon of the present is being continually formed, in that we have continuity to test all our prejudices. An important part of this testing is the encounter with the past and the understanding of the tradition from which we come. Hence the horizon of the present cannot be formed without the past. There is no more an isolated horizon of the present than there are historical horizons. Understanding, rather, is always the fusion of these horizons which we imagine to exist by themselves. (Ibid.: 272)

Curiously, Susan J. Hekman, in agreement with Richard Rorty, suggests that only Heidegger and Gadamer are overtly anti-foundational as they shift the focus from the Enlightenment's preoccupation with epistemology to ontology. To quote:

what the anti-foundational philosophers suggest is not a search for truth conceived apart from history and culture, but, rather an examination of the relationship between human thought and human existence ... an endeavor that falls under the rubric of the sociology of knowledge ... divorced from the enlightenment assumption of the distinction between objective and subjective knowledge. (1986: 9)

In the scheme of Gadamer, hermeneutics enables for 'natural human capacity' in the universal process of understanding. It is here that an 'I-Thou' relationship owing to the effective historical consciousness facilitates a 'fusion of horizon'.

Thus far, the brief synopsis of the hermeneutics underlines the significance of life experiences, existence, expressions, being, understanding, pre-understanding, historical consciousness, inter alia. All of these terms could be conveniently put under the category of tradition. But then, later developments in hermeneutics also cast aspersions on the validity of tradition. As Habermas says,

. . . we have good reason to suspect that the background consensus of established traditions and language games can be a consciousness forged of compulsion, a result of pseudocommunication, not only in the pathologically isolated case of disturbed familial systems, but in the entire social systems as well (1985: 317).

Habermas elaborates on the power that a native speaker commands owing to the creativity of natural language (vernacular of the native). This is power over the practical consciousness of men. It can be used for the purpose of obfuscation and agitation as well as for enlightenment. This inherent power equation yields a 'systematically distorted communication' with symptomatic unintelligibility. Habermas calls it 'pathological disturbances of speech', taking cues from Freud and Lorenzer. It requires reason and rationality which Habermas considers free from any prejudice and liberating humans from repressive consciousness. It is an explicit acquiescence to the Enlightenment that Habermas exhibits, which is not unstinted as he in agreement with Gadamer denounces the 'monological self-certainty' of any scientific enterprise. Nonetheless he argues:

The Enlightenment knew what Hermeneutics forgets: that the conversation which according to Gadamer, we 'are' is also a nexus of force and precisely for that reason (it) is not a conversation...the claim to universality of hermeneutical approach can be upheld only if one starts from the recognition that the context of tradition, as a locus of possible truth and real accord, is at the same time the locus of real falsehood and the persistent use of force. (ibid.: 314)

If I juxtapose Habermas with the female singers of Fulhara, the crisis of the critical hermeneutics and overall Enlightenment thinking bursts asunder. The prejudice against prejudice, which Gadamer detected in the epistemological foundation of the enlightenment, is articulated not only in Habermas but also in Ricoeur. The latter attempts at thrashing the methodological grains dispersed in the hermeneutic philosophy. However, in order to respond to the poser of the critical hermeneutics, Ricoeur reeks of an epistemological bias. For him the aim of hermeneutics is discourse that is, and can be, inscribed and rendered into a text. Writing is more meaningful than speech, as Ricoeur says in agreement with Plato, 'writing was given to men to "come to rescue" of the weakness of discourse, a weakness which was that of event' (1981: 199). At this point, it is useful to briefly refer to the celebrated synthesizing of all strands apt in interpretative sociology. Giddens's 'New Rules' suggests, 'hermeneutic, I wish to claim, does not find its central range of problems in the understanding of written texts as such, but in the mediation of frames of meaning' (Ibid.: 64).

Possibility of Holistic Hermeneutics

A recognition of the long trajectory and vast contribution of hermeneutics humbles a reader. Cobbling together the various strands while keeping the field of Maithili-speaking village in perspective enables for a field hermeneutics. To begin with, it is essential to share a tale from the fifth chapter of the *Brihadaranyaka Upanishad*.[15]

Once upon a time, three disciples of Brahma (a mythological character who appears as teacher in this tale, is otherwise god of creation) namely god, demon and human (three characters with their respective characteristics) spent years under his tutelage. They fulfilled the prerequisite to prove their competence to learn the greatest lesson. The satisfied teacher agreed to impart them the lesson. First came god and begged for it. The teacher uttered only one letter 'D'.[16] The receiving disciple, god, interpreted it as 'D' for Daman (meaning dominate sensory desires, else god will fall prey to the abyss of desires). Responding to god's interpretation the teacher said, yes, you understood it correctly. On human's turn, the teacher yet again uttered the same letter 'D', and the disciple considered it pointing to Daan (meaning, charity/philanthropic submission/ parting with one's possession else human will fall prey to avarices). Responding to human's interpretation the teacher said, yes, you understood it correctly. Demon too received the same utterance, 'D', from the teacher and construed it as Daya (meaning, kindness/non-violent attitude/caring and compassionate outlook else demon will be rampant in destruction). And the teacher did not rebuff it either. Responding to demon's interpretation the teacher said, yes, you understood it correctly.

Shankar, the ancient philosopher, renowned for his treatise on *Adwaita* (doctrine of non-duality), points out two features underpinning the act of understanding and interpretation by the disciples. First, each of the three disciples analogically indicates a distinct property/feature/sociocultural constitution. Each thus propels a distinct interpretation of the utterance 'D', and each is hence correct as the teacher affirms in each case. Second, each has fulfilled a common prerequisite; in this tale each disciple observes celibacy and affective-devotional proximity with the teacher. Hence, despite difference of dispositions, each of them is able to relate to the utterance of the teacher. A one-point observation with regard to the afore-mentioned tale is: How does the teacher know and understand all three disciples' validity of understanding? The answer lies in the dialectics of ontological epistemology and epistemological ontology that we encountered in the previous section in the perusal of Giesteswissenchaften. A further endorsement emerges from the Upanishadic lessons.

Shankar argues,[17] 'Intellect resides in *hridaya*'. The translated equal of *hridaya* is heart. But in Shankar's scheme it is not merely a biological organ. It can be rather construed as a category of skill, which thrives in an amicable union between reason and emotion, intellect and affectivity, objective and subjective. Thus, so confidently the Upanishad argues 'Only heart knows the truth'.[18] In yet another insightful adage, *Eko Aham Bahusyam*[19] one yearns for and endeavours to become many, the Upanishad points out my existential joy and fear arising from my ontological being, despite my transcendental tendency. It is a significant paradox that constitutes my realm of being, understanding and meaning.

To draw a conclusion, in order to understand and interpret one has to realize oneself, existentially and ontologically. While the knowledge generated thereby has epistemological relativism, it is ontologically transcendent. In implication, it transcends the divide of subject and object because talking about the self is also talking about the so-called other, and vice versa. The alleged epistemological relativism is thus nullified, as all understanding is in terms of probabilities. The transcendental tendency of the above-mentioned hermeneutic conclusions are by no means merely a theological illusion. At this point, it is imperative to take note of the critical realism that perceives humans in terms of meta-reality, and describes transcendence as an everyday feature. It is, categorically, in contrast with the conventional notion of transcendence as an esoteric philosophical conceptualization. Bhaskar notes, 'Transcendence, transcendental identification in consciousness and transcendental agency are indispensable feature of all human being, social life and indeed a necessary condition for any human act at all' (Bhaskar 2002: 10).

The non-dual—Bhaskar's 'transcendental self'—resides beneath the duality and heteronomy of the visible world and its people. This self is connected with everybody else by the virtue of residing in the 'cosmic envelope'. An important rider is, 'Although we are all connected at the ground state, at the cosmic envelope, we can only act in the physical world from we are and we are unique, bounded and clearly demarcated, concretely singularized beings' (Ibid.: 14).

Furthermore, 'you cannot live in a non-dual state, but you can minimize the splits in your being and you can eliminate inconsistency with your ground-state as that you are effectively a whole autonomous being' (Ibid.: 110).

Thus, placing Bhaskar, alongside Schleiermacher, Dilthey, Heidegger, Bultmann, Gadamer, and the Upanishad, there develops a sense of holistic hermeneutics. They all suggested one thing in common—Be one with your 'field' in order to talk about them, not only epistemologically but also in terms of being. Thereby, do not only seek for their meaning, also do a constant appraisal of what you as a researcher mean. In simpler words, do not divide the pursuit of knowledge into the domain of heart or mind. It indeed only occurs when the dichotomies dissolve. By *holistic hermeneutics* in this wake I mean a philosophical discourse that puts the subject and object of a research, the researcher and the researched, the subjective and the objective, in one paradigm. To understand this paradigm, a researcher has to become both the disciples and the Upanishadic teacher. For the latter knows the validity of diverse interpretations of a single utterance.

Becoming of Being in the Field: Methodology of *Being*

Looking at a researcher through the above discursive prism it is obvious that the researcher's being is itself a perpetual subject of research. In the interactive framework of the field a researcher is shaped by external influences while carrying out a well-defined research plan. The structure of research receives constant tweaking and twisting while the researcher undergoes a process of becoming. The holistic hermeneutics, a juxtaposed book-view and field-view, surfaces when I make myself a subject of perpetual analysis in the field. All my experiences since the day I began to visit villages in the Maithili-speaking region became my data for methodological investigation.

This was the note on which I began on a journey back to Fulhara. On the way I stopped over the place called Singhia to buy some sweets for the children who had called me *mama*. This was a token entry for a guest in the domain of informal relation. As soon as I reached, I was yet again given the regards meant for a guest. But then I proactively entered the inner part of the household to meet Baby and *maami*. I intended to drive home the message that a guest who is also maternally related to almost the whole village can walk in any time and make his informal presence. I began to roam about the village in a loosely tucked dhoti and kurta. For no reason I began to frequent the barber shop to get a shave or my hair trimmed. Most importantly, I was now willingly listening to anybody willing to share a story, even apparently useless and boring ones. The utilitarian logic that 'only a certain kind of story told in certain ways is useful' began to recede. I still carried my camera, which I put to use only when very necessary, and ensured that it would not cause a throwback to my 'guest' status. Now I was all ears as a listener and all eyes as a beholder. This was however not enough because I knew 'to be is to do', and 'to do is to be', the crux of my hermeneutic lesson. Thus, I took to errands and chores that came my way, such as milking the cow in the cowshed alongside the *aangan* of *maami's* house. I undertook some interesting errands: getting fodder ready for the cow every morning and evening, visiting the field whenever *maami* went to check the crops, accompanying Radha to the *kirana* (grocery) shop and to other households where she went to deliver a message or something. My favourite chore was to accompany Radha every evening to *Kansar*, the many-mouthed hearth under a small thatch roof without walls where women/girls went to get their rice or maize parched. My association with Radha located me in the matrix of everyday life of the village, while roaming around with her father Putur roped me in the informal socio-political, and economic spheres of the village. Most important for me was my association with Radha and her mother Baby which ushered me in the informal-emotional-cultural interiors of the village. Baby was a *sewika* (worker) in the *Angan Baadi* branch of Fulhara. She took me along wherever she went and introduced me as her younger brother. I was gradually established as a quiet younger brother of Baby in the circle of women. My simpleton appearance and keenness to listen to the folk drew me closer to them. I earned their confidence by providing them with necessary advice as and when the need arose. I began to think that I was one of them despite the differences in upbringing and my intellectual interest in the song culture of the village. Not very surprising, as I felt, it was perhaps always within me, underneath my intellectual outfit, which required only a bit of effortless self-realization.

Becoming of Being. *Courtesy*: Author.

This realization was still laced with shock and awe. But they all seemed to be essential hurdles in the process of learning as to who I was. Meanwhile, I also acquired an orientation to the body clock of the village. It amounted to a following of the 'early to bed and early to rise' dictum. This meant that I began to catch the rural acoustic early morning consisting of the chirping of various birds, the folk tunes, and devotional songs aired by the Darbhanga branch of All India Radio, early breakfast (*chura-dahi*) with an excessively sweetened tea, etc. The solar cycle was the cycle of everyday life for literate as well illiterate folk in the village despite the presence and references to watches, clocks, and cellphones. It defined almost everything; I got defined by it. A range of apparently meaningless actions began to appear intelligible. Curiously, the intelligibility seemed to be closely linked with feeling. It is felt in the first place, and only thereafter translated into the domain of the intelligibly meaningful. Thus, activities such as dropping a bit of tea on the earth before consuming it, responding to the sound produced by domestic lizards or to the moos of the cow while carrying on domestic chores, singing while carrying out everyday drudgery, gradually seemed to make sense. It was not as simple as Weberian Verstehen, for mere empathizing hardly amounted to the meaning the folk attached to various things that were said and done. The Dilthean 'life expression' in tandem with 'life experience', as found in the field, presumed the researcher to have it experienced in the first place. Truly, understanding is as much an inward process as an outward one. But understanding was a precondition for interpretation. And to do so as a researcher I had to find my seamless location in the 'ontologico-existential matrix' of the field. My routine tea session at the tea shop in the village where news and views overlapped neatly, my freewheeling conversations with the barber who sang *Parati* every morning, my venturing into the crop-laden field of the village with kids while accompanying them on various errands, my frequent visit to the neighbouring households as a man for whom every elderly man was a *mama* and every elderly woman a *maami*, such actions defined my being, translated me from a researcher (outsider) into an intimate knower (insider). The evolution was not fake as I laughed when they laughed and I wept when they all did.

Emotional unison was an evidence of my becoming one of them—something Martin Heidegger called *Dasein*, 'Being-there and Being-in'. As soon as attained, the state of this Being curtails the circuit of subjective speculation as well as bland search of rational meaning. The 'fusion of horizon' foreclosed the separation of 'I' of the researcher from the 'We' of the field. Yet the significance of the 'I' is never destroyed, neither is that of the 'We' compromised. Thus, for example, when Manorama Devi or Sulekha Devi sang a simple devotional song, I could fathom her tacit attempt to be self-referent and glean her 'self' located in the context of the collective. I could also figure out her biography intertwined with the songs she sang, and that her biography became a slice of the sociocultural history of the folk. Similarly, I got a sense of my own biography being constituted and reconstituted at the intersections of Manorama Devi's renditions. Every now and then I learnt that I resembled not only Manorama Devi, but also so many of those who I, as a rational researcher, would have reduced into mere informants/respondents. The folk so became a mirror reflecting my own variegated images. Thus, I realize that only *holistic hermeneutics* enables me as a researcher-observer to perceive the link between the cosmic envelop consisting of the folk as well as me at once. A Brahmin woman or man, a little child, a cobbler, a barber, a mallah, a musahar, may be singing different songs. But the distinctions notwithstanding, they all tend to remind themselves as well as their direct/indirect listeners that there is a cosmic whole, that they are variegated images of heteronomy, and that they can transcend them through practices of everyday life. To understand, interpret and put them into words, it is imperative for me to realize my own quotidian ability of transcendence. Only then can the sobbing in the middle of singing, reminiscing about an event of life alongside the rendition of a song, reluctance to sing certain songs on certain occasions, and refusal to deliver crystal-clear meanings make sense to me.

Notes

1. I have put *being* in italics for two reasons: one that it is not the being of the researcher in isolation, which can slip into intellectual atomization in the course of research and especially in the act of understanding and interpreting; two, the idea of being emerges when the experience in the field is merged with the reading of the hermeneutic philosophy along with meditation upon the insights from the Upanishad, the *Gita*, and the transcendental realism of Roy Bhaskar (2002).

2. I am using the notion of *field* with Pierre Bourdieu (1975) in mind, alluding to the basic configuration of the *field*, that it exerts relational power on the visitor. Bourdieu and Loïc J.D. Wacquant (1992) discuss the dual nature of the field, consisting of configuration of forces; and site of struggle to maintain or transform those forces. It serves the purpose of underlining the field as a site of contestation, be it among the agencies embedded in the structure of the *field* (which is Bourdieu's interest), or between the researcher's world view and that of the field.

3. See Marcus 2012, followed by Zenker and Kumoll 2013.

4. By field-view I mean the interpretative skills of a researcher inclusive of the categories and concepts, perspectives and stances, intellectual and emotional strengths that emanate from a web of social relationship with the people, their institutions, beliefs and practices, and surrounding of the universe of study. The terms such as field is used only to make it easier for academic readers who can make sense of an argument if and only if terminologies from research parlance are used. Otherwise, the field never remains a technically conceived universe for a researcher. Thus, the most honest expression, for such a field by such a researcher, would be 'the village where I lived'.

5. Foundation, here, semantically refers to the structure that supports further building. On the other hand, foundation used in the compound of 'anti-foundation' refers to the philosophical tenets of the Enlightenment and the concomitant methodology, positivism in empirical social sciences. For more along this line, see Hekman 1986.

6. The surname Misra is pronounced Misar in Maithili. Puna Misar is the father of my facilitator Putur Misar. Though the latter is known in village for his own identity, I continued with the practice of asking for the household by the name of the eldest.

7. On a lighter note, I drew an instant conclusion that most of the villagers who go to the field to defecate are never clean as one *lota* can hardly suffice, and thus they are all sources of some or other epidemic.

8. Putur rescued me from the embarrassment by spinning attractive lies, that I was a professor in a university in Delhi, and was in the process

of writing a grand book on Maithili songs and the village culture, that I earn more than anybody in the village, that I owned a big house not only in the district-town but also in Delhi, and also that I am unmarried at my age due to some family reasons rather than matrimonial ineligibility.

9. By 'emotionally truthful' I mean to refer to the communicative ability of the folk that expresses emotional intent without any qualms. Thereby, the singing of folk songs is actually a vent of the emotional underpinnings.

10. Anthony Giddens (1976) puts M. Weber and Wilhelm Dilthey together and argues that they both failed to defend against a charge that Verstehen generates only hypothesis and not verified knowledge. While the positivist social science benefited from this allegation, the qualitative social science researches and particularly interpretative sociology suffered. It is not until Martin Heidegger and Hans-Georg Gadamer that the subjective meaning of the actor could find an acceptance in the realm of objective enquiry.

11. Giddens points out that Dilthey resorted to this term with an intention to represent J.S. Mill's term 'moral sciences'. Only in approximation does it mean Hermeneutic philosophy.

12. Etymologically, Hermeneutics is related to the Hermese (the messenger god of the Greek). They had to be conversant in the idioms of gods and mortals in order to understand and interpret.

13. I am referring to Johann Martin Chladenius with an intention to touch upon, albeit very briefly, the posterity of the hermeneutical problem in question: the being of the seeker of understanding.

14. This particular stance seems to characterize the whole of twentieth century hermeneutic philosophy, in the works of Dilthey, Edmund Husserl, Heidegger, Gadamer, and Apel. It is also important to note as to how it redresses the adverse impact of the Durkheimian stance that reads: the whole is not the sum total of its parts.

15. This tale and the following discussion on it emerged in conversations with a few Brahmin priests and literate residents in Fulhara. It is presented in italics, and without claiming textual veracity of it. However, it offers an important insight for the discussion in this essay. Upanishad literally means sitting near (the teacher) and learning. The claim about the number of Upanishads varies from source to source, indicating a range of 108 to 200. However, two of them have been counted as the most prominent, *Brihadaranyaka Upanishad* and *Chandogya Upanishad*. *Brihadaranyaka Upanishad* means sitting in the great forest (with the teacher) and learning; see http://www.britannica.com/EBchecked/topic/266312/Hinduism/59824/The-Upanishads, accessed 14 April 2018.

16. D, the Roman equivalent of the Sanskrit letter *D* is phonologically more or less same, though the etymological significance and deeper connotation vary.
17. *Yad Hridayam Hridayamiti Hridayashtha Budhdhi Ruchyata;* all translations are by the author, with the help from a teacher of Sanskrit and resident of the village named Pundit Ugrakant Mishra.
18. *Hridayen hi Satyam Janati.*
19. This particular adage is accompanied by *Dwitiyat wai bhayam bhawet* and *Ekaki na ramte.* It means, I fear an existence apart from me, and, I dislike being only one, respectively. The resolve of this tension is *Sa dwitiyam echhet*, meaning, hence I want somebody apart from me. The wisdom is singularly expressed in *Eko aham bahusyam*, meaning *I am one yearning and becoming many.*

5

Mithila, Maithili and Maithil: Field in Historical Context

Ancient or not, mythology can only have an historical
foundation, for myth is a type of speech chosen by history:
it cannot possibly evolve from 'nature' of things.

—ROLAND BARTHES (1989: 110)

A critical reading of many versions of the cultural history of
Mithila, that this essay seeks to present, amounts to bewildering
understanding. The thickness of the cultural history of Mithila
could be summed up in one frequently heard exclamation: 'Mithila
is great!' The dubious platitude however solicits an optimally
agnostic approach to the historicity of Mithila. A few recurrent
motifs in the history of Mithila support the proposed agnosticism.
First, it has a history largely based on conjectures and inferences.
The history of ancient Mithila hinges on the texts of the Vedas, the
Brahmins, Smritis, and Buddhist Jatakas. This delivers a historical
account that is irretrievably entangled with mythical narratives.
Second, Mithila has a humble history, without centrality to war
and conquest, which is a regular feature in the usual history texts.[1]

Though there are instances of aggression on the part of Mithila's
kingship, they are not of the kind that could be an attraction in
the royal annals. The kings were by and large themselves men
of letters engaged in scholarly (philosophical, literary, poetic)
pursuits. Instances of aggression by kings in Mithila tell tales of
seemingly 'un-royal' escapes. History has it that any bid at carving
out a politically sovereign Mithila eventuated into a debacle for

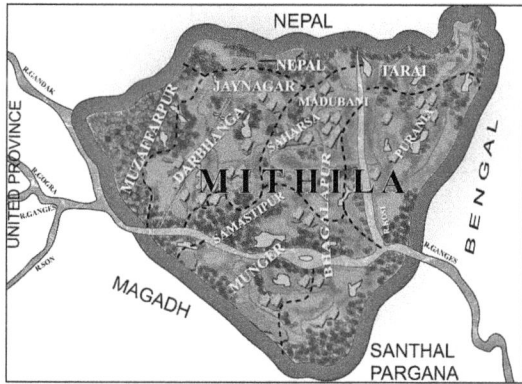

MAP 5.1: Illustrating the Dialects and Sub-dialects of the Bihari Language
Source: *Linguistic Survey of India*: Indo-Aryan Family Eastern: Specimens of the Bihari and Oriya, collected and edited by George Abraham Grierson, Office of the Superintendent, Government Printing, Calcutta, India, vol. 5, pt. 2, 1903. *Courtesy*: Nehru Memorial Museum & Library.

the dynasty. The third point is a gateway to a larger discussion on the idea of Mithila as a politico-cultural region and Maithili as its language. It is about the indefinite landmarks that shift throughout the history of Mithila, and definite speech-marks that create an intelligible idea of the sociocultural region. It invites us to ponder upon the modern debates on Mithila and Maithili whereby certain conflicting streams of thoughts emerge. All these key issues flagged in historical context become important in the context of the culture of folk songs which is the mainstay of this book. The chapter, thus, becomes a meaningful precursor to the discussions on folk songs in the latter essays.

The above remarks about the historicity of the region are aptly summed up by Upendra Thakur, one of the earliest historians writing on ancient Mithila:

There are few regions of India possessing an ancient civilization, about which we have less definite historical information than the region north of the Ganges, variously known as Videha, Tirubhukti, or (after the name of its capital) Mithila . . . its history does not center around feats of arms, but around courts given to higher pursuits of learning. (1956: 1)

The essay shall delve into these recurrent motifs in history to develop a sense of Mithila as a sociocultural entity. There is a mention of various historical epochs, which is done not to present a chronological detail of war and conquest. Instead, the essay eclectically reasons through the historical meshed with mythological to propose a platitude-free comprehension of Mithila.

Mithila: *As it Were!*

In the civilizational scheme Mithila was not called Mithila. As per the *Satapatha Brahmana* (1000–600 BC) it was called Videha. If we go by the references to traditional texts such as the *Brihad Vishnu Purana*, there were twelve names of Mithila that are all 'descriptive epithets'. Out of these, only three gained in significance. First was Videha that lost its currency of usage in medieval times. Tirubhukti was the popular name of the region in the fourth and fifth century AD. Even in George Grierson's work on the languages of Bihar, there are constant references to Tirhut (a derivative of

Tirubhukti). 'The use of the appellation "Mithila" along with "Tirubhukti or Tirhut" for the whole country is comparatively very late from about the time of the installation of the Karnata dynasty in 1097 AD' (Mishra 1979: 12). On the other hand, there are multiple versions of stories to suggest the antiquity of the term Mithila. A dominant version is that Nimi, the son of a king of Ayodhya named Manu, came to this region called Videha, the 'land of sacrifices'. Nimi's son Mithi built a city and named it after himself as Mithila. Mithi, as the builder of the city, earned the epithet Janaka, the genitor of the city, and the city Mithila acquired the status of the capital town of Videha. Another version is that Mithi was the name of a sage after whom the region was called Mithila (Jha 1958).

The name Janaka has polysemy in the history of ancient Mithila. It appears like a prestigious laurel accorded to anybody who created something extraordinary. It is also a family name for a creator. The king named Siradhwaja, the father of Sita, has a suffix Janaka. This, albeit, is not the Janaka who is hailed in texts and also routine talks in Mithila as a king-philosopher. The latter was Krti Janaka, a close friend of the renowned philosopher Yajnavalkya. Janaka, the father of the protagonist Sita of the epic *Ramayana*, is often confused with Janaka, the king-philosopher. They are both located in a mythological rather than the historical context, in a modern sense of historiography. Historians on Mithila resort to inferences from the traditional texts to make sense of the region and its people in the olden times. It helps in understanding the past even as it obscures many dimensions. Hence, it is imperative to be comfortable with polyphonies and confusions on the historicity of Mithila. Unless the implicit paradoxes are underscored, any historical understanding of Mithila is bound to be wishful glorification of the land and its people.[2]

Thus, on the one hand historians acknowledge the geographical map of Mithila and on the other they underline the dynamic aspect of its geography. Rivers are eternal landmarks in locating Mithila in posterity, if not history. Mixing history and posterity, it is between 25'28" and 26'52" N latitude, and between 84'56" and 86'46" E longitude. The Himalaya runs along its northern side, and on the east, south, and west the rivers Kosi (Kausiki),

Ganga, and Gandaki surround it, respectively (Thakur 1956; Mishra 1979; Jha 1958; Burghart 1993). A footnote by Thakur, however, adds to the uncertainty and augments the possibility of shifting landmarks of Mithila. It locates the Gangasagar, the Bay of Bengal where the Ganga merges into the sea, and is presently located near the Diamond Harbour in Calcutta, in Mithila. To quote, 'In ancient times, the sea extended up to the Himalaya. On account of constant siltation, Gangasagar has been shifting south-eastward. The Gangasagar referred to here (in Vishnu Purana and Shrimadbhagvat) might be somewhere near Mithila, in her south-east, in Munger or Bhagalpur or Rajmahal' (Thakur 1956: 6).

Similarly, shifting boundaries, in accordance with geographical-natural landmarks, is often associated with the changing course of the river Kosi. Vijaykant Mishra holds the dramatic shift in the course of Kosi responsible for change in the eastern boundary of Mithila (1979: 8).[3] Likewise S. Jha suggests, 'it is difficult to fix the boundary lines of Mithila, except on the north, where the Himalayas are immovable' (1958: 1). This is perhaps the reason why any work on Mithila in recent times encapsulates its boundary in the vastest possible demarcation. R. Burghart (1993) writes:

the country of Mithila extends northward from the river Ganges across Bihar and into Nepalese Terai from where the Siwalik foothills of the Himalayas emerge from the plain. Its western and eastern frontiers are ritually demarcated by the Gandaki and Kosi rivers whose headwaters originate on the Tibetan plateau, collect in inner Himalayas and turn southward across the north Indian plain to meet the Ganges. Between Gandaki and Kosi other rivers and streams such as Baghmati, Lakhandei and Kamla drain the southern flanks of the Himalayas and head southward across the country, playing every year on the hopes and fears of farmers. (Ibid.: 763)

In this wake, sight may not, but sounds travel unimpeded in Mithila, suggests Burghart. The speech marks rather than landmarks of Mithila thereby acquire centrestage.[4] The following section will adjudge this by looking at the sociocultural components of the region through various historical epochs.

Post Vedic and Pre-Moghul Mithila

Thakur (1956) suggests that an examination of the sociocultural structure of Mithila in ancient times unfolds a paradoxical relation between society and intellectual spectacles. It seems the principle of purity and pollution governed social tenets vis-à-vis Maithil's social conduct, allocation of roles, and ascribed status. The Maithil Brahmins enjoyed unstinted royal patronage and remained unrivalled 'drinkers of soma', the embodiment of sacred knowledge. Social stratification, the *Satapatha Brahmana* indicates, acquired tenacity along caste lines in the post-Vedic age; Thakur argues, 'it was a mid-way between the laxity of the Rgveda and the rigidity of the Sutras' (Ibid.: 73). An oft-cited example that associates caste mobility and intellectual prowess is the instance of the philosopher King Janak, who apparently switched from the Kshatriya varna to that of Brahmin through the teachings of his friend Yajnavalkya, the Upanishadic philosopher. It is however not an indicator of a rule on interchange of caste. The luxury of changing caste seems to be for a king rather than for all and sundry. Similarly, another oft-cited example of women scholars such as Gargi and Maitreyi does not represent a rule for the knowledge pursuit among women in general in Mithila.[5] In a similar vein, while men could pursue polygamy women could not. Let alone ordinary women, Thakur says, 'womanhood in the higher orders is more truly represented by helpless Sita than by the stronger minded women' (Ibid.: 79).

Alongside the privileged existed the common men and women living on agriculture, grappling with both natural calamity (mostly famine) and sociocultural humiliation. While the privileged indulged in philosophical discourse, 'the common people, however did not understand those abstruse theological and philosophical speculations, (and) they were stuck to the worship of the deities of the Rgvedic period' (Ibid.: 95).

The period of the Brahmanas that intervenes the period of the Vedas and Upanishads is termed as the 'age of sacrificial ceremonials'. Thus, religious practices across caste groups were rife with rituals and superstitions. 'The Hindu theory that religions do not come from without but from within, was ridiculously ignored' (Ibid.: 96). No wonder Brahmins, skilled in priestly jobs, occupied centre stage in not only royal circles but also in everyday life in society. An interesting setback for the preoccupation with *karma-kanda* (rituals and superstitions) was ushered in the Upanishadic

age. The epitomizing instance to account for this point, Thakur
cites, is when Janak Videh, the king philosopher, a friend of
Yajnavalkya, 'refused to submit to the hierarchical pretensions of the
Brahmanas and asserted his right of performing sacrifices without
the intervention of the priest' (Ibid.: 97). The excellence of the
age stemmed from the genius of philosophers like Yajnavalkya,
Gautama, Kapila, Vibhndaka, and Satananda. Ironically, the best of
the Upanishadic age turned out to be the reason for its downfall.
'Their extreme moral, philosophical and religious outlook was
responsible for the dying out of their fighting genius' (Ibid.: 60).
As depicted in the Buddhist and Jaina literatures, the Videhan
kings renounced the world and became ascetics without caring
for their kingdom and people. Thus, the glory of the Upanishadic
age which made the elite aware of the limitations of the Vedic
rituals, conducts, and priestly dominance, was coupled with an
abdication by the elite of their socio-political responsibilities.
The glory of the age was subdued by the unrest among ordinary
people. It was around this time that Buddhism and Jainism found
space in people's world view. In fact it had a precursor in the
Upanishadic age. As Thakur notes, 'the doctrines promulgated
by Yajnyavalkya in the Brahdaranyak Upanishad are in fact
completely Buddhistic'[6] (Ibid.: 105). The Vedanta philosophy was
sidelined, as Mithila became part of the Vajjian confederacy of
oligarchic republic in 600 BC.

The seat of power during this period shifted from Mithila to
Vaishali, and the latter became the hub of new ideas that defined
sociocultural conditions.[7] Caste-based hereditary occupations
were in decline although not very dramatically. Thakur notes, 'A
Brahmin lived as an archer, a carpenter, a craven guard, a snake
charmer, an agriculturalist, hunter and carriage driver without
incurring social stigma' (Ibid.: 129). The stronghold of Brahmins
in the Videhan territory, nevertheless, did not diminish as it was
still away from the epicentre of Buddhism. Buddhism and Jainism
could not ameliorate the basic social structure that promoted
slavish dependency of the downtrodden. In fact, the status of
women slipped further down. Buddha himself had nursed deep
disdain of women. In Buddhist thought any inclination towards
women was equal to 'falling into the mouth of tiger' or 'under the

sharp knife of executioner' because their bewitching beauty robes men of their heart. Yet Buddha allowed women in the monasteries only to regret it later as the cause of the downfall of monastic system. The diminishing social legitimacy of Buddhism and power-puffed postures of the Vajjian republic posing a threat to Ajatshatru of Pataliputra together inflicted a setback for the Vajjian state. The Magadhan commanded reigns and Mithila ushered in what historians call a 'dark age'.

The centre of political gravity shifted to Pataliputra. Vaishali and Mithila were provinces of the Mauryan Empire. In the passage of time a Brahminic reaction led to the breakup of the Mauryan Empire. The assassination of the last Mauryan King Brahdaratha by his general Pushyamitra Sung, a Brahmin from the Bharadwaj gotra, was a decisive moment. Pushyamitra established the Sung dynasty (187–151 BC), supported by Maithil Brahmins of Mithila. This was the moment when there emerged a politically 'militant Brahminism'. After a long passage of political upheavals, many invaders appeared on the scene including the Kanvas, Andhras, Parthians, Kusanas, Guptas, Palas, and many short term invaders. A new era dawned only after 1,400 years of political trials and tribulations as the Karnata King Nanyadev founded the Karnata or Simraon dynasty (AD 1097), thus proclaiming an independent Mithila. It also slipped into the hand of Vijayasena of Bengal for some time until Gangadev, son of Nanyadev, reclaimed Mithila by pushing back Vijayasena's *sena*.

Historians record that the Karnatas were skilled in intellect as well as in polity and warfare.[8] Due to its geographical location and strategic position Mithila was protected from Muslim invasions for long. It was during the reign of Shaktisimhadev that Muslim rulers began to sharpen their fangs against Mithila. Shaktisimhadev was a cruel despot and to check his autocratic power his ministers had forged a council. Later, a system of greater significance emerged during the rule of Harisimhadev, often cited as a social reformer king in the history of Mithila, who introduced Panji-Prabandha. It entailed classification of people on the basis of merit (caste-based but also incorporating significance of achievements). A decisive blow to the dynasty was struck in AD 1324 when Ghyasuddin Tughlak on his way back from Bengal, attacked Tirhut (Mithila).

King Harisimhadev entered (or fled to) Nepal along with many Maithil Brahmins. While the last Karnata king of Mithila founded a new dynasty in Nepal, Muhammad Tughlak renamed Tirhut as Tughlakpur and swept almost the entire north Bihar. In Mithila, the Sultan made Kameshwara Thakur a vassal. This came to be known as the beginning of the Oinwara or Sugauna dynasty. Mithila was, during this rule, internally independent and externally dependent on the Muslim Sultan. Any deviations from the direction of the Sultan wrought havoc for the king of Mithila. The fraught history of the Oinwaras encompasses an unstable rule, toppling and displacing of rulers, but an almost continuous and unhindered flourishing of literature and scholarship.

The renowned poet Vidyapati seems to be a chronicler for the entire dynasty, though he was closely associated with the King Sivasimha as a 'friend, guide and philosopher'. Before this, in the reign of king Bhawasimha, Gonu Jha emerged as a household name, an excellent humourist scholar.[9] The chronicler Vidyapati wrote eulogia for almost each king of the dynasty, but his role acquired overt political significance only when Sivasimha refused to abide by the Sultan. Sivasimha was vanquished by the force of the Sultan and his wife Lakhimadevi was restored to the throne only due to Vidyapati's intelligent mediations. This was, evidently, a precedent that a widow ascended to the throne. Lakhimadevi was herself an erudite scholar of Sanskrit literature. She continued the legacy of the Oinwara kings and her patronage to Vidyapati was at an all-time high.[10] The noteworthy part of Lakhimadevi's scholarship was the Sanskrit verses she wrote to parody and condemn the *bikauas* (literally meaning saleable). The latter sarcastically alluded to the Brahmins who sold their daughters and sisters in marriage to the ineligible matches. Her critical commentary on this offensive social practice of the Brahmins seems peerless.

The Oinwara's decline was gradual and due to varied reasons. It weakened post-Sivasimha and branched out into two tiny and insignificant dynasties. Historians admit the unavailability of adequate records on the later part of the Oinwaras. Summarily, on the ruins of the Oinwaras petty zamindars controlled Mithila and paid regular tribute to the Moghul Emperor Babar. Not confirmed, but one Maithil Kayasth Majumdar, one Majlis Khan, and some others were immediate successors of the Oinwaras.

From Mughal to the Company

Nasrat Shah of Bengal (AD 1519–32) decimated the Oinwaras and thus ensued a hiatus fraught with anarchy. Until the ascendance of Babar as the Moghul emperor, Mithila remained an annexure of the independent kingdom of Bengal as Nasrat Shah had broken treaty with Delhi. Mithila as well as other parts of Bihar were detached from Bengal with the arrival of Akbar. Tirhut was included in the *subah* or province of Bihar under the Mughal governor. It was during this time, when Man Singh was the governor of Bihar and Bengal, that Akbar decided to install Mahamahopadhyay Mahesh Thakur, a man of letters from Mithila, as the ruler of the region. Thus in AD 1556–7 started the reign of the Khandavala, the last major dynasty of rulers in Mithila. The Thakurs continued the tradition of patronizing and engaging with the Sanskrit scholarship. One of the admirable consequences of the royal tradition of patronization during the reign of King Mahinath was the poet Locanakavi. The latter was celebrated for his erudite approach to music and literature, manifest in his magnum opus *Rajatarangini*. It was during this dynasty that a military Mithila also came into existence. Succeeding Narpati Thakur, who was allowed by the emperor to build up a robust army, his son Raghavsimha became ambitious. He was friendly with the Nawab of Bengal Aliwardi Khan. He was the only ruler known in the political history of Mithila who changed his surname from Thakur to Simha and thereby changed his caste, from Brahmin to Kshatriya. Subsequently, argues Mishra (1979):

> the 'scholar' king of Mithila assumed the role of 'warrior' king . . . they came to be respected, feared, and counted in the public life of north eastern India, the imperial authority lay nominally in over the whole of India, but it appears that the kingdom of Mithila functioned as more or less independent sovereigns. (Ibid.: 98)

Umanatha Bakshi and Gokulanatha Bakshi were the commanding officers of the national army of Mithila, trained by one Sardar Khan. King Narendra Simha, the greatest among the warrior kings took the military-trained Mithila to its zenith. The army participated in several expeditions and helped the Mughals suppress an invasion by the Afghan adventurer Mustafa Khan.

They were also employed to deal with the aggressors from the neighbourhood. Bhumihars of Champaran dissented against the king of Mithila and were suppressed at Bettiah by the invincible army. The seemingly invincible military of Mithila met its end. It started with Pratap Simha and was completed in Madhav Simha's reign. It was when the loyal commanders such as the Bakshis and others were not paid heed and the kingship entered the permanent settlement with the British. The colonial intervention, transformative toward agrarian structure and centre of rule, did not affect the sociocultural arrangements. In 1786, Tirhut, with headquarters at Muzaffarpur included Darbhanga Raj. Darbhanga itself became the headquarters in 1867.

The later kings of this dynasty, mainly Lakshimshwarasimha (1878–98), Rameshvarasimha (1888–1929), and Kameshwarsimha (1929–62), are known for their support to the further development of literature and philosophy.[11] The legacy of supporting traditional education assumed a novel face as an inclination towards English education surfaced. It was however not a story of English superseding the vernacular. In the beginning of the nineteenth-century Maharaja Chhatrasingh extended support to Hindu educational institutions. Later, his son Rudrasingh made huge donations for the establishment of the first ever Anglo-vernacular school at Muzaffarpur. The schools run by the royal administration were better off in popular perception than the colonial schools. Meanwhile, the system of wards administration came into effect and the education of the minors of the landholders of Mithila was conducted by the colonial administration. The introduction of English education to the public was not easy and smooth, as Jata Shankar Jha observes, 'all efforts on the part of the government to spread English education in the district of Tirhoot had failed ... the region being a stronghold of orthodox Brahmins it resisted the introduction of a foreign language in the domain of learning' (1972: xvi).

The entry of English education in Darbhanga is synchronized with the accession of Maharaja Lakshimishwar Singh to the throne. By 1871, a private Anglo-vernacular school came up in Madhubani with support from both the royal family and the British government. Lakshimishwar Singh also introduced entrance examinations and competition in schools, leading to employment. No tuition fees were collected by the Raj even though the British government was interested in it. Interestingly, Maharaja Rameshvar Singh was categorically in favour of orthodox Sanskrit learning, perhaps as an indigenous response to the growing popularity of English education. A modernization of education, instrumental supremacy of the Western, and a recasting of the traditional had begun in the popular consciousness of the Maithili folk. The modernity of Mithila was furthermore visible in the crystallization of class in addition to the entrenchment of caste groups. The formation of an elite class, without a displacement of the hierarchy of purity and pollution in the caste structure occurred in Mithila too (Jha 1992). But this did not wipe out the sociocultural possibilities in nineteenth-century Mithila. The liberal, modern, and progressive scheme of thinking persisted alongside the knowledge and practice of traditions. This is the reason why Harimohan Jha, a literary genius in modern Mithila, experimented with a new character of Khattar Kaka and presented fictional, philosophical, and critical discussions on the caste mores, blind belief, and unreflective canonization of ancient epics such as the *Ramayana* and the *Bhagvad Gita*.

Meanings of *Being Maithil*

In the backdrop of a sketchy historical account it is interesting to configure sociocultural and religious arrangements in the region. For politico-administrative purposes, Mithila was called Tirhut while in sociocultural configuration the region of Maithili-speaking people continued to be known as Mithila. It is not homogenous as far as sociocultural structure is concerned; neither is it so in a religio-philosophical sense. Such heterogeneity is despite the fact that the orthodoxy of Brahmins has been predominant. The diversity of sects within the Hindu fold articulates the possible conflicts and negotiation among sociocultural groups. Speaking primarily about orthodox Brahmins, Mishra says, 'A Maithil generally has the three fold mark on the forehead representing the following symbols—the horizontal lines, marked with ashes (*bhashma*), represent devotion to Siva; the white vertical *chandana* representing the faith in Vishnu and the red sandal paste or vermillion representing veneration for Sakti' (1979: 125).

In addition to the trinity of Siva, Sakti, and Vishnu, the Maithil also worship the puranic reincarnation of Vishnu and their consorts. Worshipping Siva exhibits the elementary form of Maithili religious life, and hence Siva seems to be probably the oldest god of Mithila. The Maithil make earthen *lingam* (the various shapes of Siva made of clay). In every household Siva has been worshipped in the form of earthen *linga*. Umpteen Siva temples in Mithila, mostly low in pomp and appearance while high on importance, dot the religio-cultural landscape.[12] Such is the depth of the influence of Siva-worship that almost every scholarly work, poetic-literary and philosophical, expresses devotion to Siva. *Nachari* and *Maheshvani*,[13] the poetic compositions of Vidyapati and others in praise of Siva, dominate the oral-acoustic surroundings of Mithila. The most recent addition in the conglomerate of god and deity is Chandra (moon)—the ornamental associate of Siva. Maharaja Hemangada Thakur, of the Khandavala kula, started and popularized it and thus the celebration of Chaurchanda (worshipping *chandrama* of *chaturthi*: moon on the fourth night in the month of Kartik in the lunar calendar, roughly in the roman month of October), became a folk festival. Worshipping Sakti is equally important as the belief goes that Sakti blesses with *siddhi* (realization of the aspired).

Scholars have been influenced by Sakti. Vidyapati's predecessor Devaditya, Madan Upadhyay, and even Vidyapati himself[14] were a few celebrated worshippers. A sacred place for Gasuani (the goddess) in the household is a ubiquitous feature in Mithila. Any auspicious occasion begins with a rendition of *gosaunik geet*, songs invoking the blessings of the deity. Pertaining to Sakti-worshipping are several works in tantra.[15] Diverse instances in everyday life reflect influence of tantra (Sakti). The devotion to the goddess is mostly in tantric scheme. *Aipan* (Alpana/tantra), a design made on the floor with the wet powder of rice made by women on any auspicious occasion is a good example. Besides, the *jog* songs meant to attract husband, *joga-tona*, and *jhaad-phoonk* (magic charm) express the synchrony of tantra and belief in the goddess. The names of people such as Tarachand, Tara Charan Tantradhari,

Khadagdhari, Adyacharan too carry a sense of devotion to the goddess. Needless to say, the belief in *dakini* and *dayan* (witches who possess magical power), Kumari Puja (worshipping, feeding, and gifting virgin) fit into this scheme too. The traditional headgear called *paag*, which every Maithil man dons even these days on special occasions bears tantric character. The red dot of vermillion or red apparel is the most common sign of the Sakti-tantra influence.

Scholars also highlight the tantric character of the Maithili script and the geography of Mithila. Even families and villages are dedicated to Sakti. Names of some of the villages such as Harinagar, Mangrauni, Koilakha, Uchchaitha, and Bangama resonate this devotion. The geographic proximity to Nepal and Tibet is said to have caused the relationship between tantra and Sakti, and the deeper influence of it on Maithil everyday life. This influence mainly refers to Buddhism and its absorption into the Hindu fold. It is said to have been absorbed in mainly two ways—by assimilation of tantra form into Sakti worship, and by incorporating Buddha as one of the ten reincarnations of Vishnu (Mishra 1979). Chandeshvara had specified a day to worship Buddha in his scholarly work *Krityaratnakar*, and Mahayana Goddess Tara is a sought after deity among the Maithil worshippers.

The absorption of the Buddhist influence is not a simple tale, as there are historical evidences of discursive confrontation between the orthodox Brahminic scholarship and the Buddhist thinkers. When Mithila was not a hub of political activity and Vajjian confederacy was the centre of power, a strong Maithili opposition to Buddhism was in the making. Seer-philosophers and logicians from both sides dared each other in philosophical debates. 'For example, if a Buddhist logician defeated a greater Nyaya or Mimamsa thinker in a great public debate, attended by learned scholars from every part of the country, his fame at once spread all over the country and he could secure a large numbers of followers on the spot' (Thakur 1988: 509).

According to the *Nyaya Sutra* of Gautama, and Vatsyayan's commentary, Udyotkara challenged the renowned Buddhist logician Dinnaga (AD 500). In AD 984 Udayana wrote *Nyaya Kusumanjali*, questioning the Buddhist conceptions, especially of

the non-existence of god. Around seventh century AD another
Buddhist scholar Dharmakirti emerged in popularity; he retrieved
Dinnaga's philosophical arguments from the discursive ravages. But
around the same century Udyotkara, Kumaril, and Shankaracharya
were making their intellectual, philosophical, and social headway.
As soon as Shankaracharya defeated Mandan Mishra, a Mimamsa
scholar in Mithila, Vedantik philosophy reached a peerless height
and an immense following of Shankaracharya ensued. It engulfed
the whole of India and left little scope for the Buddhist scholars.
Towards AD 1200 Ganesha Upadhyay propounded Nava-Nyaya,
yet another milestone in the history of philosophy in Mithila.

In sum, no other religion, not even Islam despite the association
with the invaders, than Buddhism aroused the philosopher-logicians
of Mithila. The primary tenet of Buddhism that advocated a 'no
idolatry, no priests, no karma' theory and aimed at radical change
in structure was more serious a challenge for the Maithil think
tank than the Khilji, the indirect Mughal ruler. Nor were the
British the instigators for the Maithils. The rejection of Buddhism
was not uni-linear, as there is clear evidence of acceptance too.
It is difficult to deny the presence of Buddhism, particularly due
to the presence of the Mahayana deities and tantric practices.[16]
Buddhist-tantric practices were twofold, and they are hitherto
present in various parts of Mithila. One was called the *vama-
marga*, belonging to the Aghora, a cult that practices penance at
the cremation ground with unusual (socially tabooed) means.
The other is *dakshina-marga*, practiced through the means of yoga,
within as well as without the household.

The Aghora tantra inspired awe and fear amongst the rulers
as well as the ruled in Mithila given its extraordinary ways of
seeking self-realization. The Aghora tantric allegedly indulged in
debauchery, fraudulence, and exploitation. Moreover, it fell victim
to Muslim attacks and could not explain people's misery in the
face of the plight. A rechristened version of tantra entered in
Maithil Hinduism in the form of art and aesthetics, providing
depth and dimension of meaning. There was, additionally, yet
another way in which Buddhism impacted Maithil society. As
Purnendu Ranjan (1988) informs, many Brahmins came to join
the Buddhist monasteries and began to follow the doctrine. The

discursive upheaval that left Buddhism in intellectual as well as social tatters discouraged its Maithil followers. They decided to return to the Hindu fold in around the thirteenth century. But they were given only secondary/lower status in society than that of a Brahmin. Thus, they were called Bhumihars, a caste of landowners in Mithila. The Bhumihar Brahmins turned their monastery into *thakurwadis*, a Maithil term for divine abode, in an attempt to compensate for their lost glory.[17]

Arguably, the decline of Buddhism was also due to its stress on ascetic life, detachment from women and household. On the contrary, the traditional social structure of Mithila encouraged ascetic pursuits within the non-ascetic format of living. Thus, we find that all the scholars, poets, logicians, and philosophers of Mithila were men of families with worldly existence, as it were. No wonder, then, the celebrated scholar Jyotireshvara Thakur in his treatise *Varnaratnakara* expresses contempt for the ascetic cults. Second, Buddhism along with Jainism also brought about a focus on heterodoxy in the traditional space of Brahminic orthodoxy (Ranjan 1988). These religions were set on decline after the thirteenth century, without much following, but the idea of heterodoxy and thereof culture of dissent was persistent in the tantric, Nath panth, and Siddha cults. This tradition of heterodoxy made it possible for the Kabirpanth to bloom in Mithila. It began to spread in Bihar in the seventeenth-century. Bhagoda, one of the disciples of Kabir, established the first ever *math* (monastery) at Dhanauti, presently in Saran district of Bihar, at the fringe of Mithila. Another disciple Jagudas founded a *math* at Andhrathadi in the district of Madhubani and Basantpur in the district of Samastipur in Mithila. Ranjan suggests that as a dissent against the caste structure, 'intermediary castes and some lower castes and even some Muslims, became members of the panth (the sect of followers of Kabir), which flourished under the guidance of its institutional base—the maths' (Ibid.: 5).

There were four *acharya gaddis* (the oldest *maths*) in the region, in and around the Samastipur district of Mithila. Rosra, now a district in the region of southern Mithila, has been the most active of all the *maths* until very late. Curiously, there were Brahmin followers along with the followers from the lower caste groups who were initiated into these *maths*. The example of a *math* at Rambagh in Purnea town, founded by a Brahmin who renounced his caste status, is oft cited. Some Brahmins who turned to Kabirpanth called themselves *Sat Kabir*. The spread of Kabirpanth was not even and consistent, yet its presence was much felt. So much so that Ramanandi *math*, that pursued Vaishnavism and was assumed to be a Hindu alternative to Kabirpanth, emerged under the royal patronage. It could not obliterate the dynamic pockets of Kabirpanth in Mithila. In the late nineteenth and early twentieth-century, Kabirpanth assumed a greater fillip as a reformist organization. It also joined in the attack on Brahminical traditional ritualism. While the reformist crusade was confined to townships, the practices and beliefs of Kabirpanth were more popular and effective in villages.

The above synopsis of the socio-religious configuration of Mithila suggests of an interesting blend of orthodoxy and heterodoxy in Mithila. It is not hyperbolic to say that the trajectory of religions, though largely dominated by Brahmins' ritualistic Hinduism, includes other denominations of faith and practices too. Furthermore, the religions of the people were a little more than animistic as the folk worshipped natural objects as well as Siva, Sakti, and Vishnu. There was no Maithil Vaishnavism but poets composed in praise of Lord Vishnu.[18] Apart from these, the Maithil also worshipped natural objects (flora and fauna) such as Surya (sun god), Tulsi (Basil), Naag (snakes in general and Cobra in particular), Moon (in lunar cycle), etc. The temple of Surya from the Oinwara era at Kandha in Saharsa district suggests the existence of a possible sun-cult. Another image and inscription in the Andhrathadi in Madhubani district also confirms the practice of sun worship among the Maithil.[19]

The above perusal of sociocultural history of Mithila suggests that the region has been entangled in socio-religious philosophy of orthodox and heterodox nature. It has shaped up a tradition mixed with many influences, and hence it is not surprising that the folk world view too resonates a mix of philosophical concerns.[20] More importantly, this also explains the reason why Mithila, Maithili, and Maithil are not monolithic categories.

There is an intellectual pitfall attached to the usage of the nomenclature Maithil.[21] Mithila is hastily associated with Maithil Brahmins. In an elaborate footnote, however, Mishra attempts to correct the notion arguing:

... some people are under the impression that the term 'Maithila' means 'a Maithil Brahmin' only. No doubt, the term Maithil is found in medieval literature to indicate a scholar of Mithila, who was mostly a Brahmin ... but commonly speaking and also historically this is not quite correct. The word 'Maithila' and 'Tirubhukta' are very often found quoted or referred to side by side with the term 'Maithila' used for a Kshatriya ruler, for Kayastha musician, or clerk or even for persons of the so-called untouchable class. (1979: 284)

Thus, considering the innate polyphony of the term 'Maithil', there is little scope for reducing the category into only Brahmins of Mithila. Despite the predominance of Brahmins in Maithil religio-cultural and socio-philosophical configuration of Mithila, Maithil is not an epithet for any particular caste group. It is also incorrect to perceive Maithil Brahmin as a homogenous category. The uniformity is only at the level of exterior social life. Mishra argues:

We learn from traditions and certain other references found in ancient books, that the Maithil Brahmins were first divided into two main groups— one (who were) living on the eastern bank of the river Kausiki (also called Kosi) and other on the southern ... those who lived on the eastern bank belonged to the higher hierarchy of Brahmnas, when looked form the point of view of purity of blood, merit and scholarship, while those who lived on the western bank were of lower grades. (Ibid.: 285)

The division is deeply etched in the collective conscience of the Maithil. Thus, there is a common tendency to look down upon Brahmins as well as non-Brahmins from the west or south as culturally inferior. This is very rife in common sense perception and often matrimonial matchmaking entails this kind of discriminatory scheme. As a thumb rule, however, a Sanskrit phrase diminishes the exclusivity of Maithil: '*Mithilayambhavah Maithilaha*' (one who lives in Mithila is a Maithil). In this regard, Mishra points out in a footnote, 'the right view is to regard every person who lives within the geographical limits of Mithila or Tirubhukti a "Maithil" irrespective of caste, creed and language.

Linguistically however, even the Magdhans may be called Maithil as Grierson and some of the modern linguists hold.[22] (Ibid.: 285)

Along these lines the Maithil social structure explicates rules and regulations keeping in tune with the ancient textual injunctions from *Yajnavalkya Smriti*, Patanjali's *Vyakaran Mahabhashya*, and others. They are aimed at karma to direct the course of *janma* (birth). Rules of marriage are crucial in this regard. No wonder from Jyotireshvara to Vidyapati and Vacaspati, every scholar has described the folkways involved in the process of marriage. Most important in this regard is the classification of Brahmins, on the basis of *janma* and karma. The systematic classification under the patronage of the Karnata dynasty King Harisimhadev was known as 'Panji-Prabandha'.[23] It was (and is) an 'institution of having regular genealogical records of the families of Mithila in order that matrimonial relations may necessarily and without much trouble may not take place within the prohibited degrees' (Ibid.: 290). As a guess, the institution came into existence in Sake 1232 (AD 1310). It consists of three broad categories of Maithil—the Shrotriya: rigidly devoted to the performance of *Nitya karma* (daily religious duties) and acquired knowledge of *sastras* (scriptures) following the birth in the Brahmin family; the Yogya—literally, 'capable' of becoming Shrotriya by pursuing and emulating the Shrotriya karma and thereby rising in the status (it also includes befallen Brahmins who status declined due to some inferior actions); the Jayavara: meaning common people of society, largest in number and consist almost entirely of non-Brahmin groups.

The sense of flexibility, as far as a rise in social status and mobility is concerned, is only in principle. Following the injunctions from the *Yajnavalkya Smriti*, the matrimonial principle is supposed to be the sole means for such a rise in status. It is negated under the prescribed rules of marriage, for it is mandatory to observe the *gotra and pravara* (subdivision within gotra) variation. 'A girl and boy can have the adhikara (right) for marriage when the paternal side of the bride has no relations within the sixth generation and from the maternal side up to the fifth generation' (Ibid.: 293). This was to be adhered within caste-fold and outside gotra-pinda. Marrying a daughter in a higher status family, *kulin* or *bahlamanush*, became a source of social evil, as the so-called *kulin* or *bahlamanush* married girls from families of lower status for monetary and material benefits. Such *kulins* were contemptuously called *bikauas*[24] (vendors). Apart from the two categories of Brahmins, on the basis of geographical east-south location, and Shrotriya, Yogya, and Jayavara of the Panji-Prabandha, they are also categorized according to surnames. Some of the well-known surnames are Acharya, Pathak, Upadhyaya (Jha) or Mishra for the learned Brahmins; Kumar, Simha or Thakur for ruling class Brahmins; Khan, Raichaudhury, Mander or Mandala for administrators; and Goswami or Gosain for those who attained *tantric siddhi*. While some surnames emerged in association with scholarship on Vedas and ancient texts, others evolved under the historical condition of the Muslim rule as derivatives of diverse occupations. Additionally, there are the Pachchima Babhans or Bhumihars[25] who were petty zamindars (landlords) and guessed to have descended from the mix of Kshatriya and Brahmin origin. Commonly found surnames of Bhumihars are Mishra, Pathak, Singh, Thakur, Sharma or Rai. Yet another category of lower-status Brahmins is that of those who officiate the *antyeshti samskar* (the last rite, post-death, associated with cremation and post-cremation rituals). They are called by various names such as Kantaha, Mahbrahmana or Mahapatra. While they are the respected people to have food, before anybody else, as soon as *shraddh karma* (cremation rites) is over, they are not considered auspicious for other occasions. Last, there is the Bhatta Brahmins, the bards who visit the rich and are capable of singing their *virudavali* (eulogy). Similarly, the Sakadvipin Brahmins are occupationally *vaidya*, traditional health experts in indigenous herbs and medicines, who are mostly found in Gaya and Samastipur districts.

Among the Kayasthas, there are mainly two groups, the Karna Kayastha and Pachchima Kayastha. The Karnas are supposed to have come to Mithila with the founder of the Karnata dynasty, King Nanyadev. They shared a higher socio-political space with the Brahmins, wore the traditional Maithil headgear *paag*, and earned repute in doing accounts. Nevertheless, they had lower ritual status and they did not wear the *yajnopavit* (sacred thread),[26] nor recite the Vedas. Names of the Maithil Kayasthas were suffixed by surnames such as Thakur, Raut, Datta, Chaudhury, Das, Mallik or even Majumdar. The Kshatriya or Rajput, valued *kula* or *vamsha* (descent). Some such *kulas*, as the *Varnaratnakara* of Jyotireshvara[27] shows, are Paramar, Chauhans, Kacchhavahas, Chandelas, Baisvara, Guhilas or Bhatti.

The meaning of being Maithil is hence not to be reduced to one or the other category of Brahmins. It is heterogeneous, consisting of diverse categories of Brahmins and other caste groups. In the configuration of Maithil identity, other caste groups such as Dhanuk, Chamar, Dusadha, and musahar[28] too have to be factored in. In a similar vein, the language that helps to identify the Maithil is varied, although it is uniformly called Maithili.

Maithili: Neither *Junglee* nor *Bihari*

The colonial recordings pose a question on the linguistic validity of Maithili. What is Maithili, whose language is it, where is it found/spoken are questions that arise as we proceed. Is it one particular language or there are diverse variants within it? Can it be lumped with other dialects of the region and relegated to the fictitious categories such as Bihari?[29] Is a search of Maithili somewhat akin to a wild goose hunt, like it was for a language called *junglee*? This section engages with these questions to aid in understanding of the development of the language.

Mithila is not eternal; Maithili is not eternal either. They surfaced in a historical context as elucidated in the previous section. In this scheme, Prakrit (700 BC), Apabhramsha (AD 700–1100), and Avahatta (AD 1100–1300) precede Maithili. The Magadhi Apabhramsha was widespread in Bengal, Assam, Orissa, Uttar Pradesh, and Bihar. The earliest form of Maithili is traced to roughly around 1097 and corresponds with the founding of the Karnata dynasty, following the decline of the Pala dynasty in the Magadh region. Notwithstanding the *de facto* beginning of Maithili in this age, it could not be effective in literary circles until the Oinwara dynasty ascended to the throne. For long time, though, it was not called Maithili. Avahatta or Mithila Apabhramsha were the known names for the language of the region, known as Tourtiana (Tirhutia) in the colonial records. The standard form of Maithili evolved to the fullest in the middle ages when the Khandavala *kula* was at the helm of power. Vijaykant Mishra (1979) mentions that Mr. Colebrook noted in *Asiatic Researches* about a language by the name of 'Mithelee' or 'Mythili' in 1801. However, the language remained doubly named, some calling it Maithili while the others continued with the name Tirhutia. Sir Asirkin Perry called it Tirutia and clubbed it with Bengali while Sir Joan Bims called it Maithili and clubbed it with Hindi. Grierson is hailed for establishing the name of the vernacular Maithili in 1880.[30] It is interesting to glance at the early phase of Maithili language for two reasons. One, it detects the poetic tradition that supported the growth of Maithili. Two, it also shows a switch from the language of the literate scholars (intellectual elites) to the language of the masses. It is indeed important for a research on oral tradition of Mithila as it underlines the intricate relation between the classical and the folk. Historically, the early Maithili literature (1300–1600) coincides with the Karnata kings Nanyadev and Harisimhadev, thus, encouraging the development of the Maithili school of music around AD 900–1300. The first ever literature,[31] though disputed in clear linguistic origin, was *Charyapada* (or *Caryapadas*) in proto-Maithili dialect midway between standard Maithili and standard Bengali. These were the *padas*, the songs of the Buddhist saints. S. Jha suggests that:

as a matter of fact the language represents a proto-Maithili dialect of the Chikachiki area of today, an area which lies midway between the regions of standard Maithili and Bengali. Naturally, such a language is expected to have points of similarity and difference with both, standard Maithili and Bengali; though for obvious reasons, especially grammatical, Chikachiki still remains a Maithili dialect.[32] (1958: 36)

The *Varnaratnakara* by Jyorishvara Thakur is the earliest undisputed work in the vernacular, although it is not entirely distinguishable from Bengali. Alongside setting up the poetic convention in Maithili language, the *Varnaratnakara* presents a rich social anthropological account of Mithila. Curiously, the *Varnaratnakara* does not mention Mithila Apabhramsha, the language of the book itself, in the long list of languages presented in the book (Jha 1958). There is an obvious ambivalence towards the language of the region in the time of Jyotireshvara Thakur which begins to disappear by the time of Vidyapati. The former was guided by the dominance of Sanskrit, which did not recognize Mithila Apabhramsha. On the other hand, Vidyapati's works in the genre of *giti kavya* (ballad poetry) took Maithili poetics to its initial heights. It is with Vidyapati's[33] work that Avahatta Maithili assumes a status independent of Sanskrit. Therefore, Vidyapati is credited to have founded the trend of writing in *desil bana* (desa bhasha/ vernacular of people). His works such as *Kirti Lata* is of historical significance too as he describes the Muslim invasion and the sociocultural space shared by the natives of Mithila and the newly converted as well as the outsider Muslims. Another work by the title of *Kirti Pataka* describes the battle between the Oinwara King Sivasimha and Muslim invaders. Besides, Vidyapati is, hitherto, celebrated for writing poetry on love and devotion. Many poets and scholars, both contemporaries and successors of Vidyapati, took to writing in Avahatta rather than writing in Sanskritized Apabhramsha. Amritkara, Chaturbhuj, Govinda, Bhishma, Laknhima, and Chandralekha, are oft-mentioned poets who followed Vidyapati's footprints. The vernacular also incorporated the Muslim influence as loan words from Arabic and Persian figured in the then compositions. *Varnaratnakara* and *Kirti Lata* have such loan words like tuluk (Turk), *tir* (arrow), *pyaju* (onion), *ohda* (post), *mouja* (village), *adab/adaf* (respect), *dewan/diwan* (minister), *tabela/astabal* (stable), *sadar/sadr/darwaza* (main gate).

The standard form of Maithili became the language of not only everyday speech but also the official lingua franca of the royal court of the Khandavala *kula* dynasty. From about 1860 Maithili was banished from the official landscape when Darbhanga Raj and the British reigned indirectly. It remained only as a medium of speech in everyday life, and a subject of studies and surveys. The linguistic survey of India conducted by Grierson recorded a bewildering diversity within Maithili. Seven broad variants (dialects of Maithili) are the standard Maithili, the southern, the eastern, the Chikachiki, the western, the Jolahi, and the central colloquial. Of these, according to S. Jha (1958), only three have received distinctive attention: Chikachiki of south Bhagalpur, which uses expressions *chika* and *chiki* frequently; Jolahi, the language of Muslims of Mithila, called so because the majority of Muslim community is *jolahas* (weavers); Khotta, the language of

Malda, spoken as far as the Mahananda River in the east. On the basis of these variants, the official geography of Maithili-speaking folks consists of the districts of Darbhanga, Muzaffarpur, Purnea, Monghyr, and Bhagalpur in the state of Bihar. It is also present in mixed forms in the eastern part of Champaran, eastern part of Patna, and northern part of Santal Pargana districts. A variant of Maithili is the language of people in the Terai of Nepal, on the border of Bhagalpur and Tirhut divisions, and, non-Bengali residents of Malda and Dinajpur in Bengal. Thus, other coexisting languages are Bhojpuri, Bengali, Nepali or Kura, Magahi, and non-Aryan languages of Santali and Munda. No wonder that Mithila is recognized for abundant speech-marks, which refers to territorial autonomy of a language that enables the speakers to operate in diverse registers. The distribution of language is not uniform and thereby in each micro-region the lexical, syntactic, and phonetic features may vary. Thus, we get an exemplar fusion between Maithili and other languages.

Any formulation on the historicity of Maithili is not devoid of a reference to the relationship between Maithili and other Indo-Aryan languages. A historical example is the relation between Maithili and Bengali. The relationship gave birth to a language of poetry in Bengal known as Brajabuli in which Rabindranath Tagore composed his verses. Similarly, the *Sukumar Sahitya* of Nepal carries the influence of Maithili, and poetics and drama in medieval Orissa and Assam used Maithili linguistic codes. This is in addition to the relation Maithili has with other languages of Bihar such as Magahi and Bhojpuri. So, as Burghart suggests, 'an ideal map of the Aryan languages of India would therefore present to the eye a number of colours shading off into each other' (1993: 771).

Even in terms of the scripts of Maithili, the relationship of languages is evident. S. Jha (1958) encapsulates some scripts of Maithili: Maithil or Tirhutia script, allied to Bengali and Assamese script, used largely by Brahmins and Kayasthas; Devanagari, which is actually the script of Hindi, has influenced the writing and speech in Maithili or Tirhutia; Kaithi, resembling Gujarati script, belongs to the semi-literate and also heavily used in revenue and law courts in Mithila.

This is, however, not to negate the distinction of Maithili. S. Jha argues:

(so) it is really an independent language and can not be included in either Hindi or Bengali as one of the dialects of either of these, and that on the basis of lexicography only. All these languages being of Aryan origin naturally have in them a predominance of words of Sanskitik stock. Mostly such words are common to Hindi, Maithili and Bengali, though it may well happen that the same word has different meanings in the several languages. (Ibid.: 20–21)

The confusion with regard to 'what is real Maithili?' spilled through the colonial and postcolonial times as well. Grierson's work on Maithili language discloses it and Burghart captures it in analytical fashion, as he argues, 'In 1911 Maithili is Hindi in its wide sense because it is not Bengali; from 1951 Maithili is Hindi in its wide sense because it is important that the national language be the main language in as many regions as possible' (1993: 788).

During the company rule of the early colonial period, poorly understood Maithili (Tirhutia) was thought of as a dialect of Bengali and of eastern Hindi. Even in Grierson's linguistic survey, spanning 1903–28, there were many notions of Maithili. When the lingua franca of upper India gained in currency, Grierson began to deem Maithili as a *gaonwari boli* (rustic speech) that intrigued him and his fellow administrators in British India. An orientalist-philologist by training, Grierson focused on Maithili of the literate and mostly Brahmins. As a result, Burghart notes, 'Maithili Pundit's "chaste Maithili" became the European Philologist's "standard Maithili". By implication, the Maithili spoken outside the *Panckosi* (the micro region of Madhubani) became variant forms, which were classified as "dialects"' (Ibid.: 775).

In a fairly phased survey, Grierson initially considered Maithili as an independent language because it was mutually unintelligible with Hindi and Bengali. But by the same token of mutual unintelligibility, Grierson revised his conclusion and put Maithili with Magahi and Bhojpuri as yet another dialect of Bihar. These dialects of Bihar, he thought, belonged to a language group, a philological prototype, which he proposed to be called 'Bihari'. Criticizing this convenient conclusion, Burghart argues, 'it seems preposterous that Maithili, Bhojpuri and Magahi speakers could all speak variant of a language, of the existence of what they are unaware' (Ibid.: 778).

The census of 1901 agreed with Grierson on Maithili being a dialect of Hindi rather than of an unheard language 'Bihari'. The ritual decennial census continued with this clubbing even in postcolonial India, for example in the census in 1951. In the midst of these developments, Maithili became nearly non-existent on the political map of isoglosses.[34] Commenting on this Burghart argues, 'in sum, a language cannot simply "not exist"; rather it is made not to exist, and in the techniques of exclusion linguists play as significant a role as their layfolk' (Ibid.: 762).

It is important to understand that Maithili speakers intend to perpetuate the dichotomy of chaste/standard and rustic Maithili in sync with the official documents. It establishes the dominance of one kind of Maithili speakers over the other. Against this, it is imperative to put Burghart's nuanced observation that the landscape of Mithila, replete in speech marks rather than landmarks, is resonant with rustic Maithili. For, 'It cannot be said that rustic Maithili is in any way a simplification of chaste Maithili, for the grammar is equally complex . . . the difference that emerges is largely one of style as a result of the big and little castes taking different sorts of vocalic and semantic decisions' (Ibid.: 768–9).

Maithili Folk Songs

It is in this context that Maithili folklore ought to be understood. The polysemy of the terms such as Mithila, Maithil, and Maithili enriches the domain of Maithili folklore too. Mithila is replete with folklore, often understood in a taxonomic manner (Mishra 1949; Singh 1993; Jha 2002). Of all other, folk songs are central and often part of performance associated with rite of the passage. The most heard category of songs in rites of the passage is known as *samskar geet*. The category includes songs for birth, *mundan* (tonsorial rite), *upanayan* (sacred-thread giving ceremony), and marriage. There are varieties of categories of songs. Pankaj Jha claims there are more than 150 different categories of songs. *Parati*, *Sohar*, *Baagabni*, *Tirhut*, *Jog*, and *Uchili* are a few of the prominent ones. Ramdev Jha argues that there are songs for the event of death as well, which are often not sung by women.[35] Besides there are caste specific folk songs and ballads, such as the Salhesa songs of the Dusadhas, the Deenabhadri of musahars, the Loric of Yadavas, the Jat-Jatin of mallahs, etc. All the available compilation of songs begins with *gosaunik geet* devoted to the household deity.

In the song culture of Mithila women have a predominant role, though songs associated with folk plays and epics are generally sung by men (Jha 2002). Commenting on the Maithili song culture and its association with women Edward O. Henry remarks, 'in Mithila the women's songs provide a concrete expressions of tendencies that distinguish Maithili culture from that of other parts of India' (1998: 415). It is hardly surprising then that most of the compilations of songs in Maithili are addressed to the Maithil women, cutting across age groups, caste, and class. Various collections of songs published by the Maithili Akademi (Patna) and others have a direct reference to 'Maithil Lalna',[36] meaning Women of Mithila (See Devi 1980; Anand and Anand 1997; Mishra 2004; Umapati and Mishra 2004). In his introductory note to the compilation of songs by Kameshwari Devi, Mohan Bharadwaj writes, 'This is an interesting paradox that uncultured songs are rendered on the occasion of the rites which are meant to culture individuals.'[37] This paradox accords superiority to women as they execute *lokpakshiya kriya* (folk activities) of the rites though their songs. The *lokpakshiya* is no less important than the *dhrmapakshiya* (religious aspects), which are executed by the pundits in rites and rituals. The songs pertaining to the *lokpakshiya* are equivalent to the hymns and mantras chanted in the *dhrmapakshiya*. No wonder, Maithil scholars connect Maithili songs with *saamgaan* (songs/ hymns form the *Samaveda*) (Henry 1998; Jha 2002). Henry suggests that the Vedic style of singing is retained in the singing of Shrotriya Brahmin women. The interface of the classical (textual tradition) and oral (folk tradition) seems to be explicit in the song culture. There are many songs with names of a poet inserted at the end, such as Vidyapati's. They are all, not written by Vidyapati. Jayakant Mishra argues, 'the insertion of the poet's name (or any name he chooses whether nom de plume of himself or the name of the guru) appears to have been practiced in the old and the medieval periods throughout the length and breadth of upper India' (1976: 77).

This however should not rule out the possibility of the transformation of classical poetry into folk songs as there are evidences of women singing Vidyapati's *gosaunik geet* (songs in devotion to mother goddess). An acknowledgement of women's prominent position in the song culture of Mithila also discloses the problem of an academic-scholarly approach to the treasure of songs, which often amount to mere classification of songs. Henry points it out by noting:

Women most often classify wedding songs according to the name of the ritual or ritual stage in which they will be sung, but some times according to the ritual alluded or referred to by the song text. Classification is thus not watertight, and singers occasionally disagree about the genre to which a certain song belongs, or create hyphenated categories on an ad hoc basis. (1998: 418)

It ought to be admitted that classification, to which most of the approaches to songs resort to, does not suffice for the purpose of understanding the text and context of the songs. Moreover, women's songs also divulge a treasure of meanings. Especially certain categories such as *Samdaun* and *Sohar* are pregnant with philosophical meanings. In them, 'the poetry is more literary, and the message more philosophical than that of most women's songs'[38] (Henry 2000: 88).

The next essay will discuss in detail mythological icons and their relation with the protagonist of a song. *Samdaun* songs, which are sung while bidding farewell to daughter after her marriage, very strongly present this association between the mortal and divine. Henry draws an interesting parallel between death and the farewell given to a daughter who is leaving for her in-laws' home, saying 'the removal of bride is a metaphor for death in many songs, the nirguna bhajans in particular' (1998: 427).

Henry points out the dialogic structure of devotional folk songs in which the benevolent as well as malevolent mother goddess is praised. But the dialogic structure is an abiding feature in many other songs too. And the depth of meaning, which Henry perceives in *Samdaun* songs can be unearthed in other categories as well. Songs of everyday life, especially *Parati* that are meant to be sung in the morning without any special occasion by individual singers in the space of household, as well as songs of the Nirgun kind are extremely philosophical in terms of the meanings that are enunciated.

Conclusion

This essay attempted to establish the historical emergence of polysemy of the terms such as Mithila, Maithil, and Maithili. Such an exegesis helps in overcoming the platitudes vis-à-vis over-glorification of a cultural region. The historicity of Mithila underlines a perpetual interaction with myth. The meaning of Maithil and Maithili too appear heterogeneous and non-monolithic within this framework. The shifting geography along speech marks, making landmarks less significant is an important lesson from this historical narrative. In the backdrop, the next essay unfolds the Maithili folk songs, situated in the calendar of events and everyday life encountered in a particular village. Thus, the next essay shall seek to be more particularistic than the foregone one on historical background of the larger context of Mithila.

Notes

1. It is important to reset the notion of history at the outset of this discussion. Here history does not mean what positivistic historiography suggests of the craft. History of a cultural region is invariably enmeshed in mythology and located in the domain of tradition(s). Hence, the following discussion, based on the perusal of historical writings and some first-hand observations does not claim to present a perfect historical account. It rather is an endeavour to make sense of what the region was and how it has passed through historically recorded as well as unrecorded milieus.

2. Invariably every piece of reflection on Mithila, academic or otherwise, underpins an overtone of glorification of Mithila, Maithili, and Maithil (who inhabit Mithila). While there is no denial of the sense of pride in Mithila being a seat of scholarship, art, and religion, this does not foreclose a possibility of a critical engagement. In many personal conversations I found that scholars from Mithila do not tolerate the idea of Mithila as a myth, because for them myth, opposed to reality, is a lie.

3. A geologically verified explanation on the continually shifting Kosi river is given by Wells and Dorr 1987.

4. The section toward the end of this essay deals with the language Maithili and debates the issues related to it. The essay intends to explore and establish the intricate link of Mithila, its people, Maithil, and Maithili.

5. Upendra Thakur mentions as to how Gargi and Maitreyi attained knowledge that was not available for Katyayini, another wife of the same philosopher.

6. One should, however, not confuse the basic differences between the ancient philosophers of Mithila and Buddhism. Thakur draws attention to the criticality in philosophical enquiry and of world view, common with Buddhism and *Brihadaranyaka Upanishad* of Yajnavalkya.

7. Seemingly, the well-to-do in Mithila emulated the new religious ideas. An example of this is Mallinatha, the nineteenth Tirthankara of the Jains, who was a princess of Mithila, daughter of the then ruler of Mithila King Kumbha. It is by no means an evidence of socially deep-rooted Hinduism being substituted by Jainism, though influences in part cannot be denied.

8. King Nanyadev wrote *Natyashastra* compiling and commenting on multiple genres of music associated with theatrical performances. Ramsimhadev too is known for having contributed to sacred literature.

9. These two historical characters, belonging to the Oinwara age, Vidyapati and Gonu Jha, are very significant because of the constant references made to them in the oral tradition of Mithila even in contemporary times.

10. It is an unusual historical fact that most of the royal authority of Mithila did not contemplate any revenge even though the arrogant Muslim rulers vanquished them. Instead, they continued with their peaceful pursuit of scholarship and care for the subjects.

11. In the popular lore of Mithila, the later kings of the last dynasty, hitherto, have an esteemed place and they are often remembered in association with diverse temples constructed by them. In the Raj precincts, now the campus of Lalit Narayan Mithila University, there are a number of well-maintained temples where people throng for religious purposes, and unwittingly thank the last Maithil kings too. One of such temples, called Shyama Mai Mandir is said to be built on the remains of Maharaja Lakshimishwar Singh.

12. The list of such temples is fairly long, comprising Kapileshwarsthana, Madaneshwarsthana, Sitanatha (Jaynagar, Madhubani), Hariharsthana (Janakpur, Nepal), Bhairavnatha (Rajkund, Muzaffarpur), Haleshvara (Sitamarhi), Chandeshvara (Darbhanga), Kusheshvara (Hirni, Darbhanga), Singheshvara (Madhepura, Saharsa), Budhanatha (Bhagalpur), Ajgavinatha (Sultanganj), Sundarnatha (Purnea), Kamadanatha (Darbhanga), Goivinatha (Monger), Ksiresvara (Kauradi, Nepal), Ugranatha (Bhavanipur), Mukteshvarnatha (Ganauli), and many others.

13. *Nachari* is the devotional hymns in praise of Siva, and *Maheshvani* is songs depicting marriage of Siva and Parvati/Gaura.

14. The famous poem of Vidyapati '*Jay-jay Bhairavi Asur Bhayauni . . .*' is sung in every household as a folk song.

15. To name a few are Vidyapati's '*Durga bhakti tarangini*', Govind Thakur's '*Puja paddhati*', Devanatha's '*Tantra kaumudi*' and '*Mantra kaumudi*', Narsimha Thakur's '*Tara bhakti*', etc.

16. I need to quickly mention a famous pilgrimage, Ugratarasthan located in the village Mahisi, in district Saharsa. The main deity of the temple Ugratara is a testament to the assimilation of the Mahayana goddess into the Hindu dharma. Besides, the temple also has some of the rare statues of Buddha being worshipped by the visitors as various manifestations of the Hindu god Siva.

17. Many Bhumihars in Mithila hitherto call themselves Bhumihar-Brahmin and have kinship relation with Brahmin families. There is contestation about the explanation on the becoming of Bhumihar.

18. Vidyapati's poetry, indeed, bridges the difference between Siva and Vishnu, by using the word *harihar*. Others wrote in praise of Vishnu without making Vishnu the ruling deity of Mithila.

19. In this regard it is important to mention that the festival of Chhath is important in Mithila as much as elsewhere in the northern India. The ethnic politics behind the festival has been prominent in recent times.

20. The historical account in the previous sections vouches for the observation and wisdom that philosophy of Mithila, a cultural region, ought not to be seen in separation. One reason that they are enmeshed, and the other reason is that most of the overly glorification of Mithila is based on the exclusive talk of Maithil philosophy. Even historians are susceptible to this tendency. Thakur and Vijaykant Mishra are seemingly no exception as they present philosophy and history of Mithila as separate. As a matter of fact, philosophy of Mithila makes better sense in the historical context.

21. When asked, any professor of Lalit Narayan Mithila University would like to wax eloquent on the glory of Maithil and by this term, they would simply mean certain groups of Brahmins.

22. The linguistic question would be discussed in a separate, following, section, as it presents great deal of complexity, expanding and enriching the category of Maithil.

23. Brahmins and Kayasthas of Mithila have, to some extent, maintained the tradition of Panji-Prabandha. Panjikar or hereditary genealogists go on annual tours to register the changes, death of old and birth of new members, and marital alliances and kinship-expansions.

24. There is unanimity amongst the scholars, as Mishra's reference to Girindranath Dutt quoted by H.H. Risley in *The People of India* shows, about the Maithil origin of Kulinism. The Brahmins of Bengal

borrowed the system of Kulinism, in a rather more degenerated form. There is, however, no concrete historical evidence or systematic research to establish it.

25. In the foregone section, Purnendu Ranjan was cited to offer a glimpse of the origin of Bhumihars as those who converted to Buddhism and then reconverted to the Hindu fold. The *District Gazetteer, Darbhanga* supports this probability. Besides, there has always been a mild conflict between Brahmins and Bhumihars, with the former denying the superiority of socio-ritual status. But, caste groups become almost one in Muzaffarpur of Mithila, suggests Mishra.

26. This is disputed now as the Kayastha, as well as many non-Brahmin caste groups, conduct the sacred thread-giving ceremony during weddings.

27. The *Varnaratnakara* of Jyotireshvara Thakur is a major reference to understand the demographic constitution of Mithila.

28. For a brief recognition of multiple caste groups in Maithil identity, see Mills et al. 2003. Also see Narayan 2003, which adequately aids in understanding the culture of dissent in Mithila arising from the performances of lower caste groups.

29. Bihari is the philological prototype proposed by George Grierson to club all the three languages of Bihar—Maithili, Magahi, and Bhojpuri. Scholars have expressed logical reservations about this proposition. Second, *junglee*—literally meaning wild—was a fictitious language of the Punjab province. Grierson obviously could never locate it in his survey.

30. The scholars of Mithila are unanimous in paying tribute to Grierson for establishing the vernacular language as Maithili in the survey records. So much so that, there is a Grierson Chowk, a junction on the merger of diverse roads, in the Madhubani district of Mithila, as a token of respect to Sir George Grierson. But the feeling of reverence is not unequivocal, for Grierson finally ended up considering Maithili as part of a language group which he called Bihari. The Maithil scholars often laugh at the alleged slip of Grierson in creating a language group, which allegedly does not exist.

31. An ambiguity in this regard, S. Jha mentions, Vacaspati's ninth century AD commentary on the Sankarbhasya, on Vedantsutra, known as Bhamati, as an oldest work in Maithili, though with an overtone of Sanskrit.

32. S. Jha also mentions the arguments of Rahul Sankrityayan, which held the language of the Caryapadas close to Magahi. To quote, 'Sankrityayan maintains, the writers were living either at Vikramshila (which is in the east of Mithila), or at Nalanda (which is not very far from Maithili speaking tract)' (1958: 36).

33. The two linguistic regions, Bengal and Mithila, have claimed proximity with Vidyapati's poetry. He is also known to have influenced the famous Bengali Vaishnava poet Candidasa—celebrated in Bengal and Assam. Not least, his poetry in praise of lord Siva, known as *Nachari* found pride in the historical work *Ain-i-Akbari*.

34. R. Burghart refers to Grierson's search of a speech in the south of Punjab which he called *junglee* (wild). He never found it because everywhere he went he was told 'yes, we know junglee very well, you will find it little further on'. Grierson's Bihari, metaphorically, is synonymous with *junglee*.

35. Songs of Kabirpanth/Nirgun are considered songs of death. Anima Singh (1993) mentions three such songs in the end of her compilation of 1,012 songs. Other compilations published by local publishers do not mention any death song.

36. In editorial words, Ratneshwar Prasad Singh addresses 'Maithil Lalna' as a target group of this compilation. This book consists of songs recollected by Smt. Kameshwari Devi (1980) who learnt these songs from her grandmother during her childhood. Herself an illiterate, she wished to publish these songs so that it could be preserved. According to her, the literate women are exceedingly forgetful of these songs.

37. Mohan Bharadwaj, in Kameshwari Devi (1980), says, *Eeektaadbhutvirodhabhasisthitiaichh je manushya ka susanskrit karaywalaanushthanakawsar par asanskritgeet gao ljayetachhi*. Here *Asanskritgeet* refers to the folk songs in contrast with the classical religious texts.

38. Edward O. Henry's works (1998, 2000) are concerned with the performance of songs and the inherent musicological structure. The musicological findings of Henry suggest that there is a distinct sonic characteristic of Maithili folk songs of women, with unique melismatic surge, melodic style, and unregulated unison of singers in the performance. Henry also refutes Grierson's thesis that there is largely a singularity of melody in each genre.

6

In Fulhara: Sound and Sight in a World View (Part I)

Arriving at a world view presupposes a holistic view of the spatial-temporal structure of the society. This essay engages with sociocultural events through songs, and practices in Fulhara, the micro-context within Mithila. Pieced together in totality, the songs of Fulhara, their renditions, and associated actions disclose a set of folk knowledge central to this essay. The attempt is towards drawing a complete picture without any claims of the exhaustiveness of details in the limited space of an essay.

To reach Fulhara, one has to board at Samastipur Railway Station a local passenger train bound for Saharsa. Alighting at Nayanagar station, one has to take a 4 km. bumpy ride on a horse-drawn carriage. The roadway is easier and shorter for one who is starting from Darbhanga. The 50 km. journey comprises a comfortable 40 km. stretch to a subdivision called Singhia, and a rickety 10 km. ride via Dudhpura bazaar to Fulhara.

Way to Fulhara. *Courtesy*: Author.

Living in *Fulhara*: A Synoptic View of Everyday Life

Bricked pathways crisscross the whole village, with regular ditches at places where the bricks have given away. Fulhara is flanked on the one side by Deodha, a village comparatively larger in size and population and by the river Kareh-Bagmati on the other side. Sprawling around the village are tracts of agricultural fields of the villagers. Season-specific crops, at various stages of growth, glisten in these outstretched fields on a sunny day of the season. Bordering on the fields are *gachchi* (orchard) with trees of *aam* (mangoes), *kathar* (jackfruit), leechi/litchi (*Chinensis* in Latin), and *jamun* (*Syzgium cumini* in Latin). Bamboo groves also dot the topographic landscape in the fields as well as inside the village. Rustling bamboo leaves, and winds causing rift of tall bamboo trees, producing an eerie sound, orchestrate the sound of solitude. Reserves of water, mainly ponds of all sizes, are interspersed all over. If not *makhana* (fox nuts), these reserves are full of fishes, snails, and other aquatic creatures. A *makhana* planted reserve looks clad with large, circular-spiked leaves afloat on the surface of water as if the entire space is a green-leafy landmass rather than a pond.

As we move toward the human inhabitations we come across humans of all kind of physical appearances—some sturdy and some haggard, some wheatish and some fairly dark in complexion. Pigments of skin however do not determine the social group one belongs to despite a Maithili saying that 'doubt a black Brahmin and a fair Chamar for their lineage'. The people don a variety of clothing—kurta-pyjama, dhoti-kurta, shirt-pant, lungi-ganji, saree-blouse, and salwar-kameez—some with an ostensible stain of time and some without a single streak. Before specifying the categories of groups, it is interesting to lay out the spatial locations of the village.

It is a fairly small village in terms of spatial coverage, but it is densely populated and neatly woven with *gullies* (alleyways). Some of the *gullies* are too narrow to let two men pass side by side. Walking in a single file in those earthy passages one gets a feeling of claustrophobia that defines the spatial structure of the village.

This is mainly in those parts of the village where the lower caste folks reside. The passages are relatively broader in the part which the Brahmins inhabit. Narrow lanes can be found even within the parts inhabited by the Brahmins. These lanes connect one house with the other and one lane with the other. As per a rough estimation, provided by the village elders, which corresponds approximately with the official records, the overall population in the village is about 5,050. The demographic distribution consists of 1,500 villagers belonging to the Dusadha caste; 1,000 of Brahmins; the Dhanuk and Koeri together also comprise about 1,000; 500 of the Chamar caste; 1,000 of Kayasthas and Banias put together; and a small bunch of 50 people belonging to the Dom caste. The latter are situated towards the northern end of village, at the periphery, as outcastes. Interestingly, Brahmins' inhabitation is also toward north of the village, but it is not the fringe of the village. In the centre of the village are situated the Bania (known by the surname Poddar) households, while the Koeri live towards the south, Chamars towards the east, Kurmis and Dusadhas towards the west of the village. Every house in the village, regardless of whether it belongs to an upper caste or lower caste family, has a small or big exterior called *dalan,* which is meant to accommodate guests. There are half-dried, almost abandoned wells outside the *dalan,* especially adjacent to some of the household of the upper caste folk. These are apparently the houses of the zamindars of yesteryears. These wells are now the source of children's horror tales. The main source of drinking water is the tube well that is

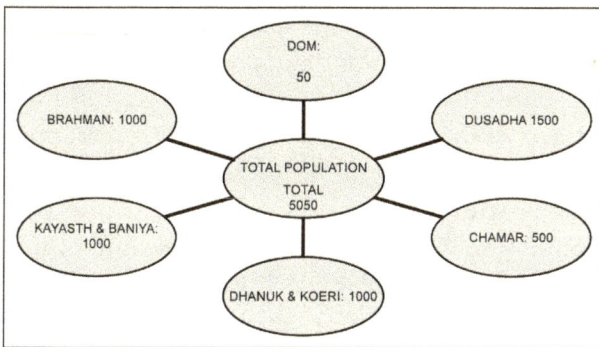

Caste-Distribution. *Courtesy:* Author.

found in every household of the upper caste families, while it is
unevenly found in the lower caste household clusters. Tube wells
are a great leveller and connector as we get to see common tube
wells in the village where people of any caste can fetch water.

Toward this end, even some of the benign business outlets play
significant roles. There are three spots in the village where a *kirana
dukan* (general grocery store, selling everything of basic needs)
is situated. At the junction where the pathway to Fulhara meets
the road to Deodha, is the main chowk of the village is where
one kirana dukan is located. There are a couple of *paan dukan*, a
sweetmeats shop, a cobbler at a corner, a carpenter in the centre,
and a puncture repairer at the end of the road. The other spot
of the shop is inside the village, along the pathways surrounding
the locality of the Brahmins. Toward the interior there is a *paan*
shop, a tea shop in a thatched hut, and a simple bamboo structure
that functions as a barber's saloon. Not far from the tea shop are
two general stores and a shop for fertilizers and seeds. Villagers
buy seeds and fertilizers from this shop only to fulfil an urgent
need; the bulk of the purchase of seeds and fertilizers is preferably
done in the nearby Dudhpura bazaar. The best destination for
buying anything in bulk is the Rosra baazar, a new district, nearly
5 km. away. One *kirana dukan* is oddly situated towards the end
of the village on the bricked pathways leading to the Dudhpura
baazar. Last, one *kirana dukan* is in the midst of the lower caste
inhabitation. All these shops are sites to get updated on the latest
gossip of the village. Needless to say, folks from across caste groups
meet one another casually while passing by and exchange notes
of well-being too. There are two state government schools in the
village, a middle school at the main chowk, and a primary school
toward the end of the inhabitation of the lower caste from where
begin the tracts of the field. Right amidst the government schools
one finds tuition centres, which almost have the look of a proper
school. The centres hold classes every morning and evening
without conflicting with the timings of government schools.

Though there are innumerable sites of religious festivities, on
occasions various trees (mainly peepal/boe) become the object of
reverence of the folk. The main temple called *thakurwadi* is on the
bank of a pond where every Tuesday, as well as on other auspicious

occasions, villagers organize *kirtan* (collective devotional singing by the men folk). The *kirtan* brings together participants from across caste groups, except the outcastes such as the Dusadha and Doms. The Dusadha have a separate *thakurwadi* in their residential area. On special occasions the villagers conduct *ashtajam*, an eight-day kirtan programme in which they repeatedly recite the name of the god who is to be thanked for the fulfilment of a wish. Such an occasion brings about a modest crossing of caste lines and anybody who is known as a *kirtaniya* (efficient singer of *kirtan*) merrily participates. There are some renowned *kirtaniya* in the Dusadha and Chamar caste groups.

There is another place of worship known as Brahmsthan, which is a small temple built under a huge *bargad* tree. Women gather here to invoke and make offerings to the *Brahman devta* on special occasions such as any rite in the household or after the fulfilment of a wish. Curiously, every upper caste household has a place for the *Brahman devta*, as *kul devta*, the god of the clan. This is found in the lower caste households too. The village elders inform that earlier the village had only one single Brahmsthan where the folk, across caste groups, gathered to make their offerings. *Brahman devta* who is the presiding god in the Brahmsthan is also known as *budhaa baba*. The deity is iconized in a godly statue saddled on a horse inside the simplest structure of the temple underneath a fairly old banyan tree. The *Brahman devta* of Brahmsthan does not refer to Brahmin caste. It is a folk deity transcendental of caste identity. Hence, all caste groups throng the Brahmsthan. The Dusadha too visit the Brahmsthan even though they operate with an alternative religiosity. They have their priests who conduct slightly different rituals than that of Brahmins and other upper castes. They worship Raja Salhesh, a legendary character, whose story is on the tip of the tongue of the villagers across caste groups. Interestingly, the Dusadha under the instructions of the officiating priest from their own caste, also perform *Satyanarain puja*. The latter is a ubiquitous *puja* observed across groups.

Doms, an outcaste group associated with the menial job of digging toilet and cleaning filth, seldom go to any temple other than the Singheshwarsthan, which is located in the neighbouring village of Deodha. At this specific temple, Doms from far and wide congregate once every year to worship the legendary character Singheshwarsingh.[1] They sacrifice pigs, cook at the site, eat and drink local liquor, and dance through the night. They make sure that nobody from non-Dom caste groups participates even casually in the festival. Many villagers stated that every year the annual festival invariably ends with the Doms fighting and injuring one another.

The religiosity visible in everyday life renders every household as a site of religious operations. A *tulsichaura* (the basil plant on a raised platform, with the shape of Hanuman carved on the outer surface and smeared in vermillion) is something that can be found in every household. Men and women both pour *jal* (sacred water) every morning in the plant while they look at sun with squinted eyes. The sacred *jal* is water filled in a clean brass pitcher after bathing. This is the usual scene in the households across caste groups except that of the Doms. Women, especially, are attached to the *tulsichaura* and lit *diya* (earthen lamp) and *dhoop* (incense sticks) every morning and evening. Of course, when women worship they sing. They actually sing while doing anything, even while working in the field. Men and women both indulge in the agricultural drudgery of sowing and reaping, of harvesting and carrying the crop home. But the sonic effect in the field is mainly attributed to women who break into songs at any juncture of their work.

The main crops in the fields of Fulhara consist of lentils of all kinds (*moong, arhar, masur,* and *chana*), the rabi crop (wheat, maize, pea) in summer, spices (coriander, black chilly, turmeric, ginger), and sunflower in summer as well as in winter. The specific crop in winter is kharif (paddy, maize) and sugarcane. Most of the upper caste folk get the agricultural work done by the lower caste folk under their supervision. The payment for agricultural labour is invariably in kind and occasionally in cash. For reaping 10 bundles of paddy the labourer may get 2 bundles, or for assisting in the thrashing of the 100 kg. of wheat the labourer may be given 5 kg. of the thrashed wheat. For other tasks the villagers have cows and buffaloes at the *khuta* (tether). It is a local idiom to express the prestige of a household: if a household has a *khuta* with a cow or buffalo that produces milk every day, it is considered a marker of prosperity for the household in the village common sense. It is a part of the daily chores in every household to arrange for timely fodder for the cattle, collect and clean their dung, and milk them at the right time. Women take onto themselves to clean and gather the cattle dung in a corner of the cowshed, which they knead and smash onto the wall to make *goitha*, a fuel made of cow dung mixed with husk. Women also smear a bit of fresh cow dung on the unplastered floor as a sign of auspiciousness on religious occasions. In wealthier households, where men are not available to do the chore themselves a servant is deputed. There are families, in upper caste as well as among lower caste groups, where men go out to do official work in the daytime. Before leaving for work, and when they return in the evening, they serve the cattle. Men who have no work to do outside the village spend their afternoon playing cards in the *dalan*. The tea shops also become places for playing cards, winning and losing, in the afternoon. Men and women while away their afternoons differently. Women may indulge in sewing and embroidery, sieving, and winnowing. For men the sonic companion in the afternoon is the transistor airing songs and intermittent news bulletins. Women themselves provide with melodic company to their work. There are also many who while away their afternoon by taking a siesta.

Everyday life in the village is neatly woven with the notions of time and sound. Every morning, the villagers wake up slightly before sunrise, responding to the twittering of birds and the mooing of cows. Sparrows and mynas begin to sonorously fill the atmosphere before crows start cawing. It is considered virtuous if people leave their beds before the cawing of crows reaches their ears. Elderly men and women wake up by three or four in the morning during summers and by four or five during winter. Youngsters wake up by around six and seven after their parents have set the tone for the morning. A far-removed loudspeaker in the temple blares some devotional songs that gently waft across the village. At some *dalan*, a radio airs devotional songs in Maithili from the Darbhanga station of the All India Radio. Long before this, about five in the morning, while passing by a *dalan*, or *aangan* we get to hear elderly men and women of the village softly singing a specific category of folk songs called *Parati*. At this hour when

the darkness of night is on the way out and the effect of light is
sneaking in, when the village is yet to wake up to cause the rural
din, the early morning songs are audible enough no matter how
ordinary the manner of singing. As these songs are not associated
with any big ritual event, they are not sung with a sense of display,
and are audible within a short expanse.

With the crack of dawn, life begins to roll on the path as people
are seen running toward the field with a *lota* or any small container
filled with water. Women too do the same, almost stealthily and
slyly. The intention is to evacuate in the *khet* (fields), *gachchi* or
bansbitti (bamboo groves). The places are never completely filled
with excreta as the discharge is biodegradable and becomes soil
in a couple of weeks. But the stench wafts in the air and becomes
unbearable during extreme summer and in the rainy season. Some
households also have the most primitive form of toilet, with a
long whole dug in the earth and slightly raised platform of bricks,
on which women sit with perfect aim to relieve themselves. Such
a toilet is covered on three sides with bamboo and leaves up to
the height of human body. Some households, especially of the
zamindars of yesteryears, have relatively proper toilets. But then,
men from these households too are seen frequenting the fields
for the purpose of every day bowel-evacuation. It is considered a
new trend to have proper toilet.[2] The visible run to evacuate also
surfaces at twilight as the day draws to a close.

The day sets in with the mellow and crimson morning sun
turning sharply bright. Everybody is bathed, ready for *jalpan*[3]
(breakfast), and leave for work. Children are exceptions if there is a
holiday or they have not started going to school yet. The pond and
the tube well are the two options for bathing. Mostly, it is the tube
well where everybody bathes. Women bathe in the covered parts
of the *aangan* and men have no qualms bathing in the open. In the
lower caste inhabitation, we also catch a sight of women bathing
collectively in the open with their saree reduced to skimp body
cover. Women generally bathe later than men and children after
finishing their routine chores of cleaning and cooking. Elderly
women and widows bathe early in the morning. Men and women
bathe their children with utter religiosity, scrubbing their whole
body with soap. By the time the cows begin to moo for fodder

and are ready to be milked, breakfast is almost ready, except milk that is yet to be boiled. The sound wave of the village by this time carries a film song from a remote radio, or from a megaphone blaring a Maithili chartbuster. Post breakfast, while children are off to the school and men are to their destinations within or outside the village, women stay home unless they have something specific to do outside. If it is the time of season when agricultural activity is at the peak, with either sowing or reaping, women may go to supervise work in the field, especially when men are away. Around this time the sound of the village becomes sparse, while some urchins fight at a street corner, a passer-by pedals the bicycle away or a woman calls out for her son who has ventured out in the noon to play with his friends.

Taking a walk in the village in the afternoon is a distinct experience. By late afternoon, people gather at different gendered spaces: men at the *dalan*, tea shops, and frontal area of a *kirana dukan* to play cards; and women gather to gossip in somebody's *aangan*. Some women would be squatting with tresses unwound and a little girl (of age nine or ten) would be searching for lice in the woman's head with her fingers moving nimbly through the parting of hair. If it is winter, the bevy of women will be busy multitasking in such a gathering, knitting yarn and glibly talking about neighbourhood matters. In case it is a household of a woman where an auspicious occasion of the rite of the passage for anybody belonging to the family is afoot, the gathering of women will be seen helping in the preparation and also singing off-and-on. If it is a household, that has recently witnessed any rite of the passage, the women will discuss the bygone with glee of success and glum of some amiss. It is never a vacuum of ideas or issues for them. But it is not always a sight of 'everything's fine', for this is where disagreements emerge and bickering ensues. It is more frequent and uninhibited among women in the lower caste inhabitations, while the upper caste women keep the acoustic manifestations of the fights low unless it is a fight among relatives on the issue of grave injustice and humiliation. The quarrel could be on a range of issues: children hitting each other, abusive behaviour, neighbourly envy, breach of trust, encroachment on each other's field, and sexual allegations, etc. Some become an issue of major rage and some die a natural

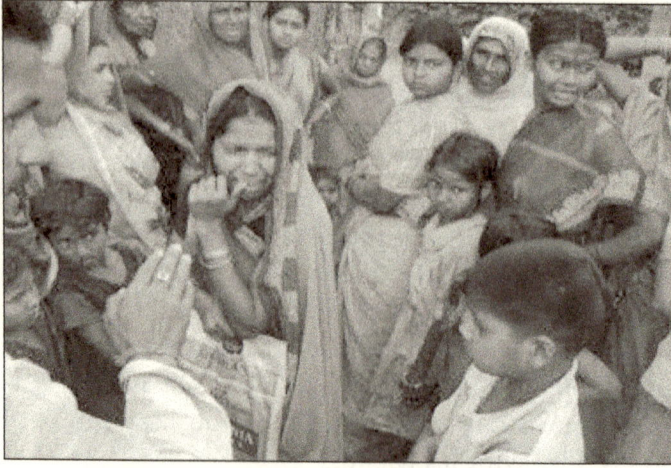

A Sight of Quarrel. *Courtesy*: Author.

death. Some reach the nearby Thana (police station) and the
district court, while some are solved at the village level. More
often men folk show a condescendingly dismissive attitude toward
bickering and quarrelling initiated by women. If, however, the
fracas flares up into a fight based on the issue of family prestige,
the men folk vigorously join in. At times, it amounts to an issue of
the village to be discussed in the panchayat in front of the village
elders, unless the trusted elders resolve it within or without the
family. But many of them become too violent, which occasionally
leads to bloodshed. There are innumerable cases pending in the
courts pertaining to issues that started with disagreements and
informal bickering, and the ensuing process of interventions by
the village elders. The afternoon is as much responsible for setting
the tone and tenor of the village life. Toward early evening, when
disciplined children slacken and parents get back to the rest of
the day, the soundscape of the village rises considerably. Some
men gathered at the *dalan* will ask a passer-by as to how their day
was and all that transpired through the day. If the passer-by is free
enough and feels like spending some time with the fellows, he or
she will join the gathered men for a while, else they will answer
from the pathways in an audible voice without staying back. These
are some of the rare moments when men and women cross each
other's spaces. Some men, on the way back from the field, may

be herding oxen back, and the tinkles of the tiny bells around the neck of an ox speechlessly suggest the farmer's day has ended. This is when some of the tired men can also relax for a while by the roadside and gulp down a clay-glass full of *taari* (a local toddy, the secretion from the palm and date tree, fermented and sold by a particular caste group called *paasi*). Though everybody says it's a drink of people from low-income and lower-caste groups, it seems popular across caste and class. Those who have sufficient money also tend to buy a bottle of Indian-made foreign liquor (IMFL). Some drunken men, but not all, return home singing aloud or even abusing folks. Women from both upper and lower caste households always resent the consumption of intoxicating beverages by men. There is, however, one intoxicating item which seems culturally accepted for consumption. Tendril plants of *bhang* (cannabis) are ubiquitous in the village. The villagers select the best of kind and dry the leaves with care for cleanliness. In the evening, mostly during summer, men make the paste of *bhang* by rubbing the leaves in between two pieces of rocks with black pepper and other dry fruits, if available. Men swallow the rolled paste, generally in the evening, with a raucous hailing of lord Siva, in the belief that consumption of *bhang* brings an ecstasy that only the god, the creator and destroyer, can enjoy. Some men also smoke *ganja* (marijuana), yet another plant belonging to the same botanical family. Women do not oppose the consumption of these intoxicants unless its consumption affects the general effectiveness of the men's abilities. The consumption of *khaini* (dried tobacco leaves rubbed with lime before consumption) too is socially accepted. There is a strong folkloric attitude toward *khaini*, and one proverb reads *assi chutki nabbe taal, takhan dekhu khaini ke haal* (eighty rubs of thumb and ninety times tapped winnowing makes a solid pinch of *khaini*). There is also a popular song in Maithili, in which a nephew asks his maternal uncle for a pinch of *khaini*, in order to show that consuming in his company would keep their relation ticking. In winter, some men cultivate *khaini, bhang*, and *ganja*, especially for their personal consumption, apart from out of agro-economic interest. Men folk also grow *paan* (betel leaf) in the kitchen garden. Consuming *paan* is culturally significant. A folk saying suggests that a man who gets his lips reddened by the *paan* juice is destined to receive conjugal love! The folk also count *madhu* (honey), *paan* (betel leave), *makhana* (fox nut), and *maach* (fish) as being specific to Maithili culture.

Women and children contribute to the sound and sight of twilight too. Young girls frolic to *Kansar*, which is a place where five-six joint hearths are put together under a thatched roof by the *kansarin*, the owner-woman of the *Kansar*. Women visit her in the evening to get their grains parched and puffed. The visiting girls chitchat about village trivia while ladling the clay pots in which they have put their grains mixed with warm sand for puffing.

Women, in the meanwhile, wind up everything else as they go about preparing dinner. They light clay lamps at the *tulsichaura* and inside the home where the household deity is placed, dovetailing it with recitations of some of the devotional folk songs. Children come back from their play, which is largely hide and seek, or touch-me-if you can, and settle to study under the open summer sky (or in the veranda during winter and autumn) huddling around a dimly lit lantern. Sometimes they sit under a dimly lit electric bulb as the electricity supply in the village is intermittent. Men are also around, at the *dalan* or in the neighbourhood, unless some late evening agricultural work is on in the field during

An evening at *Kansar*. *Courtesy*: Author.
Note: Women and girls waiting for their grains to be puffed
at Kansar, while the Kansar-owner women are at their job
providing with skilled services.

the season of harvest. The quietness of evening descends on the village by seven in the summer or five in the winter. Except the sound of the *kirtan* in the temple especially on days like Tuesday or any other day of significance, continues till late. Or it could be the last news bulletin on the local station of All India Radio at a *dalan*. An occasion of festivity, such as Krishnashtami or Sivaratri, is when people are awake until late to celebrate. In the month of *falgun* (around February-March of the Roman calendar), the time of spring, people walk around even in the thick of the night. They move door-to-door and sing songs of *falgun*. Generally, the whole village retires by eight in the winter and latest by ten during summer. Lanterns that were lit in the evening dangle from the hook of the veranda inside as well as outside the house until morning. In the thick of darkness of the moonless night, the light of lantern is the only anchor for cruising eyes during summer. But on the nights when moon showers silvery beams on the village, human eyes are not dependent on lanterns alone. For dark nights people also depend on the battery torch; in fact, they sleep with a torch at hand. Nowadays Chinese models of battery torches are popular among villagers. They are sold by hawkers who procure these and other such electronic goods from Nepal. Summer nights have the added attraction of innumerable glow-worms, locally called *bhagjogni*, beaconing human eyes on the pathways. Winter nights, which are mostly foggy, have a special sound in the background as foxes howl in the fields, and add to the eerie nocturnal silence of the village.

In the Calendar of Festivity

In Fulhara like in other parts of Mithila, the folk follow the pan-Maithil *panchang* (the almanac with dates in accordance with the movement of the moon, sun, and planets), which indicates the auspicious days for religious festivals and rituals. Many such days are month-specific, while a few are to be observed throughout the year or for half of the year. The onset of festivals begins with the month of Saon (सावन, roughly corresponding to July-August) when monsoon renders summer wet and humid, and snakes begin to crawl out in full folk view. Saon is the month to worship Siva

and his consort goddess Parvati/Gauri. Women folk in particular
consider the month auspicious, for it is in this month that they
start to observe fast every Monday (*Sombari*) and worship Siva with
various objectives, including to seek protection of their husbands
or to find a right husband. The day of *Sombari* is a mini festive
occasion involving older and younger girls, and also boys who
get the joy of accompanying women (mother, sisters or aunts) to
the temples. Both men and women also undertake a strenuous
journey to a distant Siva *linga* to offer water and milk to it. There
is popular *kamar-yatra* toward the Babadham, a famous temple
located in Deoghar, now in Jharkhand, or any other destination
within the region of Mithila itself. In the month of Saon the
folk also celebrate Nag Panchami where they worship snakes
in general and a particular snake, mythically called Bisahara, by
offering milk and corn. In this very month falls the festival of
Raksha Bandhan, a pan-north-India festival that celebrates the
bond between brothers and sisters. The most important festival in
this month is Madhushravani. It is held in a household where a
wedding took place in the previous year. This is a festival where
women of the locality are invited to participate in the folkways
and storytelling for thirteen to fifteen days, involving the newly-
wed couple, at the natal home of the bride. Every year one or
more household celebrates Madhushravani in Fulhara. Women
sing innumerable songs on this occasion, starting with *gosaunik
geet* (song in praise of the mother goddess), *gauri ke geet* (songs
in praise of Gauri, the consort of Siva), *bisahara ke geet* (songs in
praise of the Bisahara, the snake goddess), and songs associated
with rituals such as *aankhimunawwal ke geet* (blindfolding the eyes
of the bride), and *temi-dagba ke geet* (dabbing the lit-wick on the
thighs of the bride). The bride's family receives gifts from the
family of the groom.

The month of Bhado (the month of rains) offers the occasion
of Krishnashtami (the birth of child god Krishna) and Anant (to
invoke prosperity and dispel pathos). The most important festival
in this month is Chaurchanda,[4] which is celebrated in every
household, across caste groups. The day is astrologically significant,
for it is believed that it was on this day that the moon received its
blemishes. Worshipping the moon and Ganesh, devotees pray for

their wishes to be fulfilled. The preparation for this festival fosters happiness among the entire family as new wheat is washed, dried, crushed, kneaded, and fried with jaggery to be served as offering. Children are excited about it, women prepare it, and men folk participate religiously in this festival of the dark evening.

The month of Ashin (roughly September–October) is popular all over north India for Durga Puja. In the villages of Mithila the month is also known for other festivals such as Pitarpaksha, which involves worshipping dead ancestors, the father and the teacher of the clan, and Jitiya where women observe a fast for twenty-four hours without even drinking water, wishing for the long life of their sons. A famous Mithila-specific festival called Kojagra in the month of Ashin is a major attraction in Fulhara as well. On this day a newly married groom receives a bundle of gifts from his father-in-law. On the evening of Kojagra every household worships the goddess of prosperity and celebrates by eating dishes made in milk. The celebration entails women drawing *aipan* (the tantric design made on the floor with the paste of rice and vermillion) and cleaning the house with fresh cow dung. The most prominent festival in the following month of Kartik (October–November) is Deepavali, the festival of lights. But in Fulhara, like any other village in Mithila, Bhardutiya, Sama Chakeba, and Chhaith are also highly popular festivals in this month. Bhardutiya (Bhrati Dwitiya in Sanskrit) is the day when sisters invite their brothers, adorn them with betel leaves, nuts, and flowers and feed them the special food they cook. In return they get gifts and also a reassertion of the mythological assurance that their lives would be full of joy. On this day every household in Fulhara has a special preparation in which elderly women help young siblings to celebrate emotional bonding, by singing the songs on their behalf, arranging for the play, and sweetmeats. Sama Chakeba too has a similar import involving siblings and women of the household. Every night women sit together to sing songs, relating stories of Sama, the daughter of Krishna, who was cursed to become a bird, and in pathos her husband Chakeba too became a bird. Sama's brother Samb did penance to rescue her from the curse and also destroyed the sinister design of Chugla who was eyeing Sama. Women also sing songs, in which the real life actors, brothers and sisters, are named and transformed into the protagonists of the songs,

> *Sama khelay gelhu phallan bhaiya ke angana*
> *Dalwa lay gel chor*
> *Ek muththi kharhi ho bhaiya*
> *Seho phuki karah e jot . . .*

> In the courtyard of my (name) brother, I went to play *sama*
> My baskets and all my dolls
> A thief stole away
> Light a fistful of straws, o brother!
> Spark the light, and catch the thief . . .

The motif of the song underlines a sister's dependence on her brothers for protection of her belongings and happiness. Sisters invoke brothers to catch the thief and recover the stolen wherewithal of play and pleasure. Every night, following Bhrati Dwitiya till the full moon night, women and children celebrate this festival with folksy fanfare. The most auspicious festival of this month is Chhaith (also called *Pratiharshashthi* or *Chhathi*, literally meaning sixth), which is popular across caste groups. With doubly-aimed devotion, one to the sun god and other to the goddess Chhathi (who is otherwise not known in the Hindu pantheon of deities), the devotees seek for various kinds of wishes to be fulfilled. The festival involves stringent preparation. The person who is the main worshipper has to observe a fast for thirty-six hours that commences with a special dinner on the night of the Panchami. Before the sunset on the sixth day, everybody in Fulhara surrounds the pond of the village to worship the sun god. This is repeated on the following morning before sunrise as well. Children wear new clothes, like they do on Durga Puja and Deepavali, and burst fire crackers. Alongside these festivities, women sing numerous folk songs against the deafening megaphones that air similar songs sung by a one-time popular folk singer Sharda Sinha and some of the new singers. A song says:

> *Apne ta jai chh ho bhaiya des re bideswa*
> *Hamro le labiha bhaiya gahum sanesba*
> *Aabigelay ho bhaiya chhathi san baratiya*

Gahum ta chhai bahin badd re mahagaba
Chhodi dahinge bahin chhathi san baratiya . . .

You travel far and wide, o brother!
Bring me some wheat in gift for me
As approaches the festival of *Chhathi*
Wheat is, but, so very dear, o sister!
Leave the *vrata* this time, you . . .

The song reveals a dialogue between brother and sister; the latter requests the former to bring wheat as a present for her so that she can make *prasad to* offer to *Chhathi*. Though the festival does not seem to be free from caste structure, a song suggests otherwise:

Domin beti sup nene thaad chhai
Uga ho suruj deb arghakerber
Ho pujankerber
Malinbeti sup nenethaadchhai
Nirdhan-kodhi sup nenethaadchhai . . .

Standing in the pond is the daughter of a sweeper
So is the daughter of gardener
And also the destitute and leper
All beseech the sun god
Awaiting the crimson rise
For favour and blessings
And so please accept our devotional offerings . . .

Social hierarchy finds a way to seep into the festival and the banks of the pond exhibit divisions along caste lines, with the upper caste on one side and the lower caste on the other. The levelling effect of the worshipping does not alter the social structure of caste. If at all, the mitigation of the caste division is only instantaneous and spiritual rather than concrete-empirical. The manifest behaviour and mode of conduct of the upper and lower caste devotees testify to the differences. Even the quality of fabrics they wear (the cotton saree of saffron colour) and kinds of offering they make vary across caste lines. Curiously though, devotion of the lower caste devotees is visibly more excruciating. Many of them come prostrating all the way from their home to the bank of the pond.

In addition to these spectacular festivities, there is a low-key festivity in the month of Kartik called Devotthan Ekadashi. It marks the beginning of a day-long fast on the eleventh day of every month throughout the year. This is very peculiar of Maithil, especially the Brahmins who tend to observe this fast by invoking various gods of the pantheon without specifying any single god. A similar fast is performed on every Sunday of a week called *raibbrata*. It is observed with minimal rituals while invoking the sun god and wishing for health and prosperity. These observances of austerity and fasting seek to underline the everydayness of religiosity in the village. The month of Maagh (January–February) opens the festivity with Tila Sankrant which is generally known as Makar Sankranti in north Indian and has an almost fixed date of 14 January every year. Like any other village, Fulhara gears up on this day with people bathing at the earliest possible time in the morning, while battling the challenging chill of the wintry month. The special food on this day, a fascinating attraction for all age groups, includes *lai murlai*, *tilkut tilwa*, *chura-dahi*, and *khichdi* in the evening. Other festivals in this month, popular in Fulhara as in other parts of Mithila are Narak-Niwaran Chaturdashi (observing total fast, without even drinking water the whole day, by devotees who worship Siva), and Vasant Panchami (worshipping the goddess of knowledge). Narak-Niwaran Chaturdashi is yet another peculiarity of Maithil festivity, while the latter is famous all over north India.

The month of Falgun (March–April) is famous for Holi, a festival popular across north and central India. Almost a week before the day of Holi the youth of the village, mostly belonging to the lower caste, take out regular procession in the evening while singing *jogira* (a genre of reciting funny lines on the beat of a tin drum). While the youth sing *jogira*, the male elders surround them enjoying the performance and clapping for them. Women catch a glimpse of it from the window; young girls pop out to have a slice of the fun and report to the older women of the household. The *jogira* culminates with *holika dahan* (the burning of piles of wood to mark the defeat of a mythical monster) on the night before the day of Holi. Early morning on this day, women cook some special dishes, especially *maal-pua* (made of flour, mixed with milk and banana, and fried in ghee), a curry of mutton/chicken, and a special curry of jackfruit and *dahi-bada* (a dish in curd). Women play among themselves using powdered colours while men go out in the alleyways, chowk or to the *dalan* of other men to exchange colours and smear mud on each other. Kids also start roaming about with friends since early in the morning after eating the special dishes cooked at home. With the gentle wind of the month, the proverbial *falgunahat*, the soundscape on this day carries the intermittent crescendo of *Holi hai* (it's Holi) or *Bura na mano holi hai* (do not mind it, for it is Holi today) against the background of the beat of tin drum. Clusters of male folk roam about playing and singing songs; at chowks shops play songs from Hindi films or albums in Bhojpuri and Maithili on loudspeakers, tape-recorders, and transistors. Men visit every household and sit at the *dalan*. Women of the household take pride in sending their cooked items to their *dalan*. The men are also treated to *bhang sharbat*, a paste of cannabis mixed in milk). These days IMFL have replaced *bhang*. The songs on the day of Holi are mostly sung by men folk. They carry the effervescence and playfulness of the season, along with a notion of melancholia. A song, apparently incompatible with the occasion, moves emotionally, blending joy and sorrow:

Hori kai sang khelab madhab hamar bides re
Apno nai aabthi likhinai pathabathi . . .

Who do I play Holi with, my *madhav* is abroad
Neither writes to me, nor comes back . . .

Yet another festival Shivrait (also known as Sivaratri) is the festival with a twofold celebration. The diurnal celebration entails fasting and worshipping the Siva *linga*. In the nocturnal celebration villagers take out a *barat* of ghosts and goblins. Women have an interesting role in the celebration of Shivrait, like on many other occasions, of singing the folk songs of Siva *vivah*. The categories of songs they sing are *Nachari* and *Maheshvani*. While women sing these songs within the periphery of the household, men take out the procession. Most of these men consume *bhang* and *ganja*, as one of them enacts the role of Siva and others create hullaballoo as ghosts and goblins. In a *Nachari* song women seek Siva's blessings:

Kakhan harab dukh mor ho bholenath
Kahiya harab dukh mor . . .

When would you rid me of these woes
Bholenath! When will be cured these sores . . .

And, so much is the affection for Siva that they sing playfully:

Bhola nene chalu hamro apan nagri
Apan nagari ho kailaspuri
Parbatike hum tahal bajayab
Nit uthi hum nir bharab gagri . . .

Take me along to your world
The world we call *kailashnagri*
(abode of Siva, the mountain of *Kailash*)
Will serve you, and your wife *Parvati*
Every dawn, I will fill pitcher . . .

Devotion notwithstanding, they sing songs mocking the appearance of the groom Siva, when the men are out with the *barat*:

Hum nahi janal ge mai
Ehan bar narad johi louta
Dekhatahi sab paday . . .

Did we ever know! Oh!
Such a groom *narad* will fix
Awful and shocking
None stays to take risk . . .

With the onset of the month of Chaitra, the village gets ready for the festival of Ram Navami that falls on the ninth day of the ten-day long worship of the goddess Durga. There is Judshital,[5] another festival peculiar to Mithila, which has an important place within Fulhara. The rituals are household specific, inclusive of cleaning and preparing food, worshipping the *pitar* (dead ancestors) and household deity, and feeding Brahmins. Children enjoy the activities associated with Judshital, such as flying kites and organizing wrestling matches.

In addition to these festive moments that reflect the religious as well as the sociocultural structure of rural Mithila in general and Fulhara in particular, there are occasions when *Satyanarain puja* is held in some or other household of the village, on any day chosen and suggested by the Brahmin who can read the *panchang*. Almost every month some household in the village would invite everybody to hear *katha* (the sacred story told by the officiating priest that discusses the significance of this *vrata*). The inhabitants of Fulhara perform this *vrata* with an objective in mind, as a thanksgiving to god for some favour granted or to request for some favour to be granted in the future. Yet another informal *vrata* is *brihaspatibarikatha* in which a woman fasts and reads stories of the benefactor Lord Vishnu, every Thursday throughout the year. Similar is *Shanibari* observed on Saturdays. There was a time when a *vrata katha* of Santoshi Mata was very popular in the village, but its popularity has now faded. The popularity of Santoshi Mata can be traced back to a popular Hindi film, *Jai Santoshi Ma*, from the 1970s[6] (Sharma 1975).

This outline of everyday life and calendar of festivity attempts to underline the intersections of popular and folk in the Maithil world view in Fulhara. This is, however, also marked by the landscape in terms of sound and sight. In this landscape, a system of meanings emerges which is analytically discussed in the next essay.

Notes

1. The legend is that Singheshwarsingh was a Rajput by caste and fell in love with a *domin* (a girl from Dom family). He decided to claim his love publicly and struggled against the caste hierarchy. The Doms worship him as their god and meet annually to celebrate his heroism.
2. My facilitator's house did not have a toilet and they noticed my discomfort in the practice of going to the field like other men. I was provided with a facility to use the toilet of a neighbouring house, of a well-to-do family. Six months later, when I went back to Fulhara to resume my fieldwork I found my facilitator had got a toilet built. When I asked as to why they got it done so quickly, they said it was for guests like me.
3. This may include either *chura-dahi* (*chura* is crushed rice and *dahi* is curd) or *roti-tarkari* (manually made bread and cooked vegetable). *Chura-dahi* happens to be preferable in *jal-pan*.

4. Chaurchanda has an established historicity. It became popular after King Hemangada Thakur of the Oinwara dynasty began to observe it considering the importance of the moon in astrological framework.
5. Judshital corresponds with Satuain of the Bhojpuri-speaking region of north Bihar and Uttar Pradesh, and Baisakhi of Punjab.
6. The film was a blockbuster.

7

In Fulhara: Sound and Sight
in a World View (Part II)

Continuing from the previous essay, in addition to the festive occasions of singing and collective effervescence according to the calendar of Mithila, Fulhara also has other innumerable events in the sociocultural life. These pertain to rites of the passage that occasion the gathering of men, women, and children from not only Fulhara but also from other villages. Such events take place in some or other household every year. These are called *samskar* in priestly terms, and have an inevitable impact on the everyday life of Fulhara. They constitute sound and sight in the world view of Fulhara. In this essay there is an attempt to continue with the objective of the previous one and present more instances from Fulhara to draw a comprehensive picture. It attempts an interpretative understanding of the sound and sight in Fulhara, thus unravelling the key debates in the songs.

Festivity in Rite of Passage

In the life cycle of any individual there is a festivity associated with the sixth day after a child's birth, famously known as *chhathihar*. It is celebrated across caste groups without any priestly intervention. Women conduct the folk ways with the intent to protect the baby from any evil eye by smearing *kajar* (collyrium) on the baby's eyes, and sing songs from the category called *sohar* and *khilona*. The eldest of the household leads the singing and is accompanied by the bevy of women, as song goes on:

Lalna re kathi dekhi hanslain horil ke baba
Aabe bans badhal he
Hatthi dekh hanslain fallan (name) ke baba
Aabe bans badhal he. . . .

Friends, what sight triggered a laughter of Horil's father
That now descence moves ahead
Saw an elephant and burst smiling (name) that Baba
That now descence moves ahead. . . .

The celebration of the arrival of the new member in the family, especially a male child, is also a manifest preference for a son in the folk society of Mithila. If the birth of a son has an association with something morbid or undesirable, then it is expressed remorsefully through another *sohar* song:

Sita ban me khari pachhtay
Lav kush janmal yo
Jyo aaj rahtathi raja Dashrath ji
Lutayabtathi Ayodhya san raj. . . .

In the midst of forest, *Sita* regrets
Born are *luv-kush* here
Had there been, Dasrath, the king
He would have donated all his kingdom
In the midst of forest, *Sita* regrets. . . .

The song recounts the key characters form the epic *Ramayana* to express the remorse of Sita who was stranded in the forest with her newborn babies. This was after the dramatic act of Ram casting aspersion on Sita's chastity. In yet another *sohar*, women sing a criticism of the sociocultural celebration of a son and the secondary status of daughters:

Jahi kokhiya je amma
Bhaiya ke janam dehal
Tahi kokhiya hamro janam dehal. . . .

The womb that delivered my brother,
O mother!
That is where I was nurtured too. . . .

The songs from *sohar* and *khilona* dealing with child birth also convey the emotional upheaval of a new mother. Such songs underline the paradoxes involved in the process of becoming a mother:

Pahil bedan jab uthal angina me mudiya patkal he
Sasu aab nai khelayab he tora beta sang latgenma. . . .

As arose the first pang, I threw my head in *angana*
No more play of love, *Sasu* (mother-in-law), with your son
It just made me miserable. . . .

The song mentions all the in-laws and conveys what the labouring mother experiences: regret for having given into desire, having conceived, and a joyful possibility of becoming mother of a child. In the course of rendition, the singing women break into conversations and disclose the superiority of a male child. In the same breath, however, they also emotionally express the value of a female child despite the associated burden of getting her married when she grows up. Male children are valued for strategic purposes such as the socio-economic support they may lend to their aging parents.

Furthermore, yet another rite is *mundan samskar*, the tonsorial rite, of a male child in a family. The lower caste women turn up to sweep, swab the floor with cow dung, and clean utensils.

A *mundan* in Progress. *Courtesy*: Author.
Note: With mother holding the child, women singing songs, girls looking on and the barber with his scissors on his job.

Lower caste men deliver goods made of bamboo and also turn up to help in cleaning the spot where the feast takes place. The barber plays the most significant role, apart from the Brahmin who hardly pronounces anything consequential in this *samskar* of shaving the head of the child. They are all paid in cash and kind, and of course they are not always happy with the amount they have been paid or gifts they have been presented with. Women join in the preparation for the event by dyeing the *dhoti* with turmeric paste and drawing *aipan* on the floor; of course the most important role is their singing. The acoustic companion to the whole process of *mundan* begins with songs invoking the deity and ancestors:

> *Jal phool lay nautab gharak gosauni he*
> *harsit hoti bhawani barua ke aashish deti he*
> *swargahi naut pathayab ki pitar anand hot he*
> *swarg se outah pitar je ki barua ke ashish deta he. . . .*

> Inviting you with sacred water and flower,
> goddess of home ye
> Pleased is the mother, blesseth the *barua* (the child
>   protagonist) with care
> Inviting you in heavenly abode, all the ancestors ye
> Descendeth today to bless the *barua*, with care. . . .

Such songs invoke not only deities but also all the chief ancestors from at least up to three generations back for divine support to ensure fruitful implementation of the rituals and meaningful occurrence of the rite. There are many songs women sing to point out the roles of various living relatives of the child protagonist in the *mundan*, such as:

> *Kone baba chhudiya gadhaol bent madhaol he*
> *kone amma lel janam kesh ke shubh shubh hoyet he. . . .*

> Who is the father of this boy, who gotten the blade made
> Who is the mother of this boy, who delivered this hair sacred. . . .

Many songs of this genre reveal the name of the child protagonist and establish the relation between the child, parents, close kin, and the divine cosmos. A similar song relates the whole story on the selection of this day, with the help of a Brahmin priest, placing all the actors involved in a narrative context:

Rani je chalali shayangrih raja se bicharal he
raja, balak ati sukumar karab jag mudan he. . . .

The mother queen, in the bedroom, discussed it with the
    father king
The child is too tender, let's have his tonsorial rite done, on a
    day that is good. . . .

There are some peppy songs addressing the barber with pun and
humour:

Dheere dheere katihe hajma kesh,
Ke baua bad dular chhaik re
baua ke maami hajma tore debo re
ke baua bad dular chhiak re. . . .

Be tender in cutting hair, o barber
For, baby is rose of our eyes
Gift for you is the maternal aunt
For, baby is rose of our eyes. . . .

The general sociocultural tendency is to make fun of the maternal
kin through the songs. This song seems to suggest with a subtle
sexual undertone that the barber would get to have the maternal
aunt of the child if he does his job with due care and tenderness.
Not to be ignored are the songs where aunts of the child, his
father's sisters, lodge a complaint of neglect shown to them:

Kehen kathod bheliye yo bhaiya
pahile beta ke mudan kelon
bahini bidagiri bisarlon yo bhaiya. . . .

How heartless is it of you o! brother
Had have first son's *mundan*
Forgot inviting your sister o! brother. . . .

The song goes on revealing the list of compensation for the
insensitive injustice done by the brother of not inviting his sister,
the protagonist of the song. It seeks material compensation for the
brother's folly. Ideally, for the rites such as *mundan, janeyu, biyah,*
and *mrityu,* an invitation is sent across the kinship groups a month
or two in advance. Special invitations are sent to the daughters,
sisters, and aunts of the family. The daughters cry when they arrive

at their natal home from their in-laws' home. The mother, aunts, and other women join in the crying of reunion. The crying is repeated during departure as well. Apparently the former is crying in happiness of seeing the visiting daughters, while the daughter is crying at the sorrow of separation. The incoming women immediately join the workforce of the household, while men while away their time at the *dalan*, passively overseeing the event.

Janeyu, also called *yajnopavit*, the sacred thread-giving ceremony, is larger in implication and design. The main events span over three days after almost a month of preparations. Though mainly a rite in the upper caste groups such as Brahmin, Rajput, Kayastha, Bhumihar, etc., it is also popular with other caste groups such as Koeri in Fulhara. Among Brahmins it is equal to a *yajna*, the religious event in which all gods are invoked for participation through the help of Brahmin priests who are supposed to have knowledge of the Vedas. The function invariably becomes a focal point of public discussion until it is completed. Almost the whole village participates in such an event in differing capacities. A *kumhar* (potter) supplies the needed clay pots, the Dom makes the bamboo baskets available, barbers who traditionally would be the messenger are now reduced to only shaving on the day of the event. Women from the Dhanuk caste group cook and clean, and, of course, women from the upper caste households are always there for all purposes. Women sit all afternoon spinning cotton on the wooden charkha (loom) and make threads, which they subsequently colour in turmeric paste. These threads are put together in a delicate way, in six folds (or three, as per the tradition of the caste group); this is what is called *janeyu* after the Brahmins chant the hymns of the Vedas. The whole village and some of the nearby villages feast for at least two days. There is, thus, another level of preparation in this event, where all the necessary items to be cooked are gathered and catered to the guests in the feast. Curd is a sought after item in any feast in the village, and therefore the household where the event is to take place gathers sufficient amount of milk, duly boiled and kept in clay utensils to set the curd. Other sweet dishes of milk are also prepared.

The rite has manifold occasions of singing. In addition to the songs in praise of the deity and ancestors, there are songs for the main actions associated with the rituals in *janeyu*. A song that presents the scenario in narrative form is:

> *Lal piyar acchi madba paane paat chharal he*
> *tahi madba baisalah baba se 'fallan' baba he. . . .*
> *rahu rahu babu aai ahan brahman hoyab he*
> *ke lal janeyua deb ki piyar januyua deb he. . . .*

> Red and yellow *madba*, thatched with betel leaves overhead
> Sat beneath such *madba*, the father, who is such a father
> Go slow my child, you are becoming Brahmin today
> Red one or yellow one, which *janeyu* shall we give him today. . .

The story reveals the names of the father and other kin involved in helping the child become a Brahmin. There is another song sung on the same occasion that also ridicules the sociocultural tendencies of a Brahmin:

> *Baklel babhna chura dahi chatay ela hamar angana*
> *chaur deliyen dail deliyen dhelni angana*
> *ek rati non le karai chhathi khekhna. . . .*

> Idiot Brahmin, greedy for *chura-dahi*,[1] came over our *aangan*
> Gifted you with rice and lentils, you hoarded them away
> A bit of salt makes you crib about, not expected of you. . . .

The song targets greedy priests who often end up asking for more and are never content with what has been already given to them. In general women do not shy away from ridiculing Brahmins for their meanness. These women are from both sections, the upper caste—including Brahmins—as well as the lower castes. Whenever an elderly woman has to say something harsh to a young boy from a Brahmin family, she would address him as '*re babhnaa!*', which connotes criticism for the 'unbecoming Brahmins'. Women remind the men of the Brahmin caste the socially expected behaviour with attributes such as wisdom, generosity, compassion, and grandness. The feeling of offering a son to the social cause that is in the nurturance of a Brahmin is overwhelming. Hence, the mother of the child who is going through the rite sheds tears, thus marking a sense of separation. The elderly folk trenchantly remark that *janeyu samskar* is merely a lip service these days as nobody really observes the rules of chastity and austerity until marriage anymore. The show of the *samskar* is merely to assert caste hierarchy, prestige and is borne out of cultural habit rather than the process for inculcation of values.

The *janeyu samskar* is almost a prelude to the *vivah samskar* (the wedding), and hence these two events have a similarity in the ritual performances as well as songs. The wedding ceremony is a little more spectacular than *janeyu* ceremony. The process of match selection itself encompasses the whole village involving even those who do not belong to the household. An intermediary called *ghatak* (also called *agua*) facilitates the primary broaching of the proposal for both the parties. If a potential bride's side comes to visit a potential groom's side to adjudge their socio-economic status, people from every corner of the village get to know of it. Similarly, if the father of a daughter is visiting places to find an eligible match for his daughter, it is not a secret for the village. The amount and property promised in dowry is often the main attraction of the village talk, indicating the socio-economic abilities and status of the family of a giver and taker of the dowry. There has been literally no marriage without dowry in Fulhara. It is not hyperbolic to suggest that wife-givers and wife-takers are primarily dowry-givers and dowry-takers. The mathematics of a marriage entails the amount of money spent in buying exchangeable gifts, socio-economic status of the givers and takers, and the economic value of a potential groom. Once both sides accept the proposal, a plethora of preparations commence. Several rounds of shopping of clothes, ornaments, daughter's trousseau and son's wedding outfit, and also the heavily bargained shopping for the grand feast for the *barat* (the entourage accompanying the groom), takes place. Women in the household lay the groundwork of preparing for everything, from the nitty-gritty of *bidhi-bidhan* (folk ways) to the aesthetics of the wedding ceremony.

There are more preparations involved for a daughter's marriage than that of a son's for the event consummates at the bride's natal home. Most of the preparations occur where the bride resides and the entire village gears up to offer paid as well as unpaid services. One of the many activities in a wedding is writing *kobar*, a special wedding mural that women make on the wall of the

A *Kobar* Writing in Progress. *Courtesy*: Author.

private chamber in which the newly-married couple is supposed to spend nights in continuity with rituals. The humble art of *kobar* has a telling effect as it intends to convey tales of marriages of the mythological icons such as Sita-Ram, Siva-Parvati; it comprises dandy images of men and women in an ornate frame neatly populated by snakes, flora and fauna.

Songs, however, accompany the action at both the places. At the groom's household the women folk including the mother, sisters, and aunts, may sing something emotionally appealing like:

Jaahi din aaho babu toro janam bhel
ann pain kichhu ne sohay he
seho babu chalala gauri biahan
dudhba ke daam dehu ne chukaay he
dudhba ke daam amma sadhiyo nai sakachhi
posai ke daam dai de deb he. . . .

The day you were born, my grown up child
No food no water, in the labour pain, I had liked
That grown up child of mine is on the way to marry Gauri
Can you pay for the milk I gave you, is there a price?
Priceless is the milk you fed me o mother
We will however reciprocate for my bringing up. . . .

The song presents a dialogue between a son in a wedding outfit and his mother. It narrates a mother's passionate desire to possess a son and seeks his assurances that his wife would not obscure his

attachment with the mother. The son promises that his wife would
tender utmost respect and care to the mother. Curiously though,
while singing songs of happiness occasioned by son's marriage, the
mother also sobs occasionally while relating stories of bringing up
her son. On enquiry, they say these are 'tears of happiness';[2] but the
songs also echo a sense of separation. Joy that a son is graduating
in the passage of life is coupled with the sense of sorrow that he is
going to switch his loyalty to his wife. Some of the mothers of the
groom manage to articulate the potential emotional separation
that the new woman in the son's life would change the degree of
emotional proximity between mother and son. The mother and
her friends also sing songs comparing the vanity and resplendence
of the groom's appearance to that of mythological icons such as
Ram, Krishna, and Siva.

At a bride's place, prior to the commencement of the wedding,
women may be telling another story through their songs:

Sita ke dekhi dekhi
jhakthti janak rishi moti jaka jhrani nor
sita jugut var kat bhetat, othi se layab jamay yo. . . .

Gaping at Sita, remorsefully Janak
Sheds tears copiously
Anywhere if exists an eligible groom, will go get it, for Sita. . . .

Drawing a parallel between the woes of a father of a daughter
and the mythological father of Sita, the song reveals the perennial
anxieties of a daughter's parents in a patriarchal condition. It
alludes to the ordeal of match selection, dealing with the pride
and prejudices of ascribed identities and a genuine emotional
apprehension of a father about finding an eligible match for his
daughter. The dilemma whether the selected match is the best for
a daughter comes clearly again in a song, sung when women do
parichhan (receiving the groom):

Hamro gauri chhathi panche baras ke
ek so baras ke jamay ge mai
kona ke gauri sasur basti
chhathin ati sukumar ge mai. . . .

For a tenderly aged *Gauri*
So old a groom, alas!

How would Gauri live with him
So very soft and suave. . . .

When women have to criticize a likely mismatch they compare the groom with savage Siva's sordid appearance. However, by the end of the song they reconcile and recognize the divine excellence of Siva. In between the rendition of such songs, some women also exchange notes on the nicety of the groom or otherwise. On such occasions, women also recall some marriages in which the groom's father cheated the girls' father as the former turned out to be not-so-good people. Through gossip and singing, there will be infrequent instances of sobbing. Even though it is a happy occasion to have daughter married off, a sense of separation from the daughter also looms large in the background. Listening to those songs of women even the men folk, father, brothers, uncles, and others break down and start sobbing quietly. Some men, exasperated by the emotionally overwhelming moments, run off to the *paan* shop to get a change of mood. Or they scream at the women to stop generating such emotional turmoil. It however seldom prevents women from singing and touching everybody emotionally.

Way before the weeping finds an unhindered crescendo there are socioculturally defined situations for the celebration of the new marriage. The elaborate ritual underway, in the magnanimous rite of marriage, entails songs for each bit of ritual—songs for *aam-mahua vivah* (marriage of trees before the marriage of the couple to ensure that all the bad astrological effects, *graham-dasha*, is received by the trees rather than humans), *naak pakarbaak geet* (the elder sister of the would-be bride, or any other woman in sisterly relation, ushers the groom by holding his nose, in a jocular manner), *laaba bhujbak geet* (songs when the corn is popped), *othangar kaalak geet* (when the would-be groom is made to join the men of the household in thrashing the seeds in a wooden plank symbolizing act of reproducing), *saunth kaal,* and *senurdaan* (when the bride's hair is parted by her mother to receive the vermillion smeared by the groom), *bedi kaalak geet* (when the couple is taking rounds of the auspicious fulcrum made of tender bamboo trees), *kanyadaan* (when the daughter is ritually given away by the father in the company of other men), and *kobar* (when the ritually married couple is ushered by the women in the special bridal chamber). On the way to the *kobar* women sing evidently amorous songs suggestive of mythologically supported romance, such as:

> *Nadiya ke tire tire maali phulbariya,*
> *tahi mei chanan ke gaach he*
> *tahitar malin beti palanga ochhaol*
> *raja beta khelay shikar he. . . .*

> On the bank of the river, in the garden
> Stood a sandal wood tree beneath which
> Spread a bed on the couch, the daughter of the gardener
> Nearby plays hunting, the son of king, of fame. . . .

But the sense of romance is not devoid of a fear of the same, as a song speaks for the protagonist (the bride) revealing a meaningful dilemma:

> *Hum nai jebai kobar ghar humra dar lagay ye*
> *dar lagay ye, ho baba laaj lagay ye*
> *jakhne mahadeb, basaha par baisalani*
> *ange bhibhut rudra maal sobhaiye*
> *hum nai jaibe . . . humra dar lagay ye*
> *jakhne mahadeb madba par baisalain*
> *bhoot-pisach sab taal maray ye*
> *jakhane mahabed kobar mei baisalani*
> *bisdhar naag fufkar maraye*
> *hum nai jaibe kobar gahr humara dar lagay ye. . . .*

> No, I can't go to *Kobar*, for it scares me of the unseen
> Fears of the unseen and that I am too shy for this
> As *Mahadeb* sat upon his favourite ox, *Basaha*
> Ashes on his body silvered
> Garland of *rudra* too peered
> No, I can't go to *kobar*, for it scares me of the unseen
> As *Mahadeb* sat beneath the sacred *madba*
> Ghosts and goblins all roared in upbeat
> As *Mahadeb* sat in *kobar*
> Venomous cobra, dangling his neck, hissed all over
> No, I can't go to *kobar*, for it scares me of the unseen. . . .

The song has deep sexual connotations as it describes the romance with the groom from the newly-wed bride's point of view. A sexual romantic imagination within the mythological frame with reference to the most adored god Siva presents another instance of the conjunction between the social and mythological, mortal and divine, sacred and sexual, spectacular and ordinary. Women not only initiate the couple into the romantic frame, they also rejoice in abusing and teasing the newly-wed groom and his accompanying men. The *barat* listens to it with rapturous joy, even as they demand for another song despite being the targets in the songs:

> *Nij kul kamini samdhin chhinro*
> *sagar nagar eko nahi chhorlain*
> *ke thik apan paray. . . .*

> The mother of the groom, the wife of the man in red robe
> She is such a beautiful whore
> Bewitching for the whole world
> Never does she distinguish her husband and other men. . . .

Such outrageously sexual and abusive songs waft in the air along with the aroma of the food served to the *barat*. The songs are common in all caste groups with variations in tonality. Towards the end of the ritual, at the last leg of the rite of marriage, women sing songs called *samdaun*, which expresses the grief of bidding adieu to the daughter:

> *Bad re jatan se hum siya dhiya poslahu*
> *seho dhiya ram nene jaay. . . .*

> Brought up my tender daughter
> with utmost care and love
> Such a piece of my heart, Ram takes away. . . .

While singing such songs women do not shy away from venting their emotional outbursts and men more often than not slip into the same fold. The occasion of final separation, of the groom setting off for a patrilocal family with his newly-wed wife, occurs either just after marriage or after a year or three years later, as the rule suggests. Called *dwiragman,* literally meaning second marriage, it is executed with almost as much fanfare as the marriage. But the level of melancholia overshadows that of joy due to the imminent

separation from the daughter, and also an unrequited attachment
with the groom, as a song says:

> *Bad re jatan se hum ram thagi lelhu*
> *seho ram jai chhaith apan gharbe ho lal*
> *je hum janitahu ram chal jaytah*
> *panma khuway ram ki rakhitahu ho lal. . . .*

All deceit that I did to win over Ram
That beloved, deceiving me, is on his way back
If I knew he will go away
Must I have fed him nice betel leaf!

On such an occasion women's singing and weeping blend
so neatly that a choking throat and hiccups appear as musical
accompaniment to the song and add to the emotive effect. A song
reads:

> *Suga jyo posito hbhajan sunaybto*
> *dhiya posi kichhu nahi bhel*
> *ghivak ghail jaka poslahu dhiyake*
> *beta jaka kayal dular. . . .*

Had I cared for a parrot
I would have sung songs of god to it
What did I get caring for a daughter?
A pitcher-full of butter was it
like my son, I loved my daughter
Such a daughter, my dear child, goes away
Leaving this home, and us all, aside. . . .

The song articulates a protestation against the sociocultural
practice of separating from a daughter. There is a tint of resistance
to the social practice though it does not amount to its rejection.
Curiously, in such songs sobs, hiccups, and truncated emotional
narrations supersede the lyric. This tendency also characterizes
the event of death, where wailing complements other forms of
folklore.

The last rite in any biography is *antim samskar* (the last rite)
performed upon the death of an individual. There is no practice
of singing songs on the event of death. Nevertheless, there are
songs called Nirgun that are sung by some men from the lower

castes. The knowledgeable elders of the village often glibly explain this paradox by referring to an extinct institution of *Nepobhatin*, which means bardic crying, of which even many of the scholars/teachers at Lalit Narayan Mithila University are unaware. Without much historical substantiation, they narrate that particular groups of women used to be professional singers on the event of death and their songs were in the format of wailing.[3] It was largely singing while mourning. This traditional institution of singing and wailing is now extinct. There is however a practice of ritual weeping slotted on a particular day, the *ekadasha*, the eleventh day, when the *karta* (the main carrier, often the eldest son of the deceased or the eldest brother, or an equivalent kin) comes back from the site of the karma (the act of the worshipping and sending the departed soul to heaven). Prior to this ritual, the elderly women prevent the members of a bereaving family from crying and they focus on listening to the stories from the *Garud Purana*. This is prevalent only among the upper caste in general and the caste of Brahmins in particular. Singing still holds true among the lower caste: while men sing well-composed songs from the Nirgun category, women sing their sorrow out in the manner of grieving.

Antim samskar generally refers to the post-death rituals. The rituals related to death seem to begin right when the person is dying, unless the death was brought about by an accident or occurred in a hospital. There is a notion of 'good death' and 'bad death', the former alluding to dying in the household in the presence of all the near and dear ones even if the dying person was ailing. If a person has died at an unexpected turn of life, such as dying young and unwed or if a child dies, it negatively stirs the conscience of the folk. These are the occasions when recovery of the social selves of the surviving members of the family happens to be more challenging. Even in instances of bad death the folk have a tendency to subject the corpse to various rituals. In any case, the dead body is taken out from the enclosed space under the roof of the house to the open space in the *aangan* near the *tulsichaura* (discussed in the previous essay). As the news spreads that the person is about to die, or has died, the villagers start streaming inside. While men seem to be active in terms of conducting the

rite, women and kids snuggle up in corners consoling the kids
and women of the household. As part of the beginning of the last
rite, they administer some droplets of *gangajal*, the pious water of
the sacred river Ganges, stored in a pitcher in the household, to
the dying person by opening his/her mouth. Some well-to-do
families also conduct *godaan*, the donation of a calf, in the belief
that by holding the tail of the calf the dying person would have
a smooth journey from this world to the other. It is assumed that
the priest who would officiate in the rite will receive the calf in
gift. Even without *godaan*, the folk believe that a well-conducted
last rite ensures a potential liberation for a departed soul. More
often than not it is believed that *praan* (life force) is released from
the body through the mouth where the droplets of *gangajal* have
been poured. In some instances doctors are involved in the scene
to make sure that the person is biologically dead. In the instances
where no doctor is present, the folk themselves declare the body
of the dying person as being fit for the cremation process. All
this while, children and women, even some adults, stay in close
proximity with the dying person, holding the hand or feet and
caressing their head. An eerie silence punctuated with bursts of
crying and the din of hurly burly marks the situation as the dying
person is finally declared dead by the village elders. Some male
members of the household prepare the *arthi* (the bed of bamboo
sticks) to carry the dead body to the cremation ground. If the
dead were a woman, who died as a *suhagin*, her husband being still
alive, she would be decorated by the women of the household
as a bride in a new saffron-coloured saree and embellished with
other things associated with a new bride. In other instances, the
dead body would be generally covered from head to toe in a single
piece of white cotton fabric. A procession carries the *arthi* to the
cremation ground, which is generally by the side of a pond or a
gachchi. The procession consists of kith and kin and others from
across the households in the village; they all walk in the procession
chanting *Ram nam sat hai, sab ka yahi gat hai* (the god is true, and
so is death for everybody). The four sides of the *arthi* are soldiered
in turns by either the sons or other kith and kin of the dead. Some
families also take the dead for cremation to the bank of the Ganga.
Simariya, in the neighbouring district of Begusarai, is the place

where many of the villagers take the dead for a more auspicious cremation. This involves a short three to four hour bus journey. The funeral bed for the pyre at the cremation ground is set with logs at the base on top of which the dead would lay covered with logs around it. The rituals are minimal and are performed at the instruction of the Mahapatra Brahmin—a particular group of Brahmins who solely specialize in conducting the *antim samskar*, and are considered of the lowest status among all the upper castes. The pyre is lit with the help of a Dom, the outcaste who specializes in performing the defiling works within the socially structured inequality. The sound and sight are too sombre and profound at this juncture. This is where no crying or singing takes place. The entire group awaits the completion of the cremation until the body gradually turns into ashes with the bones left over. In the process of burning, a few men from the village feed the fire with more logs and adjust the funeral bed so that the flames engulf the whole of the body. The smell at the moment of burning is inexplicably heady. At last, the oldest of the household offers the leftover to the river, or if the cremation has taken place in the village the leftover is gathered in a pitcher to be offered later to the river. Including the day of cremation, the rite extends for eleven days during which the oldest son of the deceased or anyone of equivalence, who will be called *karta*, the doer, offers sacrifices and the *preta*, the spiritual remains of the deceased, is propitiated everyday at the bank of any river/pond in the village. On the eleventh day, it is assumed that the deceased has finally departed to the abode of the *pitar*, their ancestors. The *karta* returns to the household to offer gifts to the officiating priests. Gifts include the wherewithal of everyday existence such as clothes, cot, mattress, utensils of brass, gold ornaments, etc. It is offered under the pretext that the effect of the items given away would help a departed soul sustain an everyday existence in the *pitar lok*. This is the day when a ritual weeping takes place in the belief that the deceased has departed the earth in actuality, and does not exist as a *preta* hovering around the bereaving family. In principle weeping is not allowed before this day and the family is engaged in listening to the *Garud Purana* that tells the mythological tales of dying, departing, attributes of soul and impact of deeds after death, and the significance of dharma and karma. Nevertheless, weeping beyond the pale of ritualistic control never ceases in effect ever since death happens. Most of the wailing is truncated with narratives recalling the person, their deeds, and emotional associations with them. Amongst the lower caste, an often heard song sung by men folk is imbued with symbolism, such as:

Nirgun piya gela je bidesh
bhejai chiththi nai sandes
kona jebai sasurari, sunu he sajni
piya aila je hamar
bhejal doliya kahar
aab ta jebai sasurari, sunu he sajni
kari kai solho singar
bhelhu doliya sawar
auri kaanei jare jar
chhutal naihar parivar, sunu he sajni
santo kahaiye pukari
atai rahinai dui-chari
aakhir jaynai sasurari, sunu he sajni. . . .

Beloved beyond compare, went off the shore
Sends neither a word nor any lore
How would I go to the abode of my beloved, listen o friends!
As and when arrives my beloved
A palanquin arrives for me
Now likely, I will be going to the abode of my beloved, listen
    o friend!
I doll up myself
Aboard the palanquin sent for me
Gauri, within me, wept copiously
As I left the whole world of known behind
And saint said it aloud
It's a short sojourn here
Eventually, I have to go to the abode of my beloved, o friend!

The song draws a parallel between the departure of a soul from a body and that of a bride from her natal home. The elderly women would hush up any curiosity pertaining to death, but they would also speak of the limits of *deh* (physical existence), almost accepting the inevitable ending. Some of them, the widows, also regret living so long after the death of their husbands. Awaiting death is an abiding feature of elderly lives, not only due to difficulties in the socio-economic sustenance of existence, but also because they all aspire a timely death. While these women and men would like to bless their younger grandchildren with a long life (they address the kids with a word *chiranjeevi*, meaning 'live longer'), they seek from their gods a timely death for themselves. Perhaps the ambiguity about living (eternally) and dying (timely) underlines the peculiarity of Maithili world view and of its folk philosophy of living and dying. I elaborate on this in the last section of this essay.

Songs in Everyday Life

The soundscape of Fulhara, as in any other part of Mithila, would be incomplete without a mention of songs in everyday life. In addition to the songs associated with the rituals in the rite of the passage, there are songs women, and also men, sing for the onset of seasons, celebrating the motifs associated with the seasons in the span of a year. Some oft-sung categories of songs are *Chaitawar*, *Tinmasa*, *Chaumasa*, *Punchmasa*, *Barahmasa*, *Faag*, *Kajli,* and *Malar*. These songs establish the centrality of an intimate relationship with the loved ones and the painful distance that is caused by various factors.[4] A song form *Malar* suggests it clearly:

> *Sakhi re bisral mohe murari*
> *pratham ashadh tejal mohi mohan*
> *kaun bidhi khepab anhari. . . .*
>
> O friends, I am out of M*ohan's* mind
> Forsaken in the month of *ashadh*
> how do I while away the dark nights. . . .

The protagonist, the singer through these songs, tends to account for the fear of living away from the loved one who, generally equated with mythological icons, must have been beside her or him in the times of crises. By expressing a longing for the companion, in a subtly amorous manner, these songs emphasize the idea of separation. Similar is the stance in a song from *Barahmasa* that says:

Chait he sakhi fulal beli nikas kunj nebar yo
teji mohan gel madhupur hamar ki apradh yo
baisakh he sakhi usham jwala gham se bhijal deh yo
ragri chandan ang leptahu ghar je rahitaith kant yo. . . .

About the doorstep bloomed jasmine, had there been him
  around *yo*
For what err of mine, *Mohan* left me alone and went off to
  Madhupur yo
Drenched in sweat in the heat of *Baisakh* my body is helpless *yo*
Wish I had smeared sandal pastes all over, had there been him
  around *yo*. . . .

The resonant leitmotif in such songs is the love for the one who
has left for some destination for socio-economic purposes, and
also a longing for the fulfilment of the desires. On a larger scale,
these songs also reveal a longing for the ideal type of human
existence, a sense of being going through inevitable pleasure and
pain. This is recurrent in the songs from *Chaumasa* and *Barahmasa*
as well.

Apart from the songs of seasons, there are various songs
associated with the domestic chores. The mothers and aunts hum
these songs individually. The eldest daughter of a parent is almost
like a 'little mother' to her younger ones. She performs some of
the work mothers are supposed to do for the younger kids. From
changing nappies to cleaning the excreta of the baby, these little
mothers are spotted in every household and are heard singing
and humming as well. The songs on their lips are not same as
those sung by their mothers. While the elderly women would sing,
these little mothers would watch and hear them in awe, thinking
whether these songs really existed at any point of time. They find
them difficult to sing, given the antiquity of the wordings, and the
languid pace at which they are sung. They sing songs in Maithili
they have heard played out on loudspeakers, cassette or CD or
MP3 players. The little mothers, not all of whom are school-going
or may perfunctorily be on the school-rolls, are quick in learning
popular tunes. No elderly woman ever objects to their singing, and
they usually hear them agape instead. Some boys, mostly around
ten or twelve years old, become amused spectators and audiences

to their sisters' informal renditions. And when sisters are bored of being the object of attraction, they will persuade their brothers to sing some peppy songs or just dance casually for them.

The practice of young girls singing popular songs and the elderly women singing some of the well-known folk songs has a common link. All of them are open to singing songs in Maithili to the tune of some very popular *filmy* song. A seven-year old child Palak sings a song although not in filmy tune but still in a manner that is fairly new to the elderly women,

> *Oopar pahad neecha kankar*
> *he shiv shankar*
> *puja kona karu. . . .*

> The peak above and grimes beneath
> O Siva!
> How do I worship you. . . .

Following her, elder sister, twelve-year old Radha, sings as her grandmother looks on with admiration,

> *Chhoti si meri parbati sankar ji ki puja karti hai*
> *hari bag mei jaati hai*
> *fulo ki daal libati hai*
> *fulo ki kaliya khoti hai*
> *chhoti si. . . .*

> A little *parbati* worships *Shankar* unfailingly
> She goes to the sacred garden and
> toils to reach the flowering twigs,
> She plucks each flower lovingly
> The pretty Little *Parbati*. . . .

An unusual song, in Hindi, sung in Maithili tone and tenor, counts the hard work a little girl child does, such as gathering flowers, *belpatra* (*Aegle marmelos*), and sandal wood, to worship lord Siva. While singing this song, she apparently feels she is a 'little *Parbati*' (the young consort of Siva) and she has to devote herself irrespective of her age and limited abilities. Perhaps the song articulates a part of the biography of the singing child who too contributes to the running of the household. In between the song the grandmother would gently scold the girl for messing up with *bhas* and *laya* (meter of song and intonation) even though there is hardly any training in the style of singing for the folk women. Thus, for the next song another girl makes an attempt to sing as advised by the grandmother:

> *Baba johab tora batiya katek dinma*
> *bharal shishi gangajal seho sukhi gel*
> *achchat chandan mei baba ghun lagi gel*
> *johab tora batiya katek dinma. . . .*

> How long do I await for your arrival
> The bottle full of *Gangajal* (sacred water of the Ganges) has
>   dried too
> *Achchat* (pious rice) *chandan* (sandal wood) have been eaten
>   up by termites
> How long do I await for your arrival. . . .

The song divulges some of the existential concerns resembling the songs sung by the elders. It interrogates the divinity for the unfavourable social condition and reflects the intimate relation between the divine and the mundane, and the proximity between social and extra-social. In addition to these, children also sing a song that echoes contemporary concerns vis-à-vis patriotism, thus revealing the socially constructed relationship between the nation and the mythological divinity,

> *Brahma o bishnu mahesh nikla*
> *apna bharat ke harne kalesh nikla. . . .*

> The trinity of *Brahma*, *Bishnu* and *Mahesh* stride
> To rid *Bharat* (India) of her destitution, in a ride. . . .

The song recounts the effectiveness of each key god of the Hindu pantheon in the amelioration of the problem-struck Indian nation. While the elders appreciate the song, they say it has come to the children via their school education. Elders are not averse to the intervention from contemporary influences. A grandmother, of about sixty-five, sings a song while cooking the meal of the day, in the tune of a filmy song:

> *Sib jogiya gauri ke piya*
> *tune damru baja ke mera dil le liya*
> *mathe me jata hai*

jata me ganga hai
tune ganga baha ke mera dil le liya. . . .

Gauri's husband, O *Sib!* You austere saint
On the beat of your *Damru* (a small drum), you won over my
    heart
The *ganges* soaked in your matted locks
By streaming the *Ganges*, you won over my heart. . . .

On the tune of a song from an Amitabh Bachchan starrer Hindi
film,[5] this song divulges the reason why lord Siva is so endearing.
The elderly singers inform that they are not averse to new,
melodious tunes they hear in their surroundings. While some of
them are aware that these tunes belong to musical compositions
from films, many others seem ignorant of the sources. They all
however seem to believe that the tunes belong to the folk once
they have put their words (lyrics) on them.

Women, in the midst of their daily chores, do not cease to
sing songs every morning. These songs are not in the format of
performance of rituals in the rite of the passage. Each woman
sings within the household, individually, in the softest of tone and
tenor. Interestingly, men also sing these songs at the *dalan*. The
songs are from the category they call *Parati* (to be sung at *prat*,
early morning). These songs are heard across caste groups. With
religious appeal at the surface, these songs mark the existential
location of the folk thought.

A song reads:

Kichhu nai rahal mora haath, he udho
kichhu nai rahal mora haath
gokul nagar sagar brindawan
soon bhel jamuna ghat
brindawanak taruni sab kanay
jhahari jhahari khasu paat
ehi path rath chadhi gela manmohan
kai din takbai baat
saheb jaa dhari palati nai aota
braj bhel agam athah. . . .

A post-*Parati* tea (over a discussion on the songs).
Courtesy: Author.

Nothing in my reach
O *Udho*! Nothing remains with me
The whole of *Gokul*, all of *Brindawan*
And lonely bank of *Jamuna* as well
Beautiful women of *Brindawan,* sobbing and crying
Ceaselessly falling leaves
this way he passed by, atop his chariot
I remain on path, looking for it
My master! he went off, not to even turn back
the city, *Braj*, is orphaned, in glum
nothing in my reach
O *Udho*! Nothing remains with me. . . .

With freshness of morning on the face and calmness in their voice
men and women sing this while the dawn breaks on the eastern
horizon. The song represents the eternal sense of losing somebody
very dear. With reference to the story of women sharing their pain
on the departure of Krishna from the city Gokul, and the deserted
Brindawan where he used to frolic with them, the song articulates
a message that pursuit of pleasure is bound to be over. While the
singer is longing for the departed, wailing for the loss, shedding
tears, there is also a sense of the inevitableness of loss. If goaded for
a conversation, the singers tend to be reticent and offer a simple
notion: 'this is all about our lives!' Along this line there is a song:

Awadh anhar bhel
ek raghuwar binu

Darkness envelops *Awadh*
with the mere absence of Ram. . . .

There is also a song that conveys a sense of end, and of notions of judgement:

Kon gati hoyat mor prabhu
kon gati hoyat mor
janam janam hum pap batoral
kahiyo nai bhajlahu tor. . . .

What I am destined to
What will be my fate
All my life I did but sins
Never did I devote to you
Regretting now, it is too late. . . .

The song confesses an excessive indulgence that prevented an individual from sitting in meditation upon the inevitable events of living and dying. The notion of readiness to face the end is attached with a religious engagement with the divine. However, this is not beyond this-worldly existence. For the expressed belief in a song like this is that only such engagements can absolve oneself of the sense of sin and inability to face the end-unseen. This is not to suggest that sin is dispensable or a disabling factor in dealing with the unseen end. Instead, the song seeks to meditate and recognize the errors committed in the process of living. In the same breath, a song also instills the idea of negation and renunciation of the excesses of the world:

Karam ke baat nihar he udho, karam ke baat nihar
he kahe pipra pakua farat hai
kahe lati fal bhari he udho, karam ke baat nihar
he kahe murkha dhan par lotaya
kahe ke pundit bhikhari he udho, karam ke baat nihar
he kahe bagula set baran bhayo
kahe koyli kaari he udho, karam ke baat nihar
kahthin kabira sun bhai santo
dhani tohre bebhari he santo, karam ke baat nihar. . . .

Your deeds will be adjudged, Udho! Your deeds!
Why so much, a *peepal*, laden with *pakua*
why so heavy with fruits this tendril, Udho! Your deeds!
why this clinging to riches, so foolishly
why a scholar so stupid, Udho! Your deeds!
why the crane we hail for white
why the crows neglected for black, Udho! Your deeds!
says *Kabeer*, must listen and see
wealth is your own deeds, Udho! Your deeds!

The song reflects a close influence of the Nirgun devotional stance propounded by the medieval poet and social critic Kabir.[6] Some of these songs are more popular with the lower caste men and upper caste elderly women. However, almost every elderly person is aware of these songs and their meanings. While singing such songs they exhibit profundity of thoughts and perspective on life and death. These songs do not rule out the significance of the material world as the singers admit the importance of staying in this world. Some of these men who sing *Parati* without fail every morning are also into puffing marijuana every evening or even consuming toddy; yet they express the finitude of indulgence in their songs. It is not only said but they also believe that life is all about acknowledging and accepting these limits. By doing so, as they would put it, they look forward to their journey commencing upon death.

In addition to these oft-sung *Parati* songs, there are songs from the category called *Nachari* sung in the morning. A famous song from this category, sung by both men and women, from across caste groups, is

Kakhan harab dukh mor ho bhole dani
kahiya harab dukh mor
Dukh hi janam lel dukh hi gamaol
Sukh sapnahu nahi bhel ho bholanath
Kahiya harab dukh mor. . . .

When would you free from these woes, O generous Shiv!
When would my pathos be over!
Wasn't I born in this!
Wasn't I have been languishing in this!

Never did I even dream of bliss, ho *Bhole nath!*
When would my pathos be over. . . .

Women tend to add a further nuance to it by singing the same
song like:

Nahira mei chhai ho bhola ek lakh bhiaya
aor chhai sawa lakh bhatija
eke go je amma binu soon he bhola nath
kahiya harab dookh mor. . . .
sasura mei chhai ho bhola
ek lakh bhainsur
aor sawa lakh diyar
eke go jo amma binu soon
ho bhola nath, kakhan harab dukh mor. . . .

A million brothers, in my natal home
And a quarter more is my nieces
A mere absence of my mother makes all deserted though. . . .
When would my pathos be over?

By adding these extra lines women tend to draw the limits even along
the web of relationships. They would not shy away from accepting
that everything and everybody dear to one's heart separates, as
though separation were the absolute rule governing lives in the
samsara (the world of cognition). This acknowledgement does
not amount to total detachment from the endearing relationships
and social existence. They remain attached, as women would say,
like the chaff is attached to the grain until final thrashing takes
place! They, however, seek divine intervention by sharing their
woes with their gods to smoothen the process of separation. By
articulating these notions they also prepare themselves for an
acceptance of the idea of separation. While singing this *Nachari*,
women and men tend to be too soft in their rendition as though
the effect of the wording and devotional beseeching nudges them
to an experiential profundity. Nobody cries yet a sense of crying
in supplication hovers; the song stresses that life is in deep pathos
due to existential constraints and loss of myriad kinds. A rare song,
addressing the monkey god Hanuman, a character of significance
from the epic *Ramayana*, also perpetuates a similar motif,

Kani kani kahthin sita mata sunu sunu hanuman yo
Kona bisri gela humara ke lachhuman kona bisral sri ram yo
rawanak boli bisam san lagay deh gali bhel khuftan yo
kani knai kahthin hanumat sita sa humar bachan parman yo
Samudrak badha dur bhay jayat setu banhota bhagwan yo. . . .

Listen O *Hnauman*! Said mother Sita, with her eyes welling
    with tears
How has forgotten me my own *Lachhuman*, has forgotten me
    Ram too
The roar of Rawan frightens me so much I am wilting as a
    tendril tender
My words are my promises, O mother Sita! Says Hanuman,
    with tears as proof
The sea must yield a way as the god has launched a bridge
    for sure. . . .

There are many songs in everyday life from various genres, which
are not classified for any occasion. One can sing them any time at
will. These songs, sung in leisure are *Nachari, samdaun, Maheshvani,
gosaunik geet, batgabni,* among others. One such song, *gosaunik geet,*
is actually a poem composed by the medieval poet Vidyapati,[7]
which in the passage of time became a folk song:

Jai jai bhiaravi asur bhayauni pashupati bhamini maya
sahaj sumati bar diy he gosauni anugati gati tuw paya. . . .

Hail the mother, fear of monsters, who nurtures humans
    compassionately
Bless us all, we surrender to you, blessed are we, thus your
    children!

The song, in the earliest form of Maithili details the attributes
of the great mother goddess, which is applicable to both Durga
and Kali. The song reveals the benevolence and malevolence of
the great mother. She slaughters demons to protect her devoted
humans; she is a fierce destroyer as well as a compassionate nurturer.
Needless to say, the upper caste women are more comfortable
singing this song than their lower caste counterparts given the
presence of *tatsam* words (pertaining to Sanskrit). Another song
women often sing, in praise of the great mother, is:

Singh par ek kamal rajit tahi upar bhagwati
shankh gahi-gahi chakra gahi-gahi lok ke maa palti
dant khat-khat jih lah-lah sonit daant madhavti
shonit taptap pibathi jogini vikat rup dikhawati
brahma elanhi bishnu elanhi shivji elanti ehi gati
shankh par ek kamal rajit tahi upar bhagwati. . . .

Atop a lion is lotus, and upon is mother of all
Conch shell in a fist, discus in another, to protect us all
Gnashing teeth, flicking tongue, and spattered blood in her face
Drinks blood, drop by drop, reveals her colossal form
Brahma descended, so did *Bishnu*, and also it was *Shiv*
Atop a lion is a lotus, and upon is mother of all. . . .

The description of the great mother, triggering awe and fear, is a
source of assurance to all those who remember her. By invoking
her on all occasions of ritual event in the rite of the passage
as well as in leisure, the women intend to ensure her kind eyes
towards the home and family. Another song articulates a rebellion
in devotion:

Hey bhawani dukh haru maa putra apna janike
day rahal chhi dukh bhari beech bhanwar mei aani ke
aabi asha mei padal chhi ki karu hum kanike
biswamata chhi aha maa aha se manike
kotiyo nai paid chhodab haath rakhab chhanike
din prabhu hum nitya pujab nem vrata ke thanike
hey bhawani dukh haru maa putra apna janike. . . .

Rid me of my sorrow, for I am yours, o mother!
In the middle of tides you are inflicting pathos on me
Clung on to hope I am yet here, for no crying helps, o mother!
For you are mother of the world, that I believe and so does
    everybody else
I will not leave your feet and will clasp your hands, for ever
Day in and day out, I must worship you, with utmost devotion
Rid me of my sorrow, for I am yours, o mother!

In the gentlest manner the devout singer blames the divine for his
or her woes and also rests within a balmy hope that the mother
who has inflicted it all on him (or her) will help out. Another
song, sung irrespective of any occasion, in leisure, is *Nachari*:

Baba baidyanath[8] *hum aayal chhi bhikhariya*
aha ke duariya na
baba bad bad aas lagayal
humra upar hoyao sahay
ek ber daari diyo garib par najariya
aha ke duariya na
baghambar ke jhaad ochhyab
hum t damru ke saryayab
ful-dhthud todi hum layab
belpatra seho chadhayab
bhola bhangiya pisi chadhayab
sanjh-prat-dupahariya na. . . .

Baba Baidyanath (Shiv who adorns Baidyanath Dham)
I have arrived at your door, as a beggar!
With high hope of redemption, of your favour
Of a chance to serve you, for ever
I must clean your attire
I must tidy your drum
I must gather flowers and *belpatra*
I must make cannabis of your choice
From dawn to dusk, day in and out
For, *Bhola*, I have come as a beggar!

The song discloses the submission of the devoted singer to Siva,
so much so that s/he aspires to live in servility, for only Siva can
bless with redemption. Curiously enough, in another song women
voice a critique of living in servility with Siva:

Baisal gauri mone mone sochthi
bhangiya ke sang kona rahabai ge mai
baisal bhangiya, bhukhle tahal karbe ge mai
apne t bhola baba puja par baisthin
bhukhle tahal kona karbai ge mai
anchar phari phari kagat banayab
katek bipait hum likhbai ge mai. . . .

Mulls Gauri sitting quietly
How do I lead my life with the dope, *Mai* (common address
   for mother)

Such a laidback he, earns nothing
Starving me, how do I work for him, *Mai*
He meditates for hours, forgets others
How do I serve with my empty stomach, *Mai*
Tearing *anchal* (a corner of *saari*) I use for paper
Endless woes, how do I write all, *Mai*. . . .

The song blends admiration for the divine austerity as well as
the difficulty arising from the same. The intermingling of the
mythological, the sacred and eternal, with the finite social is
characteristic in such songs. The complaining tenor articulates the
agency of a devotee and the unsustainability of servility.

Interpretative Implications of the Sound and Sight

A panoramic peek at sound and sight in the Maithil world view
enables for a modest interpretative analysis. This entails sociocultural
patterns, the folkways of discharging occasional activities as well
as that of everyday life. The material interests and prerequisites
for existential survival too are revealed in it. The indices of social
stratification and hierarchy underpin this world view. More
crucially, there is a sense of contemporaneity therein: the possible
notions of change and continuity, influences of socio-historical
developments, interventions of the culture industry pertaining to
cinema and cassette industry. All of this however does not obscure a
possible continuity in motifs and meanings that belong to tradition.
The songs presented in this essay are sung by women, children and
also men from across caste groups. The differences in the kinds of
songs, the motifs and meanings are present not only along caste
lines but also across age groups. The motive behind this analysis
is not to extol a 'narcissism of differences'.[9] The difference, and
of course distinction, of the set of idioms and metaphors, of the
degree of linguistic-cultural sophistication in the presentation of a
motif, in the songs of men and women in lower caste groups such
as Dhanuk, Chamar, Dusadha, do not rule out the universality of
the meaning. Distinctions vis-à-vis diversity and universality of
meaning coexists, especially when it comes to the world view.
This coexistence of diversity and universality appears as the core

of the world view. Similarly, the persuasive bent to changes in the songs of younger folk, mainly young girls, does not separate them entirely from their adult counterparts. A quixotic rule of paradox here is that: 'we are different but we mean the same!' Hence, a constant interplay of the socio-structural and belief and practices, does not obscure the universality of meaning. Put together, the Maithili folk world view suggests of *folk philosophy* to which we return later after understanding the details of the world view. It broadly consists of a folk engagement with life and death amid the flurry of symbols and euphony of songs, expressing the intersection of life and death. Folk philosophy thereby operates on the scheme of union and separation. Constituting the core of the world view, thus, is the image of the humans always melodiously striving for transcendence without jettisoning their everyday concerns and questions.

The elements of meaning orbiting around the world view disclose the varying degree of freedom from ritualistic practices for diverse social groups. The folk ways, which Brahmin women discharge in the rite of the passage, are largely in unequivocal collaboration with the Brahminic-Sanskritic tradition represented by the pundits. This is not entirely absent amongst the lower caste or non-Brahmin caste groups. The Dusadhas have a whole gamut of religious performance in which they have a priest from their own caste performing rituals almost similar to that of the upper caste folks. Despite the ritual practices of the lower caste group, there is sociocultural flexibility about feminine articulations. And thereby lower caste women seem to be more at liberty in celebrating *here* and *now* rather than worrying about the 'proper' discharge of the rituals. Thus, in the orbit of the world view circulate ritualized as well as semi-ritualized celebrations of the movement in rite of the passage. But it would only be a half-truth to suggest that a focus on rituals writes off the celebration of the *here* and *now* for Brahmins. The songs of the upper caste women afford them an opportunity to be lewd, subversive, and amorous, celebrating pain and pleasure incurred due to the social existence, and maintaining a largely paradoxical outlook on the sociocultural notions.

Despite the variations in idioms, metaphors, and other expressive devices with an emphasis on the intervention of the unseen power (the divine authority), songs of every caste group reverberate with a concern for material situations. Similarly, weeping is commonplace despite the diversity in texts and tenor of the act across groups. An instance of raucous weeping with non-stop utterance of confounding words or the act of weeping in a hush-hush manner without any textual content has the same functional significance. They intend to render explicit the emotional intent of the folk. Weeping, or wailing, in the face of separation from near and dear ones or a radical movement in the rite of the passage, blurs the parameters of distinctions of the social groups. This is the act that, partially as well as completely, replaces songs of women. Such are the moments that force everybody to join the act as emotion comes to dominate culture. As a variant of weeping, mourning is a traditionally ritualized practice for Brahmins as they are asked to wait till a certain day, the eleventh day of *antim samskar*. But then, like non-Brahmin women, the Brahmin women and children too tend to break away from the rule as they weep every now and then in a silent manner. Some non-Brahmin men, on the occurrence of death, burst into singing as well. The text in mourning is, more often than not, independent of the styles and genres of songs. Applicable across caste groups, weeping/wailing brings about a chance for the resistance to the host of the factors, including social explanations, about the inevitableness of death. The commonly uttered words pose myriad questions: why the incident took place, why the deceased met with such a fate, why the god has been so merciless! It seems in the first place a psycho-emotional denial of the reality. But then this is not to be so simple. Paradoxically, every instance of resistance is also exemplary of a comprehension of the incident and of accepting it. The same bunch of people, the mourners and others, join in rational conversations to decide the course of action following a death. Sociocultural acceptance of the psycho-emotional resistance to death enriches culture for a more agency-oriented structuring. And thus, every individual mourner develops a sense of inevitability of the undesirable occurrence of this kind. Though not same as mourning, weeping on the occasion of bidding farewell to daughter is not less in affect and effect. It happens not only when the daughter is leaving for her in-laws' home for the first time, but also on all those occasions when the daughter arrives at and departs from her natal home. The tenacity of the action, in terms of affect and effect, is greater when the first instance of farewell occurs. Perpetual squeals of crying, rhyming hiccups, and hum of sobs envelop the surrounding so efficiently that men folk too jump in the fray. Free from any ritualistic prescription or priestly intervention, this act is also commonly found in the orbit of world view. This too tacitly underlines yet another instance of resistance to socio-structural principle pertaining to Maithil kinship, suggesting a question: why does a daughter have to separate from her natal home? It affectively underscores the interplay between structure and agency/agencies leading to a more nuanced reconciliation to the structural principle. *Samdaun,* sung across the caste groups, plays an important role in this phenomenon.

Furthermore, the differences in the ritual performance of caste groups does not establish caste factionalism. For the song culture offers a peek at both diversity and commonality. Songs, from the category *brahmanak geet* criticizing a *greedy-treacherous Brahmin*[10] is popular among both the Brahmin and non-Brahmin women. But then, a celebration of Brahminhood is also a common feature in the songs of the same category. Despite the differences exhibited in the orbit of the world view, there is a ubiquity of celebration of events of life. The rite of the passage for any individual brings about occasions for the entire folk society to celebrate and constantly reaffirm their world view. No celebration is a linear narration of joy. It is often punched with a notion of sorrow. It is a modest recognition of the pain involved in the process of becoming, as it were. Through these phases, marked by rites and rituals, men and women acquire social status and roles. Meaningful paradoxes underpin the process and junctures of progress in a life cycle. A quick recapitulation from the long list: a would-be wife is ridden with anxiety of unforeseen future with her would-be husband, the anxiety and fear recurs when she is expecting, she voices repentance for making love with her husband when in labour, a mother is anxious whether the groom is not up to the expectations, a father is anxious of finding the right match for his daughter, a mother cries with a sense of separation when her son in groom's outfit is setting out to marry the bride, a mother-in-law is filled with sorrow when her son-in-law is set to return after marriage, and the whole community expresses sorrow when a daughter is leaving her natal home after marriage. A sense of separation from the individual, who is the main subject in the rite of the passage, hovers at every juncture of progress in the life cycle. So the same women, who sing songs, playfully abusing the visiting in-laws when marriage has taken place, or mischievously promise the barber in a *mundan* to gift him with the maternal aunt of the groom, also reckon with the pangs of an individual's move toward unforeseen events. Progress in life cycle is a marker of a move towards an imagined end, and, every instance of separation is a fragment of the absolute separation at the event of death. But what has already ended, the physical being of the ancestors, the *pitar,* finds a place of prestige and reverence in the folk world view. The end of a physical being is, thus, a leitmotif upon which all rites seem to hinge; everybody unwittingly aspires to reach the destination of the *pitar lok* (abode of ancestors), almost beside *dev lok* (abode of gods). On any occasion of the rite of the passage *pitar* is invoked alongside gods, for blessing the protagonist who is progressing in life cycle through the rite and rituals. It thereby forges a connection between the dead and the living, the 'immortalized mortal' and the 'immortalizing mortal' on every occasion in rite of the passage. An ideal linear scheme at work suggests that every living being, moving in the life cycle, has to die and become an imperishable *pitar.* It is an ambitious objective that the folk recall at various junctures during rite of the passage. Everybody aspires to move in the life cycle toward *pitar*-hood, by dying a 'happy death'.[11] However, at the face value, invoking *pitar* is for their blessings for the main protagonist. The deeper meaning is that it helps recall the connection between life and death, joyous progress in the life cycle and an end of physical being in the end of the cycle.

Soteriological Seeking: Dynamics of Mortal and Divine

The songs tend to socialize the protagonists, as well as others attached to him/her, for new status and roles. They also pave the way for the eventual immortalization of the mortal. Often in the rite of the passage a human is identified with a mythological icon, a god, a sacred character that belongs to religious imagination of the folk. A father of a daughter is called Janak, a father of a son is Dasrath and similarly the daughter is Sita and the son is Ram. A mother is often called Kousalya, Maina or Yasoda. Invoking these mythological characters through songs, the folk aim at instilling an existential value in the protagonists of the rite of the passage. The unstated dictum is that the mortals are potentially immortal, that no human is devoid of sacred capability, that none of the humans is a mere biological accident in the large chain of existence. Another implication of connecting the mortal and immortal in songs is that it also mortalizes the immortal characters of mythology. Thus, Siva is no longer an abstract character from *Siva Purana*, Ram is not a mere imagination enshrined in the *Ramayana*, Sita is not just a creation of textual deliberation. Women, through their songs, give a social-cultural rebirth to these characters. Gods and goddesses receive breath and flesh, life and death as though they were indeed mortal characters. The socioculturally mortalized divinity exhibits fear as well as fascination for sexual intimacy thus marking a state of ambivalence. The social face of Sita, who is a living being, also walks into *kobar ghar* to spend the first night of sexual intimacy with her husband who has been already equated with Ram for his resplendence and with Siva for his wild virility. Moreover, Sita would also persist with her ambivalence when she is in labour and expecting her baby.

The personalization of the impersonal characters from mythology continues in the festival of Madhushravani, a peculiarly Maithil festivity. The eleven-day long festival perpetually instills identification with Gauri and Siva in the newly-wedded bride and groom. The sacred power that mythological characters are supposed to wield is thus inculcated in the bride and the groom. The power invested notwithstanding the vulnerability and fallibility of humans is not cast in abeyance. These invincible characters, in a social avatar, are acknowledged for their failure. Even great goddesses are told in some of the songs that they have failed in taking care of their devotees. The dynamic relation between the mundane mortal and miraculous divine assumes centrality in the song culture of Mithila.

Despite the systematic invocation of the sacred characters from religio-mythological texts and an identification of the same with humans, the songs articulate a sense of incompleteness. It applies across caste groups as the songs echo the aspiration of transcendence. The freedom for the celebration of *here* and *now* notwithstanding, everybody bemoans the pain of social existence and seeks divine intervention for redemption. Paradoxically, this is the yearning for emancipation from *here* and *now*! The seasonal songs underscore this paradox: on one hand they disclose the occasion of the celebration of seasonal *here* and *now* and on the other they narrate the sorrow of separation and distance from the near and dear. The songs from *Chaumasa, Chhaumasa, Barahmasa,* and *Chaita* reveal that everything is not fine despite the celebration of a new season. For diverse socio-economic reasons men are away from home. But the folk also sing such songs when all of them are together. The songs of melancholia, with or without the near and dear ones, present a truthful acknowledgement of what is real of human experience, sorrow. Even an occasion of Holi is not untouched by the songs of this note in addition to the songs celebrating the motif of freedom and playfulness. The truth of finitude vis-à-vis attachment and affection in social relationships, already disclosed in songs from the category *Samdaun* and *Udasi,* is recurrent in the passage of life. An affectionate daughter goes off to live with a new-found love interest after marriage, a very dear son emotionally parts from his mother to marry another woman, and the entirety of the rite of the passage ensuring progress in life cycle also paves the way for an imagined end. Meanwhile the constant invocation of the sacred, as though the sacred were social, ignites the aspiration for transcendence of the heteronomy of the material world. This does not, however, amount to a renunciation of the world as ascetics would have opted for. On the contrary it takes place within the situation of *here* and *now* without jettisoning the material world. These songs are testimonials to the human realization that they are not perfectly upright since they are humans; they admit the loss of virtue due to indulgence in sensuous pleasure. By articulating it candidly in their songs they attempt to minimize any sense of guilt of not admitting the limits of celebrating *here* and *now*. This is the emotional-intellectual truthfulness of the folk that is imbued in their songs. The ease behind this recognition also emerges from the fact that they celebrate the fall of their gods in their stories of indulgence. Hence, the folk's soteriological seeking surface in their songs broadly at two levels. One is apparently guided by a utilitarian motif, seeking redemption in this world. Worshipping sun, moon, snakes, Siva, *pitar*, Goddess Chhathi, various forms of the great mother Goddess Gosauni, and others in the pantheon of deities articulate this motif. It occurs on festive occasions in accordance with the *panchang* as well as in everyday life set up. Many songs, known as *gosaunik geet*, invoke Gosauni describing the goddesses' fiercely malevolent and endearingly benevolent attributes, seek her intervention to bring about a difference in the situation of destitution. These songs assume a dialogic form, as though the singer converses with the divine to complain sullenly against divine indifference. The intimacy between the devotee and the goddess is not obscured by the awe and fear of her appearance. The goddess Chhathi, who is worshipped with utmost precaution to avoid any folly of impurity, is known for her curses as well as favours. The songs relate the relationship of the devotee with the goddess inspired by her benevolence while the malevolent attribute is a reassurance of the goddess's power. The higher level of intimacy with the divine enables the devotees/singers to even blame the former for all kinds of social woes and existential crises. Siva is always commended for his kindness and generosity while songs also chide his failure to open his eyes for the devotee. The humble form of protest imbued in these songs echoes the strength of the devotees in the power relation with the divine rather than reflect mere servility towards the divine. This is, however, not devoid of the faith in the divinity against which a devotee lodges a protest.

But the seeking for redemption in this world does not end up with a simpler utilitarian motif though it seems to dominate the frame of soteriological seeking. A plea for this-worldly upliftment is for a better passage to and a place in the *other-world*. The latter is *pitar lok* where every individual seeks to reach. The songs expressing this motif are charged with philosophical overtones, revealing mainly two dimensions of human existence. One is the eternal suffering of the social humans and the other is an absolute refuge in the imagined other-world. Songs from *Parati* and Nirgun, and songs of *mrityu* imagine the other-world with the usages of idioms and metaphors of this-world. The other-world, thus, is a new home for a newly-wed bride away from her natal home.[12] It also depicts a resignation to the suffering of existence, which a singer confides in the power-within while confiding in the divine power-without. The power-without, the divine, has been already declared within humans on so many occasions in the rite of the passage through innumerable songs. It is as though every human contains a considerable amount of divinity inside, thus the more one talks to the gods the better one converses with one's own self. A process of telling the self that suffering of existential being on earth is as much a foregone conclusion as is joy.

Through folk songs, the folk society seeks to believe that death begins with the birth of an individual. It makes its presence felt at various junctures in the life cycle, associating itself with every moment of joy and manifests itself every now and then in the form of separation from dear ones. This eventuates into a finale when the physical being ceases to exist. The persons, the institutionalized individuals experiencing it are in close proximity with the divine power that is imagined inside as well as outside. They aspire to transcend the realm fraught with the woes of social existence. The folk also implement techniques of expression, such as crying/weeping/mourning in the process of transcendence, for the latter is not a complete denial of this world. Women, the mainstay of songs in the folk society of Mithila, play a significant role as they dovetail reason and emotion in the social matrix, helping even men to come to terms with joy and sorrow, and with life and death. The folk philosophy emerging from the songs and practices along with them underscores a world view that offers a totality of life, with admittance of ups and downs, resonance of both joy and sorrow, union and separation, living and dying in the same breath. It is not intellectually overzealous to draw a conclusive remark stating that folk philosophy inculcates a sense of the *art of dying* in everybody present in the socio-emotional matrix of folk society. The totality of the design of life is an allusion to the idea that every bit of life within the social framework is lived to attain a happy death, for only this can complete the circle by finding a place for the living in the *pitar lok*. It is imperative to reflect a little more on the *art of dying* that emerges from Maithil folk philosophy. The next essay undertakes a discussion on these categories in the interpretative fashion and seeks to connect the implications arising from the micro-contexts of Fulhara and Mithila with the macro-questions.

Notes

1. Maithil Brahmins are laughed at for their habit of gluttony in general otherwise. On any occasion they compete in eating the largest quantity of any good dish, especially sweets.
2. Similar sobs, expressive of the so-called happiness, was ubiquitous during *mundan* and *janeyu* too.
3. This practice seems to resemble the institution of *Rudali*. However, it is difficult to make a plausible proposition due the utter absence of any evidence.
4. As a quick mention, this motif is also called *biraha* found in poetry, songs, and folk theatrical performances. *Biraha* is a genre to narrate the anguish and pathos of separation, and has been associated with the songs of the lower-caste Chamar group. See Henry 1988 and Marcus 1995.
5. The tune of the film song, *pardeshiya ye sach hai piya* . . . used in this song is sung by a woman named Gulab Devi, age sixty-seven; she sings with the same ease with which she sings some of the old folk songs.
6. For more on Kabir's Nirgun bhakti see Lorenzen 1995.
7. A historical account on Vidyapati is in the third essay, which establishes not only his scholarly and poetic excellence, but also his contribution to the evolution of Maithili language. It stresses on the fact that he was the first ever scholar who decided to write in Avahatta, the earliest version of Maithili, the lingua franca of the common Maithil, breaking away from the convention of Maithili scholars. Many of his poems, of devotional temperament, now belong to the treasure of folk songs, especially in the category of *Nachari* and *gosaunik geet*.
8. *Baba Baijnath/Baidyanath* is another popular name of Siva in Maithili. This name especially refers to the Siva located in the district of Deoghar, also called Baijnath dham (abode of Baijnath), which now falls in Jharkhand. This song is often sung by the *kanwariyas* (the devotees who walk for miles over hills from Sultanganj filling the

pitcher with *gangajal* to the temple in Deoghar) in the month of Saon and Bhado (months of rain).

9. By 'Narcissism of Differences' I mean the excessive and hyperbolic celebration of distinction of groups. For political interests, there may be a tendency toward this excess in order to distinguish oneself from the other. This tendency is not an abiding one in the folkways, practices, and most importantly singing of songs. The underpinning nuances of the songs, in particular, overcome the distinctions of the style of presentation, usage of idioms, variety of songs, literary and metaphorical visions, and allusions to aspects of the specific groups.

10. The category of *greedy Maithil Brahmin* refers to those who never shy away from gluttony in community feasts and demand higher returns from the clients for priestly services. These are the Brahmins who emerged as power-seekers and property-makers in medieval times. See the fourth essay for a historical account on the category of Maithil Brahmins.

11. Only those who have gone through the upheavals of life—the pleasure and pain in union and separation—will graduate stage by stage, to die happily. More on the notion of happy death appears in the next essay on 'Art of Dying in Mithila'.

12. The parallel between songs for the farewell to a daughter, *samdaun*, and Nirgun songs in the category of the not very popular *mrityu geet* and the most common found *Parati,* is an attraction in the maze of Maithili songs, about which I have discussed in the previous section of this essay.

8

Art of Dying in the Maithil
Folk Philosophy

Vivah Janm Marnasya, Yada Yatra Bhawishyati

—BAIDYANATH MISHRA[1]

The strangest thing in the world is that each man, seeing others
die around him, is still convinced that he himself is immortal,
says Yudhisthira in the Mahabharata.

—SUDHIR KAKAR (1978: 35)

Yama is a deity who inspires dread. In India, talking about
him or simply pronouncing his name is avoided even today.
Paradoxically, the phenomenon of death does not cause similar
fear in the souls of Indians.

—G.G. FILIPPI (2005)

Death is the constant companion of the living.

—B.N. SARASWATI (2005)

The notion of death and dying is mainly a concern in cosmogony.
The latter is amply underlined in the classical scriptures,
mythological accounts, and rituals performed in the rite of the
passage. These aspects collectively find expression in the folklore
of Mithila. Maithili folk songs present a hint of unique cosmogony.
The songs are not preoccupied with the key cosmological questions
of the origin and evolution of universe. Instead the songs grapple

*I am borrowing the phrase *art of dying* from Geetha Hariharan (1993),
whose collection of stories presents diverse motives pertaining to death and
its relation with life.

with the notion of life and death as present in the events of life, on the special occasion of rites of the passage or through several occasions in everyday life. The songs discuss cosmogony in terms of the sociocultural imagination of death through events and metaphors of life. This however ought not to be mistaken for a thanatological preoccupation in the songs. For these songs engage with, and prod the folk to engage with, the idea of death at mainly two levels: a social imagination of death at various junctures of life and the philosophical implications of this engagement. Neither the objective-scientific attitude of thanatology nor the mythological focus of cosmogony characterizes the ideas of life and death that the Maithili songs present. Hence, the phrase *art of dying*, entailing cosmological and thanatological interests in philosophical framework is more apt to explain how these songs present death in close relation with the events of life.

This essay discusses this specific revelation in the folk songs of Mithila, which is arguably a cardinal aspect of the Maithil world view, explained and sustained by the folk philosophy. Here death is not an event in isolation—it is not imagined in merely metaphysical terms. Death is imagined through the idioms of life, and is sought for thorough indulgence in this-world. The more one engages with this-world, lives through joy and sorrow, union and separation, the better are the possibilities of achieving a happy death. The notion of happy death, conversely, connotes the end of physical existence; it appears after having gone through all the phases of life and having experienced a variety of emotions pertaining to human existence. Death here entails both an indulgence and transcendence. The act of dying thereby assumes the significance of a phenomenon, an *art of dying*, so to say. This essay engages with the complexity of this phenomenon and points out the necessity to understand the conceptual categories of dharma, karma, and moksha in the light of the folk experiences expressed in their songs without reducing death and dying into cosmological and thanatological issues. This is the way this essay underlines the possibility of pursuing folk philosophy, without succumbing to the formal-institutional disciplinary framework of philosophy. Here folk philosophy is more akin to philosophical assemblage, rather than systematic philosophy. Alfred N. Whitehead (1968) discussed this distinction, suggesting that the formal philosophy may not be able to grasp the wide array of notions and experiences present in the nuggets of insights strewn in discourses. 'In all systematic thought, there is a tinge of pedantry. There is putting aside of notions, of experiences, and of suggestions, with the prim excuse that of course we are not thinking of such things' (Ibid.: 2). Folk philosophy can be characterized with the idea of assemblage, rather than a systematic philosophy, laced with emotions, experiences, and suggestions. One of the key scholars in the field of existential anthropology Michael Jackson (2013) makes it a realizable objective as he dwells upon the experiential trope merging his self and that of the folks in the field, to engender a sense of philosophical orientation emerging from affective expressions. Along this line of reasoning, this essay pursues the category of folk philosophy, and thereof experiential, suggestive, and emotive contents.

Ubiquity of Metaphors of Death

The orientation to death is a manifestly central, though largely unstated, motif in the folk sociocultural arrangement in Mithila. Songs associated with rite of the passage put together with that of everyday life yield the notion of separation, the end of one stage and progress to the other. It unfolds both sorrow and joy; and it reveals a profound paradox: a celebration of the here and now, a yearning to redeem the situation in social existence, and an aspiration to transcend the constraints and conditioning of social existence. As a simplistic teleology every act in life, marked by the rite of the passage and rituals reveals the ability and desire to die a happy death.[2] It is evident in the rites of birth, *mundan, janeyu,* and *biyah* where the notion of the end of the physical existence finds a varied mention. The end is, thus, merely an event that has been already imagined and invoked on occasions aplenty.

Pundit Baidyanath Mishra points out an important aspect. On the occasion of a daughter's marriage and the sacred-thread giving ceremony (*janeyu*) for a son, there is a ritual that marks a symbolic death. The ritual is termed *aabdhik shraddh. Shraddh* is the ritual performance post-death that seeks to obtain a release for the departed soul from the worldly connections and a passage to the

pitar lok (the sacred abode of the ancestor's souls). *Aabdhik shraddh*
on the other hand is a death-ritual for a living being performed to
mark the termination of a particular time frame in an individual's
biography. The pundit informs that it is the death of a temporal
stage in the life of the individual. The ordinary folk in the villages
do not seem to be aware of this with the clarity of the pundit. But
they seem to have an idea that something related to the last rite
happens at various stages in the rite of the passage. This underlines
the ubiquity of death and of its metaphors despite the paradoxical
dread of death where nobody talks of it, but everybody feels
it and knows that it is there in an unknown corner. Such an
acceptance is not devoid of fear, and the fear is not detrimental to
the imagination of death. There is little hint of fear explicit on all
those occasions that mark the progress from one stage to the other
in the life span. The folk philosophy is thus in agreement with
the tenet of the *Garud Purana*, a classical text the pundits read for
the aggrieved family upon the occurrence of death, which reads,
'every actuation or realization signs an inexorable step towards
bodily death, the end of human life . . . death awaits man from the
very moment of conception' (quoted in Filippi 2005: 36).

The marking of each event, manifestly jovial and fanciful,
by a 'notion of ending-beginning' is characteristic of the folk
philosophy that underlies the folk world view. The centrality of
death, neither overtly pronounced nor entirely absent at junctures
of life, is not an unusual idea. An elite version of the same
centrality appears in the Maithil poet Vidyapati's *Kirti Lata*. The
poetic narration in *Kirti Lata* underscores the significance of *kirti*.
The latter alludes to the 'good' deeds, revealing human attributes
of being a discerning, able-minded, and active individual. This also
entails, according to Vidyapati, the ability to connect individual
egos, and create novel values while discharging the ascribed roles.
Kirti, thereby, is a literary replacement for dharma in the Hindu
world view. But it is not *kirti* and dharma in a narrow perspective.
A king on a winning spree may kill innocent people. This does
not earn *kirti* for the king, nor performs dharma, in this scheme.
Merely winning is not the criteria to judge one's *kirti*. Similarly,
merely accumulating and possessing wealth does not make for
kirti. It ought to be related to an individual's ability to creatively

respond to myriad emotions unfolding in the domain of the living. By doing so one becomes emotionally capable to relate and also liberate. The ultimate criterion is whether a *kirti* paves the way for a happy death (Jha 2005).

The centrality of death is also reflected in the practice of retiring to the city of Banaras, the mythological city Kasi where dying ensures moksha according to the Hindu belief system (Saraswati 1975). Death, however, is only an end product of the whole. The span of life, replete with actions and rendition of songs, express joyous experiences of the *here* and *now* and of the movement in the life cycle, which tend to be substantial fragments in the totality of world view. The expression of joy is never dissociated from the recognition of the end and of separation and sorrow that appear in a physical form only when the physical body ceases to exist. The sum total of this experience, as voiced in songs across categories, constitutes the folk *art of dying*. What constitutes the category of *art of dying* is a sociocultural recognition and actions to live life with emotional truthfulness. More on the category of *art of dying* and *emotional truthfulness* appears in the latter part of this essay. Suffice to say here, these coinages do not negate the notions of dharma, karma, and moksha. But these notions are not articulated in the folk philosophy as they are in the classical, Sanskrit, religious texts, which is the prerogative of the learned Brahmins. It is about living a life, while undergoing the processual demands with truthful responses to the social emotion of the individual social actors or the group(s) in the specific cultural contexts. The motif of the sorrow of separation, among various other motives, characterizes the processes in the lives of the folk vis-à-vis events in rite of the passage, calendar of festivities, seasonal changes, and everyday living. The sorrow of separation reigns higher and intervenes even the moments of joy and pleasure. Songs presented in the previous essay offer testimonials toward it.

A few slices from these songs may help in the comprehension of the arguments.[3] The *sohar* songs on a joyous occasion such as the birth of a child unfolds mixed emotions. Women reminisce on the separation of Sita from Ram as they think of the newborn son, *Sita ban mei khadi pachhtay . . .!* Joy does not eclipse the notion of sorrow and a critique of unceremonious separation. In another song women criticizing the social preference for son and neglect for daughter also voice the potential separation from daughters. They sing, *Bhaiya ke deliyen amma rang mahaliya, Humro deliyen duaaer...!* Similar is the sense when a mother sings in the company of other women a song bidding farewell to a son who is going to marry. It suggests the pain of separation, *Jaahe din aaho babu tore jana bhel...!* It finds poignant expression when a daughter is bid farewell, as women sing, *Bad re jatan se hum siya dhiya poslahu, Seho dhiya ram nene jaay...!* Similarly, the sorrow of separation from Ram is sung when the groom is about to depart from the house of the in-laws, *Seho ram jai chhaith apan gharbe ho lal...!* The pangs of sorrow find a more profound articulation in the songs of everyday life, as every song of *Parati* conveys the restlessness in the finitude of social existence and a yearning for a merger with the higher truth, be it death or the divine. A song from the Nirgun category would state the evaluation of one's own existence in the face of ending, *Karam ke baat nihaar he udho . . .!* or *Kon gati hoyat mor prabhu . . .!* Another song recounts the waning associations with the material possessions and physical existence, *Kichhu nai rahal mora haath he udho . . .!* In a similar vein, men and women would sing, *Kakhan harab dookh mor ho bhole daani . . .!* The sorrow of separation even creeps into the songs for festive occasions like Holi and songs for seasons, where the social imagery of feminine longing would be the means of expression used by both male and female singers. As the folk sing, *Sakhi Re Bisral Mohe Murari . . .* or *Hori Kay Sang Khelab Madhab Humro Bidesh Re!* The prevalence of this motif however does not obscure the indulgence in material pleasure within the limits of social existence. Social existence is, after all, the realm in which the processes of life unfold as the actors gradually move towards death. The processual features of the *art of dying* redefine some of the categories which are generic and determinant in defining the Hindu world view. We often tend to take these categories, in consonance with their classical interpretation, as a foregone conclusion about folk society. But the folk philosophy that emerges from the folk world view, stitching folk ideas present in the songs, suggest otherwise. In the process emerges an alternative version of religiosity consisting of a differing notion of dharma and karma, the integral categories of the Hindu belief system.

Dharma/Karma/Moksha, and *Beyond*

Dharma, following T.N. Madan's exegesis, 'includes cosmological, ethical, social and legal principles that provide the basis for the notion of an ordered universe.' (1991: 17). The believer aims at *purushartha*, implying attained perfection of the being by the virtue of dharma, artha, kama, and moksha. *Sanyasa*, renunciation of social activity, is a way out of this axis for liberation.[4] Building upon a similar understanding of the philosophico-religious categories of the Hindu world view emerging from the classical texts, M. Allen (1982) paints a considerably inferior position of women in the Hindu society. For Allen, dharma is the absolute guiding category for Hindu men while the women only assist the men in realizing it. This is because men aim at moksha, the liberation. Rites of the passage are also solely meant for the men folk. Hence, Allen and many others draw the conclusion that women are only a source of impurity and are not of much significance in the Hindu religious structure. While there is no denial of the instances of gender discriminations and secondary ritual status accorded to women, such readings obscure the non-ritual significance of women's status. The alleged preoccupation with the classical categories, and their taken-for-granted usage, has amounted to such conclusions.

Dharma, karma, moksha, the concepts of the ancient texts are, however, accessible only to the elite priesthood. Among Brahmins, it is only a select few who are into the profession of priesthood. Some of the priests in the villages whisper in informal conversation: 'the meaning of moksha, not an ordinary priest's concern!' So, it seems that Brahmins and non-Brahmins including the lower caste do not subscribe to these notions exactly in accordance with the classical-Sanskritic texts. The universality of these notions, therefore, largely seems to be a scholarly construction. The typicality of this understanding and interpretation is expressed when Kakar (1978) suggests that these intellectualized concepts of dharma, karma and moksha percolate down to the literate as well as non-literate masses as 'prescriptive configuration of ideal purposes, values, and beliefs'. This is evidently based on a hierarchy of values, where the textual knowledge of the pundits seems to rule the folk at the lower rungs. It generalizes and establishes the universality of the meanings of dharma, karma, and moksha. It does not entertain the possibility of the plurality of means and goals nor does it take into account the folk negotiation with these categories. Kakar mentions in passing, almost as an afterthought, 'for the vast majority of Hindus, men and women, there are traditionally sanctioned "ways" that also lead toward the ideal state. An individual may choose from among these according to the dictates of his or her temperament and life circumstances' (Ibid.: 29).

The goal of moksha may be bhakti (devoting oneself to the divine), *jnan* (by the way of intellectual pursuit) or *karma yoga* (selfless actions)—or perhaps a combination of all.[5] This formulation does not take into account what folk philosophy offers as the most important undercurrent of dharma and karma, namely *emotional truthfulness* that guides everybody, irrespective of caste and creed, in the logic of praxis. There is a combination of the 'tragic and romantic' elements in the Hindu world view, Kakar suggests. Every social actor undergoes phases of suffering while experiencing the spates of romances. It inspires the folk imagination for metaphysical destinations such as *mukti-moksha*, which is liberation from the cycle of birth and death. It does not occur, one may proffer contra Kakar, at the price of the mundane, the physical-worldly, material-sexual, and sensuous, and everything that appears transient in the realm of existence. Kakar admits in passing the possible dissolution of the dichotomies such as the 'unitary vision of soma and psyche, individual and community, self and the world, me and not-me' in the Hindu world view. This is the socio-psychic structure that manifests in the songs where the folk intend to pursue life that is oriented towards the goal of the physical end (without stating it to be moksha), emotionally responding to the events of life in the cultural framework, and expressing unity of beginning and end, of life and death. It is primarily pursued in the setup of the household (Kakar 1978, Madan 2006). But the textual and ethnographic reflections of Madan result in the dominance of the classical notion of dharma (the textually prescribed moral conduct) and karma as the rituals in the life cycle (rite-of-the passage) within the fold of *grahsthya* (household). The understanding of the ritualistic notion of karma, with reference to *samskar*, makes Madan argue, 'life-cycle rituals constitute *samskara* that is, the process whereby one is "made complete or perfect" and ultimately after death, transformed into an ancestor' (2006: 221). It is like living through everything as a human and becoming eligible for the ultimate goal. As Kakar puts it, 'it is only he who has built a house, planted a tree, and brought up a son, who is ready for the final effort' (1978: 43). These categorical notions of dharma and karma, while reducing the world view into the rituals in the rite of the passage, render the social actors into mere passive receivers and followers of an imagined cosmological goal. While dharma says 'what one should do', karma becomes a reflection of helplessness of humans—one is bound to do certain things for certain reasons (as the results of the action of past). Without denying the aforementioned dimensions of the folk world view, I intend to argue that it is not a passive acceptance of the classical-textual categories of dharma, karma, and moksha.

Folk philosophy reconciles with the prescriptive-classical notions by refashioning them, adding the liberty of expressing even those motifs that may not be congruent with the classical notions. Incongruence is not to be mistaken for a unilinear resistance or subversion of the classical categories altogether; for the champions of the classical categories also subscribe to the folk world view. The resistance and subversion, if at all, are not directed against fellow humans; it rather seeks to bring about an understanding that the sociocultural kinship ideology has limitations. This objective is achieved through the rendition of songs, and by appealing to the emotional elements present in the social structure. Hence, never do men object to women abusing men in their songs, or women ridiculing the Brahmins, *Baklel babhna chura dahi chatay ela hamar anagana . . .!* Or another song, in which women target the female kin of a groom, *Nij kul kamini samdhin chhinro . . .!* Many songs in which women ridicule the male kin in the entourage accompanying the groom, are accepted as a usual occurrence in the cultural framework. Never do men frown upon women breaking into ritual sobbing and crying either. This also entails complaints against male folk, such as a sister's complaint, *Kehen kathod bheliye ho bhiya, Bahini bidagiri bisaraliye ho bhaiya . . .!* Or

another song in which women narrate the poignant struggle
of a father in search for a groom, *Sita Ke Dekhi Dekhi Jhakhti
Janak Rishi*. . . . Men accept the sense of separation expressed in
the songs of women. In addition to these songs, there are those
instances where crying in free narrative prevails upon everybody
present in the context. Be it the departure of a son from the
paternal home for the affinal home or while bidding farewell to
a married daughter, crying appears to be the main folkloric tool.
These moments do not bring about any confrontation between
men and women; men are willing party to it instead. The classical-
Brahminic-Sanskritic notions seem to be at the mercy of the
folk for acceptance, redefinition, and reconciliation. Thus, it is
imperative to look at the folk philosophy underpinning the world
view of the folk present in the folk songs.

Anchorage of *Emotional Truthfulness*

The folk philosophy underpinning the world view conceptualizes
the categories of dharma and karma at the conjunction of existential
reality and textual injunctions, thus drawing a relationship between
ontology and epistemology. What they 'sing, say, do and are' appear
in one simple principle: be spontaneous in a situation! If at a
particular stage of life, indulgence seems to be the spontaneous
act, the folk would do it without any moral inhibition. But in the
same breath if they have to express scepticism towards indulgence
or of the limits of the socio-material existence, they do not shy
away from it. In the folk reasoning it is not contradictory to express
both unstinted devotion and a sort of belligerence toward the
divine. They follow emotion as though it were the main reason
that determines whether to perform or not. Their norms are in
sync with emotion. Thus, anger in accordance with a situation
would be considered the right action; if somebody were going
away the sorrow of separation would determine the performed
emotion.

Each song is in tandem with the situational emotion. Abuses by
women, in a situation when the *barat* has settled down at the *dalan*
of the bride's father, seem in total agreement with the situation,
and hence, the whole community relishes them. A criticism of

a greedy Brahmin is well-nigh a product of the situation. Of course, in the backdrop of the situation is a set of values about right and wrong. But these values are also in turn determined by fluid emotions as the former determines the latter. The value of indulgence is in accordance with the emotion that stems from a situation. For example, the value of legitimate sexual intimacy is inspired by the emotion of the newly-married couple. Similarly, the value of ambivalence toward the sexual union is in sync with the folk's emotional confusion about whether sexual intimacy is right or wrong. Emotion may be fluid, and hence reshaping the contingent values. This does not deny the consistence and prevalence of certain values, such as that in relation with caste and gender. In the volatility of emotion it is but natural that the notions of dharma, karma, and moksha would be a little more than what the texts of the pundits suggest. While the *art of dying* includes this axis of dharma-karma-moksha, and redefines *sanyasa* as an act of detachment while living in society and fulfilling social responsibility, it is not devoid of another lesson that the individual is the architect of their life-course with its joy and suffering, living and dying. However, it must be added here that the folk art of dying, as it emerges from the compendium of songs, is not merely a system of recapitulation and reaffirmation of the basic tenets of the aforementioned categories of the Hindu world view. The latter is conventionally perceived as a system of knowledge (belief and practices) centred upon the notions of karma (action with causal efficacy) and dharma (the righteous conduct that is supposed to guide karma). The conventional notion of dharma is echoed in oral tradition—in *katha*, the telling of scared tales, *bhajan*, the singing of religious songs, and *vrata*, the religious observation of fasts (Mathur 1991). But in the folk philosophy, and in the *art of dying*, it also connotes an alternative notion of piety in connection with emotions while acknowledging the significance of textually-prohibited actions. This ambivalence, comprising the textual and priestly as well as contextual and emotional, sets a distinction in the folk philosophy. This is in other words the importance of women's *lokpakshiya kriya* (the folk ways) parallel to the *dhrmapakshiya kriya* (the textually prescribed ways effected under the instruction of an expert/officiating priest) without any sense of conflict. The ambivalent character seeps into the philosophy, holding the classical notions and socio-emotional understanding in one breath. This not only vindicates the importance of women's role but also their not-so-*dharmik* actions. It is considered not-so-*dharmik* due to the absence of textual support; women's singing and other actions in the right of the passage do not have the support of a Veda, a Smriti or a priest-craft. However, they are an integral part in the whole of the world view and indispensable in solemnizing an occasion. The priests stop at appropriate junctures during the ritual performances and request the women to sing their songs. Occasionally, the women are slow in commencing a song and the priest will mock: 'What! Have you all forgotten your *bidhi-bidhan* (folkways)?' Furthermore, there are instances of a critical attitude not only towards the priests and the patriarch but also the divine. Songs like *Kakhan Harab Dukh Mor . . .* shake the authority of Lord Siva by chiding the divine indifference toward the destitute, or another song such as *Hey Bhawani Dukh Haru Maa Putra Apna Janike . . .* questions the great mother: why the singer (devotee) has been subject to pathos?

These are the crucial evidences of humans yearning for a better life here (in this world, *ihlok*) and better destination there (in the other world, *parlok*). In addition to these motives of the sorrow of separation, and the motif of criticizing the social as well as the divine, there is also a cultural engagement with evidently sexual intent. For *ihlok* is not devoid of the worldly pleasure and of undercurrents that run counter to the pleasure principle. This is a crucial aspect of *emotional truthfulness* too. Songs accompanying the newly-wed couple to the special chamber, *kobar*, express it all, *Hum Nai Jebai Kobar Ghar Humra Dar Lagay Ye. . . .*

Or in the similar vein, women sing songs from *sohar* to recapitulate the experience of intimacy with the husband. These songs not only explicate the sexual desire, but they also disclose the fear of unseen results of the sexual intimacy. The ambivalent attitude towards worldly pleasure vis-à-vis sexual intimacy also constitutes the Maithil world view, and is an integral component of *emotional truthfulness*.

It is this feature that defines the passage of life for the folk in Mithila, which eventuates into the final ending. But the recognition of the limits of the social-material existence and engagements begins to take place much before in the cycle. For a female child also sings a song of this kind, unwittingly, meaning something philosophically profound, like *Oopar Pahad Neecha Kankar, He Shiv Shankar, Puja Kona Karu* . . . which shows the yearning of the singer to reach the level of lord Siva or request him to descend to the level of humans, so that she could worship the lord. Similarly, all those songs elderly men and women sing every morning from the category of *Parati*, express the yearning for transcendence. A song like *Baba Baijnath Hum Aayal Chhi Bhikhariya* . . . actually seeks the blessing of lord Siva, not for any favour in this world's social network, but rather in the world of Siva where the devotee wants to be an ideal servant of the lord. It is important to note that the world of Siva is imagined in *ihlok* as well as *parlok* depending on the age of the singer.

In a situation of emotional turmoil, crying/wailing/mourning assumes a central place. The act of crying on the occasion of separation (farewell), venting the emotional resistance, cautions us to argue against any unequivocal notion of dharma and karma. It is a religious cliché to speak of the *jiva/aatma* in relation with *paramatma* and explain away death. It surfaces in the folk philosophy too, but it is not devoid of a twist in the form of ritual mourning. The latter is a temporary nullification of the belief in the category of dharma and karma. This suspension of the classical categories provides the bereaving a psychosocial preparation for the acceptance of the undesirable event. Second, while the classical texts may not mention the significant roles played by women folk, the song culture does highlight the essential emotional moorings in women's renditions of songs. It persuades the men folk to surrender to *emotional truthfulness*. The term emotional truthfulness has both communicative and non-communicative dimensions. When men give in to the emotionally heightened situation largely steered by women, it basically contains a non-communicative dimension. But non-communication vis-à-vis clarity and usage of linguistic codes does not amount to meaninglessness. In the folk world view, non-communication and non-use of phonic linguistic codes bear a similar significance to communication where intelligible codes are used. Silent pauses in between songs, or within songs, have meanings; pauses as a precursor to sobbing and finally sobbing have meanings par excellence. In the backdrop of the above discussion, the term emotional truthfulness means the parity between action and emotional disposition in a sociocultural situation beyond the narrow rationalistic judgement that emotion is a binary opposite of reason.

Emotion is a handy tool with the folk to rationalize the expression of complaints, constraints as well as possibilities, joy and celebration of desires, association with the divine, and aspiration to become one with the divine. This is not devoid of slippages, conflicts, and reconciliations. The role of emotion is experienced in every bit of action, including the evidently rational actions, in the folk context. Men folk, seldom known for crying and sobbing, tend to join—however passively—in the weeping rituals of women. This ritual of weeping replaces songs on all the occasions of emotional vulnerability. A man is made to cry on various occasions: when somebody dies, when he is about to go to his bride's place in the *barat* or when his sister/daughter is leaving her natal home with her groom. A man is also given an emotional context to feel guilty for neglecting his sisters. Equally significant is the women's scheme of emotional truthfulness that enables both subtle and overt celebrations of sexuality. It also enables one to understand the significance of the ambivalence towards not only sexuality but also towards gendered stereotypical roles based on sexual differences. These acts also entail a glorification of the stereotypical roles through an identification with some of the oft-mouthed mythological icons.

Such an identification does not merely justify gendered roles, as the deeper connotations suggest a metaphysical agenda in the folk philosophy. The metaphysical design in the folk philosophy forges relationships between this world and the other world, the mortal and immortal, the temporal and eternal, the profane and sacred, and between the magical and mundane. Women in their songs establish the identification of mortals with the divine so phenomenally that there appears the twin process of 'immortalization of the mortal' and 'mortalizing the divine/immortal'.[6] While some may hastily call this folk trivialization of the divine, the process holds a deeper connotation when looked at in the larger framework of the world view. The simpler classical truth, as it appears in *Garud Purana*, is 'the gods who dwell in all fourteen *lokas* must also be present in the body (of human)' (quoted in Filippi 2005: 9). The Maithili folk songs present a similar idea in such detail that it becomes an alternative world view consisting not only of the lessons from classical texts of the pundits but also a celebration of the indwelling divine in the mundane and mortal.

On every occasion in the life cycle the sense of an individual *being* connected with the larger *Being*, a social actor nearly parallel to the sacred-mythological actor, is melodiously imparted. It is no wonder then, a folk actor unwittingly becomes an indomitable Sisyphus ready to smile, slog, suffer, cry, and hope amidst the inevitable socio-existential absurdity.[7] The folk relationship with the divine is not a zero-sum power relation as they very often end up fighting and complaining against their gods in their songs. *Faith* is not in opposition to *reason* in this emotional scheme and hence, there is no linear resignation to divine provenance. This is not to be misread as 'death of gods' in the folk imagination, nor a total emancipation from the religious structure of rites and rituals, belief and superstitions. Demanding or making wishes in front of various deities and ceremonial fasting and offerings as part of giving thanks on wish fulfilment also reveals an engagement with gods at very instrumental level. Seeking for magic and miracle is not absent in the folk world view. It is, however, only a small fragment of the whole. Moreover, the same folk also recount the fallibility and vulnerability of the humans in the lifetime. Sin is inevitable and fall is indispensable. Thus, very many songs present a self-reflective folk recognizing that *adharm* (not in opposition to dharma though) has been done by them. That they cannot be humans without committing them; that this deviation is not actually deviation; that it is as much part of dharma; that being human means being fallible and sinful. Each *Parati* song sung every morning offers a testimonial to such suggestions. This, however, is not simply the Hindu version of the catholic confession. It is an introspective reckoning by the folk when face-to-face with the immortal whom they have already invoked within themselves on several occasions. This makes for a rounded sense of the *emotional truthfulness* that defines the category of dharma and karma in the folk world view and which assures them of a *happy death*.

Moksha, the liberation from the cycle of life and death, is a remote idea seldom invoked by the folk. Only learned Brahmins would mouth platitude on the categories of dharma, karma, and moksha. The folk are instead invested in dying happily by living with *emotional truthfulness* and seeking a position in the *pitar lok*. They all know that what is more plausible than these categories is *emotional truthfulness*. Therefore, their songs articulate an engagement with death and not moksha, life in association with the ending and not karma, pleasure and seeking for sensuous success with an anchorage of emotional truthfulness rather than dharma. Transcendence, for them, is not an absolute antithesis to the engagement with the world. In the middle of dharma and karma the person within the Maithil folk context, a bundle of relationships imbued with pleasure and pain, yearns for transcendence. Transcendence is, thus, not a hostile renunciation of the worldly—it is about understanding, accepting, and overcoming the fear of the worldly. It unfolds in everyday life. The *art of dying*, anchored with *emotional truthfulness* in the folk philosophy underlying the Maithil world view, enables the folk to admit a sin as inevitable and urges them to find liberation by being emotionally truthful about it.

Everydayness of Dying

The idea of *emotional truthfulness* underlines the palpable everydayness of dying. It rests in the folk imagination and is articulated in the songs. On the special occasion of rites of the passage it unfolds in ritualistic fashion, while in everyday life it manifests without much ostentation. The manifestation of the motive, imagination of death, and the notion of dying is starker in the articulation by elderly folk. The youngsters obliquely hint at it in their songs and the elders do not mince words about it. Maithili songs do not seem to be divided along age lines; the singing of songs like *Parati* is more common among the elderly. The songs of *Parati* are not exclusive of other songs. The motif of separation, endings, and longing for transcendence cuts across genres and age sets. Second, the spaces in everyday life for the rendition of the songs are not sealed off. When an old man or a woman sings a *Parati* song, s/he is likely to be heard by the youngest of the household who would be still in bed as the dawn approaches. Or they may be huddled with the singing elderly person, perhaps trying to figure out the significance of the songs. Similarly, in the day time, after the siesta on any summer afternoon, when an old woman opens up her kitty of threads and needle to do some seams and hems or make a rag-mat, she also tends to open up her veritable box of feelings. She would voice, in a song or even in a biographical reminiscence, the concerns pertaining to the weary end of life. What happened in the past and what is at present appear in close connection. The journey that began in the youth knew no fear in growing up and moving ahead on the scale of life. As part of the folk natural attitude they articulate clearly that the present is the natural consequence of the progression. They all perhaps know it fairly well as to what would happen tomorrow. Some may not speak it, while many reckon with their awaited death with an uncanny ease. Their story usually begins with the exuberance of the days bygone and ends with the hope of dying as successfully as they have lived everything through. They have rejoiced as well as suffered; they are ready to do the same for the last act of dying too. The sorrow of separation from the social web of relationships and the familiar domain where one did everything cannot be completely ruled out. These old men and women do have their moist eyes when they speak of the lurking end. Yet, in a paradox of humanity, they toy with the idea of dying well. Probably, this is why most of the songs on the motif of death are full of the metaphors pertaining to the events of life. The going away of a soul leaving the body behind is paralleled with the departure of the bride from the natal home or a bird escaping the prison of an intimate nest.

Of course there are problems and issues that haunt the elderly folk; these are about the dependence on the younger members of the family for existential sustenance, the duress of old age, diseases, and some sense of insecurity. But they are not a hindrance to an acceptance of the totality of life. It expresses a deep contentment and bliss when an old man sitting at the *dalan* says, *dekhlo ai jagat ke khela* (I have seen everything), though he has hardly travelled beyond the capital of the state. The travails of life, subsuming all the events of happiness and sorrow that the elderly folk have gone through, accord them a sense of satisfaction. *Eketa aab, ki ant nik bhay jay* (the only thing now, that I end up well), is what all of them long for. These expressions also occur in the background of felt dissatisfaction with the existence. Sometimes, the elderly folk do not feel happy about the present situations and wish to meet their end. Reacting to these notions, when a young man or woman would say, *budhba/budhiya, marbo nai karai chhai* (the old, hardly dies and only speaks of death), the old would offer a humble repartee *toro aihina heto* (you too would get here). Morbidity about dying is diluted by a tincture of humorous lightness and acceptance of it. Interestingly, the folk also joke about dying, as a young man would tell an older one *kahiya marbahak* (when will you die). Reacting to which the elderly folk says *nai marbo* (wont't die) or *chail jeba ta bujhiyah* (you would miss me when I die). Functionally, this acoustic surrounding prepares the folk for the acceptance and event of death.

The ease with which the acceptance of death is prevalent is also suffused with another idea—the merger of the private and public. The death of an individual in an individual household is eventually an event in/of public. Despite the significance of public, the individuality of the dying is never forgotten. Everybody surrounding a dying person would call him/her by the name s/e has been known by. Once the death is pronounced, everybody would be informed by a mention of the name of the dead person. It may be an individual's name or the social address for the same, such as *badka baba/badki kaaki/fulharawali/pokhramwali* and such like. All the surrounding kin and friends call the dead by the name, even during and after the mortuary rituals are over. In a rural set up, even a doctor who is brought to examine the dying makes it a point to mention the name. It happens when the dying is a mere patient in a hospital in the city that a doctor calls him/her a 'patient'. In such a situation, as soon as death happens the doctor calls the body dead as if it were without any significance; the kin of the dead however mourn calling his/her name and narrating personalized accounts. The private medical clinics in most of the towns in the region, which are too many to be counted, show a tendency to disown the patient soon upon the occurrence of death. The medical dispensation operates with its own institutional and administrative lexicon. The sociocultural framework, however, facilitates further relation with the dead, and follows its own timeline to initiate the cremation process.

This aspect of death and dying at the interface with modern medicine solicits an exclusive investigation on some other occasion. Suffice to say, the social, at modest odds with the medical, reaffirms the social as well as individual aspects of dying and the dead after the doctors have washed their hands off. The social consists of the network of people around the dead and the social significance of his/her being. The individual is too intricately related to the social to be extricated by medical intervention. This nevertheless does not come at the cost of the privacy and personality of the dying or of the dead. During the dying and afterwards, on ample occasions, his/her name and deeds are recapitulated by the mourners. The fit of crying that engulfs the close kin irrespective of the textual injunctions and the constant prevention by the neighbours and other social actors, is wherein the name of the dead is pronounced in the most moving fashion. Amidst hiccups and tears the crying members recall the deeds of the dead. In the frame of the social, the mourning members of the family experience the expression of their own individuality. Society lets the individuals be, as they want to be, while operating around them for reincorporation. It is almost in extension of the social provision of singing the songs individually, reminiscing the past while grappling with the present and aiming at future, and thus experiencing individual strength in the face of death. Post-death, it is not society that incorporates the bereaved individuals. Instead, the latter seemingly decide to let the social have its last word.

Conclusion

This essay drew on the songs presented in the previous essay and attempted to distil the imagination of life and death as intertwined ideas, which I proposed, can be understood through the notion of the art of dying. Dying is not an act in isolation and the ideas of it appear throughout the rites of the passage. This also refers to death and dying as a phenomenon not to be reduced into cosmogony or thanatology. The imagination of death and dying utilize the metaphors from the events of life. Thus, dying assumes an art form, which happens to define the whole course of life. Another idea that emerges from the analytical understanding of these songs and the expressions pertaining to death and dying in everyday situations is of *emotional truthfulness*. The latter is an integral component of the folk philosophy underlying folk world view. *Emotional truthfulness* is, in fact, a hinge concept behind the art of dying. It alludes to the folk tendency to be spontaneous in expressions, indulge in the mundane, discharge everything expedient, fulfil the needs of all kinds, perform ritual as well as non-ritual actions, and engage with the divine and seek transcendence. It is by the virtue of *emotional truthfulness* that folk life becomes a narrative fraught with contradictions, ambivalences, and polyphony, and a premise for the dissolution of the binary oppositions of living and dying. The classical categories of dharma, karma, and moksha are tacitly reformulated in the folk expressions. The scriptural injunctions, and classical categories, do not entirely rule the performances. But at the same level, there is also an evident inclination towards the notions laced with emotions. This is how the folk simultaneously seek both *ihlok* and *parlok*. The folk philosophy is the philosophy where reason and emotion, sacred and profane, transcendental and mundane, the social-mortal and the mythological-immortal coalesce to present the totality of life. No wonder, then, in the folk context of Mithila, life is fraught with occasional reminders of death where it appears like a much awaited event. This, however, is not the denial of the problems and conflicts in the social existence, nor is it a denial of the pain and suffering. All the oddities become a substantial part and parcel in the Maithili world view.

Notes

1. Baidyanath Mishra from the village Deodha neighbouring Fulhara, is related to Fulhara village through kinship (affinal) ties. He is renowned as a learned priest and recites Sanskrit couplets to explain the relationship of some of the major events of life, birth, marriage, and death; and their interrelated allocation on the time line. Time is

what connects all these three crucial features in the Maithil folk world view, almost in correspondence with the classical-Sanskritic view of the same.

2. I am borrowing the phrase *a happy death* from the Albert Camus's (1975) novel with the same title, in which the protagonist is verily lost in the confusing terrain of desires, longings, and restlessness, in order to arrive at an existential resolve.

3. The songs cited in this essay appear with translation in the previous essay.

4. A similar sense resonates in Hetukar Jha's reading of Vidyapati's *Kirti Lata*; the scholars of Mithila nostalgically think that the Maithil world view is in total conformity with the great tradition vis-à-vis the classical interpretations. This is typical of any discourse on Hinduism in general; it boils down to these categories for explanation. See for example, Srinivas and Shah 1968 and Das 1987.

5. More relevant is Sudhir Kakar's proposition on 'tragedy and romance' as integral components in the pursuit of life. My modest argument is that the combine of tragedy and romance brings about a different attitude towards the categories of dharma, karma, and moksha in the folk philosophy.

6. Louis Dumont (1970) describes a similar process in the structural study of a folk deity Aiyanar, a double of the Hindu god Siva, in Tamil Nadu whereby the performer is possessed by the deity. But the effect of the phenomenon is only on the expert performer, and it does not establish a larger relation of the deity with the folk in general.

7. See Camus' philosophical description of the Greek mythological character Sisyphus (2000).

9

Conclusion:
Text, Subtexts, Inter alia!

Into blinding darkness enter
those who worship ignorance.
Into as if still greater darkness
enter those who delight in knowledge
—*Isha Upanishad* (KATZ and EGENES 2015: 31)

Writing a conclusion is steeped in anxiety, to say the least. A simple expression of this anxiety is: could a work be conclusive indeed? This drives towards making the conclusion as holistic and rounded as possible. This is despite the potential acknowledgement that the onus of ifs and buts about the present work is entirely on the author. In this essay, while the attempt is to draw clear conclusions, there is also an evident urge to make it holistic enough so that the sub-theses of the book do not get marginalized. The 'sub-theses' is hopefully an innocuous replacement for a more dramatic expression such as 'subtext'. There is also a thrust to be futuristic about the conclusions as no conclusion could be conclusive. This resembles talking a bit like a masquerading prophet! Be that as it may, the conclusions presented here invite for further hypothesizing. This again reinforces the view that writing a conclusion is only a partial act to fulfil the formal structure of a book for the convenience of the readership.

The folk world view, to quote A. Dundes (1995), is not merely *men's cosmology*. The Maithili folk world view unfolds more than a cosmology of the folk, of men and women of various social groups.

Women's songs reaffirm the all-encompassing character of the world view. But the distinction between the classical and the folk seem to take a back seat in the full swing of the folk world view for both men and women from various social groups engage with the injunctions of the classical-textual tradition. When it comes to practice, the classical comes in terms with the folk on a horizontal plane rather than on a hierarchical ladder. Furthermore, in the folklore of Mithila, to borrow Franz Boas's term, we find 'people's autobiographical ethnography' significantly recapitulated by the folk and staged by the women. The autobiographical ethnography neatly accommodates mortal and non-mortal characters, historical and mythological, in a sociocultural framework. The mythological content of the folklore, especially in Mithila, accords it a synchronic character. It is not devoid of diachronic value either, and hence receives the changes in outlook under the influence of the contemporary. Myth is an ongoing speech geared to the here and now. The folk world view incorporates the *here* and *now* effect of myth, along with the centrality of what belongs to the imagined past. So the songs of women, praising Siva as though he exists in an imagined domain very close to the singer, would use the tune of the latest Bollywood blockbuster; a child will be singing a song she has heard often from the cassette; a song may depict the sexuality of a Maithil woman in comparison with the sexual orientation of a mythological icon; or a song will praise Brahma, Vishnu, and Mahesh (the trinity of gods from the Hindu pantheon) for protecting Bharat. Of course, the folk may not be always aware of the mythological implications in these songs, as Dundes suggested 'we do not see the lens through which we look'.

The world view of the Maithil folk, hence, presents a confusing array of motifs and meanings, currents and counter-currents, conflating history, biography, and mythology. This is also reflected in the engagement with the material world and a tendency to transcend it. These are present as 'life-expressions' using Wilhelm Dilthey's formulation of 'life-experiences'. To understand that which may appear rational as well as irrational, the research underpinning this book sought to overcome M. Weber's ambivalence towards the irrational germs in the actions of social actors. A perusal of hermeneutic philosophy in interaction with the field thus shaped up a methodological orientation. To know/understand was to *be*. In Martin Heidegger's term it was experiencing the self within *Dasein*—the Being there and Being in, in Hans-Georg Gadamer's notion it was a *fusion of horizon*, while in Roy Bhaskar's line it was the ontological being situated in the *cosmic envelop*. Read in tandem with the insights from the philosophical implications of the Upanishads, it was a process of ontologizing understanding. Knowledge and Being were essentially in relation and not meaningful without each other. Contextualizing the self of the researcher was not meant to obscure the critical view of the local. This is what, for heuristic purposes, is *holistic hermeneutics* where the formulation 'a guest who is a researcher' was replaced by 'a villager who is also a researcher'. This is my benign contribution to the methodological discussions in qualitative research. There has been a simplistic understanding of participant observation pertaining to qualitative researches in social anthropology and sociology. It suggested that a researcher spends a year or so in the *field* and conducts longitudinal interactions with the respondents/informants. It did not deliberate on the complexity of becoming a seeker of meaning, the process of relating to the field implicit in this method. The discussion on hermeneutics in the field could perhaps be an aid to understand why the Nuer were hesitant to answer the questions of E.E. Evans-Pritchard (1974). The typical refusal of Viramma to give clear meanings of her songs to Josiane Racine (2005) had to do with the fact that the researchers could not locate themselves in the emotional matrix in the field.

Placing the researcher in an interface with the researched led to making sense of the polysemy inherent in the key terms of this book—Mithila, Maithili, and Maithil. The cultural history of Mithila is bewildering due to its seamless interaction with mythology. The hermeneutic preparation could enable to approach Mithila, often projected in the common sense as an eternal entity, as a historically evolved category. While historians dwell upon the kingship, changes of regimes of power, and a trope of spectacular events, there are instances of inevitable influences of mythology in drawing a cultural history of Mithila. This leads to the comprehension of multiple layers of the categories Mithila, Maithili, and Maithil, and it unsettles various realms of hierarchies such as between the classical texts and folklore, and between historiography and mythology. In implication, it also disturbs the sense of superiority, which works towards the glorification of a cultural region. The pedantic Maithil scholars therefore, may not appreciate the attempt this book makes towards upsetting the settled schemes of understanding Mithila. In this background it appears meaningful to find a universe in a village, in the southern part of Mithila, often looked down upon by the Maithil of the northern Mithila, where the folk is not yoked by the cultural standards of the elite Brahmins even though there are Brahmins in strength of ownership of movable and immovable property. The selection of the village as well as the questions of research sought to invalidate the notions of purity attached to the Maithil way of living and thinking by showing influences of Buddhism, tantra, Kabirpanth, and various other contemporary popular cultural components. The sound and sight in the cultural landscape of Mithila seems to present a negotiation with various influences, sects, religions, and popular material culture. The fluidity of the folk becomes its most striking feature.

With the evident posterity of the folk openness towards the influences of time and structural changes, it would be incorrect to perceive Maithili folklore as pristine and unchanging. Little wonder then that there are number of songs sung by young girls and new brides, also by some elderly women, which belong to the cassettes and compact disc, popularized in the age of the mechanical reproduction of art work.[1] The impact of culture industry notwithstanding there is a typical phenomenon in the folk context. It is that all these songs borrowed from the cassettes and discs acquire sanctity when they are rendered by the women folk; the borrowed songs also become a vehicle of the folk motifs. In other words the aura pertaining to tradition, in particular to mythology, is attached to these songs by the act of regular singing. When a woman sings a song, be it the one she heard on TV, radio, or a cassette player, she tends to add a hum of locality and a rhythm of her own context. The folk world view refashions every song coming from sources afar. At this point it appears necessary to propose an amendment in R.M. Dorson's distinction between folklore and fakelore.[2] It is not farfetched in the context of Maithili folklore to find innumerable songs sung by the younger singers that add a sacred aura to the alleged *fakelore*. It is similar to the folk absorption of the classical, as evident in the much-known example of Vidyapati's poetry that belongs to the tradition of literature, and is yet effortlessly sung by women folk.[3] No absorption is passive in the folk context. Hence, a refashioning of the classical as well as of fakelore vis-à-vis the art work in the age of mechanical reproduction is evident in the songs. In other words, the mediated nature of folk songs is only one side of the coin; the other side is that the marks of mediation are polished by the styles and sanctity arising from folk renditions. It can be perceived as a process of *folklorization* and *re-mythicisation* of the songs and musical notes, a rechristening of the output from the factory of popular culture. These songs enter the emotional scheme of the social structure of the folk as the singers and listeners indiscriminately revel in their tune. The songs become significant in the folk world view despite their apparent sources being located somewhere away from the folk context. Hence, ideas of originality and authenticity become a dubious proposition when discussing the songs in the folk world view.

And thus, Maithili folklore and thereof world view are explicitly loaded with mythological motifs and references to sacred icons. This is so strong a feature that these songs convince the folk of the eternal nature of the folk ideas present in them. As though they were the words descending upon them from some higher domain, these songs assume religious significance. Religio-social structure consists of these songs revealing the conscious and unconscious of the Maithil society, in which relationship with the divine appears as yet another form of relationship, facilitating dialogues and forging intimate cosmic connections. It is important to note in this regard that the folk do not distinguish between malevolent and benevolent mother goddess as two opposite principles, and worship both the forms of the goddess as though they were the manifestation of the same entity.[4] Same principle works in the visualization of Siva reworking the classical imagination of the lord of destruction. In these songs, Siva is a romantic lover, a naughty child, and a generous father. *He* is despised and *He* is adored at once; *He* is feared and *He* is beseeched at once.

In the middle of these songs, the folk comprehend life and death, with a view that presents a blending of the religious sacred and social mundane. In this context, under the sociocultural ambience filled with songs and singers, evolves the practice of *art of dying* anchored by *emotional truthfulness*, shaping *folk philosophy*, as elaborated in the preceding essay. To move to the next section, it is imperative to pay attention to the category of tradition emerging from the folk context, and which warrants a reflection on the similar category present in other works.

Folk Tradition: *Neither Little nor Great*

The folk locate themselves through their songs at the intersection of the contemporary and the orally continued past. Tradition acquires a meaning beyond the categories of the little and the great traditions of India. In folk religiosity of the Hindus there is an engagement with the cognitive categories of the Sanskritic-textual Hinduism. It is imperative to note the distinctiveness of the folk religion without resorting to the binary oppositions of traditions. As Milton Singer (1975) suggests, the structure of tradition and the meaning of civilization is a process as well as a product. If it were a process, it has a possibility of *becoming* and *unbecoming*, and in the context of the folk, 'tradition' becomes an entity too large to be configured through the categories of little and great tradition. In other words, the folk are not a replica of the classical; the little tradition is not a mere receiver of the norms, rituals, and edicts that trickle down from the great tradition. This is why Raj Bali Pandey argued, 'the Samskar (sacraments), mostly being domestic rites and ceremonies, were based more on precedent and popular traditional usages than on any definite written code' (1969: 1). The performance of the sacramental rites is beyond the coded rules of the texts, while also engaging with the codes. Mostly sacraments are folksy (folk like) and inclusive of folk and classical ideas. The ancient classical texts of the Hindus describe 'what to do' and 'why to do' in order to remain within dharma and perform karma. It is due to the folk philosophy that we get to know 'how to do', and because means entails ends the whole array of issues is refashioned. Thus 'how to do' redefines 'what to

do' and 'why to do'. For example, a priest would send a message by speaking aloud towards the women of the household that now we need to do *kanyadaan*, and women of the household would be ready with the wherewithal for the rituals, along with the necessary songs. The folk philosophy determines the enactment and implementation of the textual inscriptions. Evidently, this does not rule out the authority of the textual-classical-Brahminic authority. Thus, in here emerges a novel face of the religious life of the Hindus. Acknowledging this very paradoxical relation beyond the binaries, Veena Das notes:

it was Srinivas who insisted that the religion of the peasant was as integral a part of Hinduism as the scriptures. His distinction between Sanskritic and non-Sanskritic Hinduism stressed the fact that Hinduism also existed outside the Sanskrit texts. However posing this dichotomy Srinivas failed to see that both worked with common structural categories so that the religion of the illiterate peasant might constitute the structural transformation of the religion of the sophisticated literati. (1987: 5)

It means a pre-existing recognition of the counter-currents in the Hindu dharma. But it rarely translated into an innovative way to understand the religion and practices of Hindus. Hence for Das, rites and rituals, elaborating the cognitive categories in the structure of Hindu society, came from the Puranas, and thereby an ominous classification of domestic rituals and public rituals appear.[5] But we have noticed that the extreme form of separation in the form of death or otherwise has women singing or sobbing (or ritual weeping/mourning). Beyond rituals, if we ponder upon the folk philosophy, we notice the engagement with the idea of death intricately related to the events of life. This tendency was present in the studies on the processes of changes in traditional societies. Following Robert Redfield and Singer, Mckim Marriott used the notions of little and great tradition to propound the process of Universalization and Parochialization. It is in the hierarchical scheme that movement of festivals and deities, upward as well as downward, occurs in a village society. Thus, Parochialization is 'a process of localization, of limitation upon the scope of intelligibility, of deprivation of literary form, of reduction to less systematic and less reflective dimensions. The process of Parochialization constitutes the characteristic creative

work of little communities within India's indigenous civilization'
(1967: 200).

The creativity, the transformational feature in the little
community notwithstanding, there are problems pertaining to
the implicit hierarchy of the traditional components. It disables
to perceive the processes at a rather horizontal plane, where the
folk world view, the non-Sanskritic Hinduism in interaction with
the Sanskritic one, dominates the practices and articulation of
the folk. With reference to the songs presented in this book it
is not far from comprehension that literary elements vis-à-vis
metaphors, meanings muddled with feelings and systematization
of thought without compromising on the complex ambiguities,
are present in the folk categories. Hence, the whole approach
of the proposed ethno-sociology, that emulates the methods of
positivistic science, has to be understood afresh and refashioned.
In principle, as Marriott writes, ethno-social science requires:

> building from the culture's natural categories a general system of concepts
> that can be formally defined in relation to each other; it requires developing
> words and measures that can be used rigorously for description, analysis
> and explanation within that culture; and it especially requires developing
> deductive strategies that can generate hypothesis for empirical tests in order
> that the science may criticize itself and grow. It requires doing all this in
> terms that will be analytically powerful enough to define all the major
> parameters of living in that culture without violating the culture's ontology,
> its presuppositions, or its epistemology.[6] (1990: 4)

But it is evident in the list of the conceptual categories as well
as the formulation of the processes such as Universalization and
Parochialization that Marriott has compromised on the ontological
structure of traditional society of India, while delving only into
the textual-Sanskritic epistemology. For the ontological aspect of
Indian society has to reckon with the totality of epistemology.
In other words, the indigenous knowledge system belongs to the
domain of living, praxis and doing rather than what is inscribed
in the texts. The articulation in the everyday life as well as on the
occasion of rites and rituals are more expressive of the *ontologized
epistemology*. Thus, the opposition between meaning and feeling,
rational and emotional, as well as great and little tradition is resolved.
In the folk philosophy of Mithila, as culled out from the songs,

we notice that meaning and feeling are enmeshed. To understand it one has to become what the folk is unless a simplistic reliance on the textual tradition is the desired result. They sing the folk feelings vis-à-vis aspirations, constraints, and possibilities. Their songs contain the subtlest metaphorical-literary contents as well as the bluntest usages. They are systematic without compromising on the felt ambivalence and ambiguities. Then, perhaps, Marriott is wrong along with Redfield and Singer, that it is handiwork of the 'unreflective many' in the little tradition. The folk are rather the 'reflective many' in an oral/folk tradition.

At last I would like to get back to the Kannada folktale, borrowed from A.K. Ramanujan, with which the introductory essay of this book began. The elderly woman looking for the key in the street light, though she lost it in the dark room, is a personification of the researcher who tries to understand the meaning at the cross-section of the classical and the folk. The folk wisdom in it suggests to blur the distinctions and locate the search on a plane where tradition is viewed as the process as well as the product, to settle with a lesson from Singer. In the same vein we need to evaluate the distinction between the categories of tradition and modernity in the light of the folk wisdom. The latter point to a state of being that is debatably beyond these conceptual distinctions. Neither tradition based approach, as discussed in the foregone section, nor the modernity approach divulge the intricacies of the folk wisdom.

Beyond Tradition and Modernity

The project of modernity as manifest in early sociology bred the typological binaries to comprehend social realities. They served the utility of analytical convenience. But they were also offshoots of historical and philosophical churnings in the European context and, therefore, there are evident instances of a rethinking about the binaries in the latter part of world history.[7] Such a rethinking could not see the possibility of 'contextual modernity' intertwined with tradition (Pathak 1998). The notion of contextual modernity solicits an engagement with social reality and its components that could simultaneously exhibit the features of modern and traditional world views. This accounts for the distinctions of the vernacular dynamics of modernity without succumbing to nihilist rejections of universalism and celebration of isolated cultural distinction. Contextual modernity does not operate with the schism of modern grand-narrative and postmodern micro-narratives. This is the scheme in which the conventional binaries become dubious. The categories of tradition and modernity have helped the sociological analysis in understanding society in a particular manner. But the distinction also limits the possibility of understanding complex negotiations between currents and counter-currents underlying a social reality. The most debilitating is the inherent assumption of the sharp difference between the categories, as though tradition does not exist in the realm of the modern or vice versa. And if there is any evidence of tradition in the vast literature, it is only in the form of an undesirable anachronism. Thus, one view would present the idea of 'mistaken modernity' (Gupta 2000) and would criticize the remnant of past manifest in the behavioural appearances of Indians. This is often to seek for a more rational and thereby liberating modernity in a Habermassian fashion, a putative response to the post-modern challenges. A similar urge is inherent in the idea of reflexive modernity as an answer to the critique of the Enlightenment agenda with which modernity emerged at the advent of the nineteenth century. These are the responses to the ambiguity of modernity that was the focal point in the works of the classical sociologists. Marx, Weber, and Durkheim all dealt with the possibilities and constraints in the modern milieu. They all expressed optimism and pessimism vis-à-vis the modern industrialized society. They did not realize the significance of *narratives* that were beyond the pale of their scientific-objective social science. In fact, the answer to modernity's pessimism can be found in the so-called non-scientific narratives of the people/ the folk. Interestingly, these narratives were never non-existent, neither in traditional nor in modern society. The folk have not been without their rationale and logics neither in the social world that has been perceived by the social scientists as guided by the classical texts, nor in the social world that has been established to be secular, democratic, and individual-centric. It was clearly evident in M.N. Srinivas's example of the bulldozer driver in Rampura, as he suggested that Westernization does not cancel out the possible existence of the values and practices belonging to the past. It is in this background that the critiques of modernity would stress on the idea of knowledge being contextual. So, the traditional knowledge intervening in the modern lives assumes significance. We may call that set of knowledge as traditional for our intellectual convenience. But the crucial question is whether the traditional is unalloyed by the contemporary. If the traditional were purely/merely a remnant of the past, it would not have presented forms of hybrid/kitsch. When an elderly woman sings a song of unknown origin in tune with a very well-known *filmi* song, we know it is not hybrid/kitsch. Such songs and their rendition also do not refer to a resurrection of tradition in the modern times. In simple words, it only means that certain folk ideas travel across time and space, utilizing any available means for expression, irrespective of the categories of tradition and modern.

A sociological analysis of an important event such as death in the social life offers us nothing more than pessimism about it. Yes, the modern world view cripples the social harmony with the socially disruptive events of this kind. It is more so in the age of *homelessness* where the relation with the cosmic is weakened. Death undoubtedly appears only in the way our medical establishment would like us to believe. Hence, it is an anathema in public and squeezed into the private domain. Dying is then a lonely experience. The larger socio-economic structure fosters medicalized notions of living and dying. But within the same structure we also behold the scenes of graceful death in spite of suffering and we also hear the sound of melody in the heart-ranting mourning. In the hospital set-up when a terminally ill-patient is let known about the impending end, s/he starts chanting *mahamrtunjaya* mantra.[8] Another sight in hospitals in those wards where the terminally ill patients await their ending is of the kith and kin surrounding the ailing person and reading out the verses from the *Bhagvad Gita*, *Koran*, and *The Bible*, as per one's religion.[9] It instantly refutes the medical-scientific understanding of the body and the events of life that the body is subject to. Curiously, while doctors judge the state of a patient's being by reading the test reports, the dying testifies his/her state in a more intuitive manner.

Another common instance is that doctors too begin to wait for divine intervention along with the relatives of the patients, more visible in small towns than in cities. The intersecting world views do not know the boundaries of the traditional and modern. The power of the self is invoked irrespective of the milieus; the means of invocation may change, however the goal remains the same. In the final analysis, the social action is prone to a fluid ideology unlike that of science.

In this light, it is imperative of the sociological studies to understand the world view of the folk in rural, urban, semi-urban or urban contexts, in a way that can do justice to the rich and complex experience of everyday reality. Sociological and anthropological researches have to be geared towards the folk who transform everything—from textual-classical to scientific-secular to the popular—into a congruent aspect of the folk world view. Such an endeavour would indeed require thinking beyond binaries, toward which this book has made only a modest iota of contribution.

Notes

1. See Walter Benjamin (1999) for the details of this notion, which suggests, in short, that when reproduced mechanically an art work is devoid of *aura*—the sacred effect of it belonging to tradition. Rituals of tradition are replaced by politics. However, this stance does not help recognize the re-mythicization and folklorization of apparently modern and politically motivated propagations. The singing, and of course feeling, of such songs from cassette and compact discs, rechristens them in the framework of the folk.
2. See the third essay, where the notion of folklore is discussed in the historical context.
3. Such a view can be contested with an argument like all the songs of Vidyapati are not sung by women of entire Mithila with the same ease and zeal. It is restricted to the bevy of women from Brahmin caste, especially of the northern side. Second, all the songs with Vidyapati's name inserted in the last line of the song are not necessarily written by the poet Vidyapati. Some of these songs were composed anonymously and the name of Vidyapati was inserted by the community of singers for authenticity.

4. It is a counter argument to Susan Wadley (1988) and Lynn E. Gatewood (1985) who proposed an absolute distinction between the malevolent and benevolent goddess. Gatewood suggested to the extent that the malevolent goddess has stronghold amongst the lower caste group while the upper caste worships the benevolent-consort goddesses.

5. Veena Das argues that there is a distinction between the domestic rituals and public rituals. Rituals on the occasion of birth, initiation, marriage, and for propitiation of the ancestors are domestic rituals involving women. Rituals for death are not part of domestic ritual and the domestic groups are kept at bay during their performance.

6. Mckim Marriott propounds the idea of ethno-social science on the pretext of the incompatibility of the theoretical-conceptual categories developed in the Western context as far as understanding the Indian sociocultural context is concerned. The dichotomies of Parsonian theory, for instance, cannot help explain the Indian phenomenon. But then, ethno-social science is nothing more than a mere replica of the positivistic science when it comes to conceptualization and comprehension of the social reality, and hence it is restricted to the categories belonging to the classical-textual tradition of India, as it appears in the enlisted categories presented by Marriott.

7. See Patel 2006 for a representative discussion on this issue.

8. The mantra is known for liberating the sufferer from the limbo of uncertainty in illness and get him/her either death or good health. The mantra reads *Om Trayambakam Yajamahe Sugandhim Pushtiwardhanam Oorwawik Bandhnat Mrityomukshiya Mamritat.*

9. In this regard the example of the hospice movement in the West merits attention. For details on the success and failures of the hospice, see Clark 1993.

Bibliography

Abercombie, N. et al., *The Penguin Dictionary of Sociology*, 4th edn., London: Penguin, 2000.

Alexiou, Margaret, *The Ritual Lament in Greek Tradition*, Boston: Rowman and Littlefield, 1974.

Allen, M., 'The Hindu View of Women', in *Women in India and Nepal*, ed. M. Allen and S.N. Mukherjee, Canberra: Australian National University, 1982, pp. 1–20.

Appadurai, Arjun, *The Social Life of Things: Commodities in Cultural Perspectives*, New York: Cambridge University Press, 1986.

Appadurai, Arjun et al., eds., *Gender, Genre, and Power in South Asian Expressive Traditions*, Philadelphia: University of Pennsylvania Press, 1991.

Aries, P., *The Hour of Our Death*, London: Penguin, 1981.

Bachofen, J.J., *Myth, Religion and Mother Right*, tr. E. Mannheim, London: Routledge & Kegan Paul, 1967.

Bataille, G., *Inner Experience*, Albany: State University of New York Press, 1988.

Baudrillard, J., *Symbolic Exchange and Death*, London: Sage, 2011.

Bauman, Z., *Mortality, Immortality and Other Life Strategies*, London: Polity Press, 1992.

———, 'Modernity and Ambivalence', in *Theory, Culture and Society*, vol. 7, 1990, pp. 143–69.

———, *Towards a Critical Sociology: An Essay on Commonsense and Emancipation*, London: Routledge & Kegan Paul, 1973.

Beck, Ulrich, 'Critical Theory of World Risk Society: A Cosmopolitan Vision', *Constellations*, vol. 16, no. 1, 2009, pp. 3–22.

———, *Risk Society: Towards a New Modernity*, London: Sage, 1992.

Becker, E., *The Birth and Death of Meaning: An Interdisciplinary Perspective on the Problem of Man*, London: The Free Press, 1971.

Ben-Amos, D., 'Toward a Definition of Folklore in Context', *The Journal of American Folklore*, vol. 84, no. 331, January 1971, pp. 3–15.

Bendix, R. et al., eds., *A Companion to Folklore*, Oxford: Wiley-Blackwell, 2012.

Benjamin, W., *Illuminations*, tr. Harry Zorn, London: Pimlico, 1999.

Berger, Peter, *The Scared Canopy: Elements of a Sociological Theory of Religion*, New York: Anchor, 1990.

Bhaskar, Roy, *Reflections on Meta-Reality: Transcendence, Emancipation and Everyday Life*, Delhi: Sage, 2002.

Blackburn, S.H., *Print, Folklore and Nationalism in Colonial South India*, Delhi: Permanent Black, 2003.

———, *Singing of Birth and Death: Texts in Performance*, Philadelphia: University of Pennsylvania Press, 1988.

Blacking, John, *How Musical is Man?*, Seattle and London: University of Washington Press, 1973.

Bleicher, J., *Contemporary Hermeneutics: Hermenutics as Method, Philosophy and Critique*, London: Routledge & Kegan Paul, 1980.

Bloch, M., 'Death, Women and Power', in *Death and Regeneration of Life*, ed. J. Parry and M. Bloch, Cambridge: Cambridge University Press, 1982, pp. 211–25.

Bourdieu, Pierre and Loïc J.D. Wacquant, *An Invitation to Reflexive Sociology*, Chicago: University of Chicago Press, 1992.

Bourdieu, Pierre, 'The Specificity of the Scientific Field and the Social Conditions for the Progress of Reason', tr. R. Nice, *Social Science Information*, vol. 14, no. 6, 1975, pp. 19–47.

Briggs, C.L., 'Personal Sentiments and Polyphonic Voices in Warao Women's Ritual Wailing: Music and Poetics in a Critical and Collective Discourse', *American Anthropologist*, vol. 94, no. 4, December 1993, pp. 929–57.

Brihadaranyaka Upanishad, Gorakhpur: Gita Press, n.d.

Brown, M.E., 'Women, Folklore and Feminism', *Journal of Folklore Research*, vol. 26, no. 3, September-December 1989, pp. 259–64.

Burghart, R., 'A Quarrel in the Language Family: Agency and Representation of Speech in Mithila', *Modern Asian Studies*, vol. 27, no. 4, October 1993, pp. 761–804.

Camus, Albert, *The Myth of Sisyphus* [translation], London: Penguin, 2002.

———, *A Happy Death*, tr. R. Howard, New York: Knopf, 1972.

Caraveli-Chaves, A., 'Bridge between Worlds: The Greek Women's Lament as Communicative Event', *The Journal of American Folklore*, vol. 93, no. 368, April-June 1988, pp. 129–57.

Chatterjee, P., 'Whose Imagined Community?', *Millennium: Journal of International Studies*, vol. 20, no. 3, 1991, pp. 521–5.

Chatterji, Roma, *Speaking with Pictures: Folk Art and Narrative Tradition in India*, Delhi: Routledge, 2012.

———, 'Purulia Chho: Discursive Space and the Construction of Culture', in *Folklore, Public Sphere and Civil Society*, ed. M.D. Muthukumaraswamy and M. Kaushal, Delhi: Indira Gandhi National Centre for the Arts and National Folklore Support Centre, Chennai, 2004, pp. 37–56.

————, 'The Category of Folk', in *The Oxford India Companion of Sociology and Social Anthropology*, ed. Veena Das, Delhi: Oxford University Press, 2003, pp. 567–97.

Choron, J., *Death and Western Thought*, New York: Collier, 1963.

Clark, D., ed., *The Sociology of Death: Theory, Culture and Practice*, Oxford: Wiley-Blackwell, 1993.

Crichton, I., *The Art of Dying*, London: Peter Owen, 1976.

Czarniawska, B., *Narratives in Social Science Research*, Delhi: Sage, 2004.

Dalmia, V. and R. Sadana, *The Cambridge Companion to Modern Indian Culture*, Delhi: Cambridge University Press, 2012.

Das, Arvind N., *Changel: The Biography of a Village*, Delhi: Penguin, 1996.

Das, Veena, 'Femininity and the Orientation to the Body', in *Socialization, Education and Women: Exploration in Gender Identity*, ed. Karuna Chanana, Delhi: Orient Longman, 1988, pp. 193–207.

————, *Structure and Cognition: Aspects of Hindu Caste and Ritual*, Delhi: Oxford University Press, 1987.

————, 'The Work of Mourning: Death in a Punjabi Family', in *The Cultural Transition: Human Experience and Social Transformation in the Third World and Japan*, ed. M.I. White and S. Pollak, London: Routledge & Kegan Paul, 1986, pp. 119–40.

————, 'The Uses of Liminality: Society and Cosmos in Hinduism', *Contribution to Indian Sociology*, n.s., vol. 10, no. 2, 1976, pp. 245–63.

Degh, L., 'The Approach to World view in Folk Narrative Study', *Western Folklore*, vol. 53, no. 3, July 1994, pp. 243–52.

Deva, Indra, *Folk Culture and Peasant Society in India*, Jaipur: Rawat, 1989.

Devi, M. and U. Ganguli, *Rudali: From Fiction to Performance*, Calcutta: Seagull, 1997.

Dharwadker, V., *The Collected Essays of A.K. Ramanujan*, New Delhi: Oxford University Press, 1999.

Doniger, Wendy, *The Hindus: An Alternative History*, Delhi: Penguin, 2011.

Dorson, R.M., ed., *Folklore in the Modern World*, Paris: Mouton, 1978.

————, *America in Legend*, New York: Pantheon, 1973.

————, ed., *Folklore and Folk Life: An Introduction*, Chicago: The University of Chicago Press, 1972.

Dumont, L., 'A Folk Deity of Tamil Nad: Aiyanar, The Lord', in *Religion in India*, ed. T.N. Madan, Delhi: Oxford University Press, 1991, pp. 38–49.

————, *Religion, Politics and History in India: Collected Papers in Indian Sociology*, Paris: Mouton, 1970.

Dundes, A., 'World view in Folk Narrative: An Addendum', *Western Folklore*, vol. 54, no. 3, July 1995, pp. 229–32.

————, 'Folk Ideas as Units of World view', *The Journal of American Folklore*, vol. 84, no. 331, January-March 1971, pp. 93–103.

————, 'The American Concept of Folklore', *Journal of the Folklore Institute*, vol. 3, no. 3, Special Issue: The Yugoslav-American Folklore Seminar, December 1966, pp. 226–49.

————, ed., *The Study of Folklore*, Englewood Cliffs: Prentice Hall, 1965.

Durkheim, Emile, *The Elementary Forms of Religious Life*, tr. C. Cosman, London: Oxford University Press, 2008.

Egnor, M., 'On the Meaning of Sakti to Women in Tamil Nadu', in *The Powers of Tamil Women*, ed. Susan S. Wadley, New York: Syracuse University Maxwell School, 1980, pp. 22–42.

Elias, N., *The Loneliness of Dying*, tr. E. Jephcott, Oxford: Basil Blackwell, 1985.

Evans-Pritchard, E.E., *The Nuer: A Description of the Modes of Livelihood and Political Institutions of a Nilotic People*, New York: Oxford University Press, 1974.

Feld, Steven, 'Sound Structure as Social Structure', *Ethnomusicology*, vol. 28, no. 3, 1984, pp. 383–409.

Filippi, G.G., *Mrtyu: Concept of Death in Indian Traditions*, Delhi: D.K. Printworld, 2005.

Gandhi, M.K., *The Message of the Geeta*, Ahmedabad: Navajivan Trust, 1959.

Gatewood, Lynn E., *Devi and Spouse Goddess*, Delhi: Manohar, 1985.

Gawande, Atul, *Being Mortal: Medicine and What Matters in the End*, London: Penguin, 2014.

Geetnaad, compiled and edited by Dr Vibhuti Anand and Jyotsna Anand, Patna: Bhawani Prakashan, 1997.

Gennep, A.V., *The Rites of Passage*, tr. Monika B. Vizedom and Gabrielle L. Caffee, Chicago: The University of Chicago Press, 1960.

Giddens, Anthony, *New Rules of Sociological Method: A Positive Critique of Interpretative Sociologies*, London: Hutchinson and Co., 1976.

Goddy, Jack and Ian Watt, 'The Consequences of Literacy', in *Literacy in Traditional Societies*, Cambridge: Cambridge University Press, 1968, pp. 25–68.

Gouldner, Alwin, *The Coming Crisis of Western Sociology*, New York: Basic Books, 1970.

Green, N., *Sufism: A Global History*, West Sussex: Wiley-Blackwell, 2012.

Groer, G., *Death, Grief, and Mourning in Contemporary Britain*, London: Cresset Press, 1965.

Gupta, D., *Mistaken Modernity: India between Worlds*, Delhi: Harper Collins, 2000.

Hammersley, Martin and Paul Atkinson, *Ethnography: Principles in Practice*, 2nd edn., London: Routledge, 1995.

Handoo, Jawaharlal and Anna-Leena Siikala, eds., *Folklore and Discourse*, Mysore: Zooni, 1999.

Hariharan, Geetha, *The Art of Dying: Stories*, Delhi: Penguin, 1993.

Hart, George L., III, 'Woman and the Sacred in Ancient Tamilnad', in *Readings in Early Indian History*, ed. Kumkum Roy, Delhi: Manohar, 1999, pp. 57–70.

————, 'Woman and the Sacred in Ancient Tamilnad', *Journal of Asian Studies*, vol. 32, 1973, pp. 233–50.

Hekman, Susan J., *Hermeneutics and the Sociology of Knowledge*, Oxford: Polity Press, 1986.

Henry, Edward O., 'Folk Song Genres and their Melodies in India: Music Use and Genre Process', *Asian Music*, vol. 31, no. 2, Spring/Summer 2000, pp. 71–106.

————, 'Maithili Women's Song: Distinctive and Endangered Species', *Ethnomusicology*, vol. 42, no. 3, Autumn 1998, pp. 415–40.

————, 'Social Structure and Music: Correlating Musical Genres and Social Categories in Bhojpuri-Speaking India', *International Review of the Aesthetics and Sociology of Music*, vol. 19, no. 2, 1988, pp. 217–27

Hertz, R., *Death and the Right Hand*, tr. R. Needham and C. Needham, London: Routledge, 1960a.

————, 'A Contribution to the Study of the Collective Representations of Death', in *Death and the Right Hand*, tr. R. Needham and C. Needham, London: Cohen and West, 1960b, pp. 52–70.

Hogan, Homer, 'Hermeneutics and Folksongs', *The Journal of Aesthetics and Art Criticism*, vol. 28, no. 3, Winter 1969, pp. 223–9.

Illich, Ivan, *Medical Nemesis: Expropriation of Health*, New York: Pantheon, 1977.

Islam, M., *Folklore: The Pulse of the People*, Ranchi Anthropology Series-7, Delhi: Concept, 1985.

Jackson, Michael, *Lifeworlds: Essays in Existential Anthropology*, Chicago: Chicago University Press, 2013.

Jha, Pankaj, *The Colonial Periphery: Imagining Mithila (1875–1955)*, Delhi and Patna: Janaki Prakashan, 2002.

Jha, Hetukar, *Khattar Kaka*, Delhi: Rajkamal Prakashan, 2007.

————, 'Death and Social Existence of Man', in *Voice of Death: Traditional Thought and Modern Science*, ed. B. Saraswati, New Delhi: D.K. Printworld and N.K. Bose Memorial Foundation, Varanasi, 2005, pp. 32–47.

————, *Ganganatha Jha*, Delhi: Sahitya Akademi, 1992.

————, 'Mithila Ki Darshanik Parampara', in *Bihar: Ek Sanskritik Vaibhav*, ed. S.D. Singh, Patna: Parijat Prakashan, 1986, pp. 1–9.

————, 'Lower Caste Peasants and Upper Caste Zamindars in Bihar (1921-1925): An Analysis of Sanskritization and Conflict between the Two Groups', *Indian Economic and Social History Review*, vol. 14, 1977, pp. 549–59.

————, 'Understanding Caste through its Sources of Identity: An Account of the Shrotriyas of Mithila', *Sociological Bulletin,* vol. 23, no. 1, 1974, pp. 93–8.

Jha, Jata Shankar, *Beginnings of Modern Education in Mithila: Selections from Educational Records, Darbhanga Raj, 1860-1930*, Patna: K.P. Jayaswal Research Institute, 1972.

Jha, M., *Civilisational Regions of Mithila and Mahakoshal*, Delhi: Capital Publishing, 1982.

Jha, R., *Maithili Lok Sahitya: Swarup O Saundarya*, Darbhanga: Mithila Research Society, 2002.

Jha, S., *The Formation of the Maithili Language*, London: Luzac, 1958.

Jones, W.T., 'World views: Their Nature and their Function', *Current Anthropology*, vol. 13, no. 1, February 1972, pp. 79–109.

Jordan, A.R. and F.E. De Caro, 'Women and the Study of Folklore', *Signs*, vol. 11, no. 3, Spring 1986, pp. 500–18.

Kafka, Franz, *The Metamorphosis and Other Stories*, tr. Stanley Corngold, London: Random House, 2011.

———, *The Metamorphosis and Other Stories*, New York: Dover, 1996.

Kakar, Sudhir, *Intimate Relations: Exploring Indian Sexuality*, Delhi: Penguin, 1989.

———, *The Inner World: A Psychoanalytic Study of Childhood and Society in India*, Delhi: Oxford University Press, 1978.

Katz, Vernon and Thomas Egenes, *The Upanishads*, New York: Jeremy P. Tarcher/Penguin, 2015.

Kaushik, Meena, 'The Symbolic Representation of Death', *Contribution to Indian Sociology*, n.s., vol. 10, no. 2, 1976, pp. 265–92.

Kearl, Michael C., *Endings: A Sociology of Death and Dying*, Oxford: Oxford University Press, 1989.

Kumar, Rakesh, dir., *Mr. Natwarlal*, 1979.

Kvale, Steinar, *Inter Views: An Introduction to Qualitative Research Interviewing*, Thousand Oaks: Sage, 1996.

Lajmi, Kalpana, dir., *Rudaali*, 1993.

Levi-Strauss, Claude, *The Raw and the Cooked (Mythologiques)*, Chicago: Chicago University Press, 1969.

———, *Structural Anthropology*, tr. C. Jacobson, New York: Basic Books, 1963.

Lomax, Alan, 'Song Structure and Social Structure', *Ethnology*, vol. 1, no. 4, October 1962, pp. 425–51.

Lorenzen, David N., ed., *Bhakti Religion in North India: Community Identity and Political Action*, Albany: State University of New York Press, 1995.

MacLaughlin, E.C., 'Equality of Souls, Inequality of Sexes: Women in Medieval Theology', in *Religion and Sexism: Images of Women in Jewish and Christian Traditions*, ed. R.R Reuther, New York: Simone Schuster, 1974, pp. 213–66.

Madan, T.N., *Images of the World: Essays on Religion, Secularism and Culture*, Delhi: Oxford University Press, 2006.

———, ed., *Religion in India* Delhi: Oxford University Press, 1991.

Magowan, F., *Melodies of Mourning: Music and Emotion in Northern Australia*, Santa Fe: School for Advanced Research Press, 2007.

Maithili Lokgeet, collected by Anima Singh, Delhi: Sahitya Akademi, 1993.

Maithili Samskar Geet, collected by Smt. Tarini Mishra; edited by Gopikant Jha 'Umapati', Patna: Urvashi Prakashan, 2004.

Malinowski, B., *Myth in Primitive Psychology*, Westport: Negro Universities Press, 1926.

————, 'Baloma: The Spirits of the Dead in the Trobriand Islands', *The Journal of the Royal Anthropological Institute of Great Britain and Ireland*, vol. 46, 1916, pp. 353–430.

Marcus, S.L., 'Parody-Generated Texts: The Process of Composition in "Biraha"', *Asian Music*, vol. 26, no. 1, 1995, pp. 95–147.

Marriott, Mckim, ed., *India through Hindu Categories*, Delhi: Sage, 1990.

————, 'Constructing an Indian Ethnosociology', in *India through Hindu Categories*, Delhi: Sage, 1990, pp. 1–17.

————, 'Little Communities in an Indigenous Civilization', in *Studies in the Little Community*, Chicago: The University of Chicago Press, 1967, pp. 41–60.

Mehra, Prakash, dir., *Muqaddar Ka Sikandar* (Conqueror of destiny), 1978.

Mellor, P.A., 'Death in High Modernity: The Contemporary Presence and Absence of Death', in *The Sociology of Death*, ed. D. Clark, Oxford: Blackwell, 1993, pp. 11–31.

Mills, M.A. et al., eds., *South Asian Folklore: An Encyclopedia*, New York: Routledge, 2003.

Mishra, Jayakant, *History of Maithili Literature*, Delhi: Sahitya Akademi, 1976.

Mishra, Kailash Kumar, 'Mithila Paintings: Women's Creativity under Changing Perspectives', *Indian Folklore Research Journal*, vol. 1, no. 3, 2003, pp. 93–103.

Mishra, S. 'Amar', *Maithilu Loksahitya*, Delhi: Sahitya Akademi, 2006.

Mishra, Vijaykant, *Cultural Heritage of Mithila*, Allahabad: Mithila Prakashan, 1979.

Mithila Sanskar Geet, collected by Smt. Kameshwari Devi, Patna: Maithili Akadami, 1980.

Mueller-Vollmer, Kurt, *The Hermeneutics Reader: Texts of the German Tradition from the Enlightenment to the Present*, Oxford: Basil Blackwell, 1986.

Mukherjee, Hrishikesh, dir., *Anand*, 1971.

Myerhoff, Barbara G., 'A Death in Due Time: Construction of Self and Culture in Ritual Drama', in *Rite, Drama, Festival, Spectacle: Rehearsals Toward a Theory of Culture and Performance*, ed. MacAloon, Philadelphia: Institute for the study of Human Issues, 1984, pp. 149–78.

Narayan, B., 'Documenting Dissent', in *Life as Dalit: Views from the Bottom on Caste in India*, ed. S.M. Channa and J.P. Mencher, Delhi: Sage, 2013, pp. 316–40.

Nietzsche, Friedrich, 'On Truth and Lying in a Non-moral Sense', in *The Birth of Tragedy and Other Writings*, ed. Raymond Geuss and Ronald Speirs; tr. Ronald. Speirs, Cambridge: Cambridge University Press, 1999, pp. 41–55.

————, *The Birth of Tragedy and the Genealogy of Morals*, tr. Francis Golffing, New York: Doubleday Anchor Books, 1956.

O'Flaherty and Wendy Doniger, *Hindu Myths*, London: Penguin, 1975.

Obeyesekere, Gananath, *The Awakened Ones: Phenomenology of Visionary Experience*, Columbia: Columbia University Press, 2012.

Pandey, Raj Bali, *Hindu Samskaras: Socio-Religious Study of the Hindu Sacraments*, Delhi: Motilal Banarsidas, 1969.

Pant, S.G., *He dattatreya! Kumaun ki lok sanskriti aur sahitya*, Delhi: Saraswati Vihar, 1985.

Paranjpe, M.R., *Making India: Colonialism, National Culture and the Afterlife of Indian English Authority*, London: Springer, 2013.

Parry, J.P., 'Death and Cosmogony in Kashi', *Contributions to Indian Sociology*, vol. 15, 1981, pp. 337–65.

Parry, Jonathan and Maurice Bloch, *Death and the Regeneration of Life*, Cambridge: Cambridge University Press, 1982.

Patel, S., 'Beyond Binaries: A Case for Self-reflexive Sociologies', *Current Sociology*, vol. 54, no. 3, 2006, pp. 381–95.

Pathak, Avijit, *Indian Modernity: Contradictions, Paradoxes and Possibilities*, Delhi: Gyan, 1998.

Pathak, Dev, 'Through Purdah: Social Criticism in Women's Folksongs from Mithila', *SAARC Culture*, vol. 4, 2013a, pp. 3–19.

————, 'Singing in the Veil: Redefinition and Reconciliation in the Songs of Mithila', in *Colonial and Contemporary Bihar and Jharkhand*, ed. B. Pati and L. Singh, Delhi: Primus, 2013b, pp. 157–80.

Poitevin, Guy, 'Negotiating Modernity with Symbolic Resources', in *The Social and the Symbolic (Communication Processes Volume 2)*, ed. B. Bel et al., Delhi: Sage, 2007, pp. 36–75.

————, 'People's Traditions, Assets or Liabilities IV- Politics of Folklorisation', *New Quest*, no. 153, September 2003, pp. 17–30.

————, 'Popular Traditions, Strategic Assets', *Indian Folklore Research Journal*, vol. 1, no. 2, 2002, pp. 81–109.

Polkinghorne, Donald E., *Narrative Knowing and the Human Sciences*, Albany: State University of New York Press, 1987.

Racine, Josiane et al., *Viramma: Life of a Dalit*, Delhi: Social Science Press, 2005.

Prakash, J. Om, dir., *Apnapan* (Intimately personal), 1977.

Raheja, Gloria Goodwin and Ann Grodzins Gold, eds., *Listen to the Heron's Words: Reimagining Gender and Kinship in North India*, Berkeley: University of California Press, 1994.

Raheja, Gloria Goodwin, 'The Paradoxes of Power and Community: Women's Oral Tradition and the Uses of Ethnography', in *Songs, Stories, Lives: Gendered Dialogues and Cultural Critique*, Delhi: Kali for Women, 2003, pp. 5–19.

————, 'Caste, Colonialism, and the Speech of the Colonized: Entextualisation and Disciplinary Control in India', *American Ethnologist*, vol. 23, no. 3, 1996, pp. 494–513.

Ramanujan, A.K., *Folktales from India: A Selection of Oral Tales from Twenty-two Languages*, Delhi: Viking, 1991.

Ranjan, P., 'Kabirpanth in Mithila', Ph.D. thesis, Centre for Historical Studies, Jawaharlal Nehru University, Delhi, 1998.

Ricoeur, Paul, *Hermeneutics and the Human Sciences*, tr. And ed. J.B. Thompson, Cambridge: Cambridge University Press, 1981.

Roy Chaudhury, P.C., *Folklore of Bihar*, Delhi: National Book Trust, 1980.

Sachchidananda and A.K. Lal, eds., *Elite and Development*, Delhi: Concept, 1980.

Sadiq, Mohammed, dir., *Chaudhavin Ka Chand* (The moon of fourteenth night), 1960.

Saraswati, Baidyanath, ed., *Voice of Death: Traditional Thought and Modern Science*, Delhi: D.K. Printworld and N.K. Bose Memorial Foundation, Varanasi, 2005.

————, ed., *Tribal Thoughts and Culture: Essays in Honor of Surajit Chandra Sinha*, Delhi: Concept, 1991.

————, *Kasi: Myth and Reality of a Classical Tradition*, Shimla: Indian Institute of Advance Study, 1975.

Schombucher, Elisabeth and Claus Peter Zoller, eds., *Ways of Dying: Death and its Meaning in South Asia*, Delhi: Manohar, 1999.

Schomer, K. and W.H. McLeod, eds., *The Sants: Studies in a Devotional Tradition of India*, Delhi: Motilal Banarasidas, 1987.

Schutz, A. and T. Luckmann, *The Structures of the Life-World*, tr. R.M. Zaner and H.T. Engelhardt Jr, London: Heinmann, 1974.

Seale, C., *Constructing Death: The Sociology of Dying and Bereavement*, Cambridge: Cambridge University Press, 1998.

Segal, R.A., *Myth: A Very Short Introduction*, Delhi: Oxford University Press, 2006.

Shah, K.J., 'Philosophy, Religion, Morality, Spirituality: Some Issues', *Journal of the Indian Council of Philosophical Research*, vol. 7, no. 2, 1990, pp. 1–12.

Sharma, Vijay, dir., *Jai Santoshi Ma*, 1975.

Sills, D.L., ed., *International Encyclopedia of the Social Sciences, Volume 5*, New York: Macmillan and The Free Press, 1968.

Singer, Milton, ed., *Traditional India: Structure and Change*, Jaipur: Rawat, 1975.

Singh, Gajandra Narain 'Bihar Ki Sangeet Parampara', in *Bihar: Ek Sanskritik Vaibhav*, ed. S.D. Singh, Patna: Parijat Prakashan, 1986, pp. 1–10.

Srinivas, M.N. and A.M. Shah, 'Hinduism', in *International Encyclopedia of the Social Sciences*, vol. 6, 1968, pp. 358–66.

Tambiah, Stanley J., 'At the Confluence of Anthropology, History, and Indology', *Contributions to Indian Sociology*, vol. 21, no. 1, 1987, pp. 187–216.

Thakur, Upendra, *History of Mithila (Circa 3000 BC-1556 AD)*, Patna: Mithila Institute, 1956.

Therborn, Göran, 'Entangled Modernities', *European Journal of Social Theory*, vol. 6, no. 3, 2003, pp. 293–305.

Tiwary, K.M., 'Tuneful Weeping: A Mode of Communication', *Frontiers: A Journal of Women Studies*, vol. 3, no. 3, 1978, pp. 24–7.

Tolstoy, L., 'My Confession', in *Life and Meaning: A Reader*, ed. O. Hanfling, New York: Basil Blackwell, pp. 12–20.

Turner, Victor, *The Ritual Process: Structure and Anti-Structure*, London/ Chicago: Routledge & Kegan Paul/Aldine Press, 1969.

Urban, Greg, 'Ritual Wailing in Amerindian Brazil', *American Anthropologist*, new series, vol. 90, no. 2, June 1988, pp. 385–400.

Vansina, Jan, *Oral Tradition as History*, London: James Currey, 1985.

Vatuk, Ved Prakash, ed., *Studies in Indian Folk Traditions*, Delhi: Manohar, 1979.

Visvanathan, Susan, 'Structure and Usage in "Modern" and "Primitive" Society', M.Phil. dissertation, Department of Sociology, University of Delhi, 1980.

Vitebsky, Piers, *Dialogues with the Dead: The Discussion of Mortality among the Sora of Eastern India*, Cambridge: Cambridge University Press, 1993.

Wadley, Susan, 'Women and the Hindu Tradition', in *Women in Indian Society: A Reader*, ed. Rehana Ghadially, Delhi: Sage, 1988, pp. 40–55.

———, *The Powers of Tamil Women*, New York: Maxwell School of Citizenship and Public Affairs, Syracuse University, 1980.

Wadley, Susan, *Shakti: Power in the Conceptual Structure of Karimpur Religion*, Chicago: Department of Anthropology, The University of Chicago, 1975.

Weber, M., *Economy and Society: An Outline for Interpretive Sociology*, Berkley: University of California Press, 1978.

Werraperuma, S., *Living and Dying: From Moment to Moment*, Delhi: Motilal Banarasidas, 1996.

Wells, A.N. and Dorr, John A., Jr., 'Shifting of the Kosi River, Northern India', *Geology*, vol. 15, no. 3, 1987, pp. 204–7.

Whitehead, Alfred N., *Modes of Thought*, New York: The Free Press, 1968.

Zenker, Olaf and Kumoll Karsten, eds., *Beyond Writing Culture: Current Intersections of Epistemologies and Representational Practices*, New York: Berghahn, 2015.

Index